The User Interface
Design Book *for the*
Applications Programmer

The User Interface Design Book for the Applications Programmer

Alexander Martin
and
David Eastman

JOHN WILEY & SONS
Chichester • New York • Brisbane • Toronto • Singapore

Other Wiley Editorial Offices

John Wiley & Sons, Inc., 605 Third Avenue,
New York, NY 10158-0012, USA

Jacaranda Wiley Ltd, 33 Park Road, Milton,
Queensland 4064, Australia

John Wiley & Sons (Canada) Ltd, 22 Worcester Road,
Rexdale, Ontario M9W 1L1, Canada

John Wiley & Sons (SEA) Pte Ltd, 2 Clementi Loop #02-01,
Jin Xing Distripark, Singapore 0512

British Library Cataloguing in Publication Data

A catalogue record for this book is available from the British Library

ISBN 0 471 95371 7

Typeset in 10/12.5pt Garamond Book and Gill Sans
Printed and bound in Great Britain
by Bookcraft (Bath) Ltd.

This book is printed on acid-free paper responsibly manufactured from sustainable
forestation, for which at least two trees are planted for each one used for paper
production.

Contents

Preface

Computers are no longer hidden away, used only in the back room of big corporations. The human face of shopping, banking and many other activities is being replaced by an artificial one. As this process continues, the programs that control the machines, and especially the software that deals with the human users, will have a major effect on our lives. This book is aimed at those who design computer software that people will use.

About the Authors

The authors have a wide range of experience in applications design.

Alexander Martin trained as an industrial designer. An interest in programming games for microcomputers gave him the opportunity to join a computer manufacturer as a software engineer. He spent a year as assistant editor on a computer magazine before joining a computer game publisher as an artist, designer and producer. He is currently a freelance consultant.

David Eastman started programming games shortly after leaving university, as well as producing some 'serious' financial products software. He is currently working on communications software for electronic services and the Internet. His interest in computing and interface design was triggered as much by playing bad games as good ones.

How to Find Your Way Around This Book

Whether you are an experienced software developer, or a new recruit to the army of applications designers, you will find this book of interest to you. It can be read from beginning to end, as a complete introduction to computer applications design, or it can be used as a reference book when seeking guidance on an aspect of software.

The following pages show specific areas of interest and where information about them can be found:

Interface design

Section 2 – chapters 1 to 5, 10 and 11.

Designing for GUIs

Section 2 – chapters 2, 4, 5 and 11

And these references: chapter 6 – interactive graphics, chapter 3 – input design, chapter 7 – using sound, chapter 9 – sensible defaults and settings, chapter 10 – hiding options in Menus.

User friendliness

Section 2 – chapters 1, 5, 9, 10 and 11

Designing for entertainment software and games

Section 2 – chapters 3, 6, 7 and 10.

Designing for multimedia

Section 2 – chapters 2, 4, 6 and 7.

Using graphics

Section 2 – chapters 4 and 6.

Using sound

Section 2 – chapter 7.

Development issues

Section 3.

Good design practice

Section 1.

Further references can be found throughout section 2.

Section I

First Steps

This book places a lot of emphasis on interface design. However, it would be wrong to treat interface design as a process isolated from the job of designing the entire application. So we start by taking a look at design in general, the environment in which design takes place, the tools used in development and finally how design ideas can be presented.

I

Introduction to Design

Humans can make things in different ways. The particular way that something is put together is a design. If one way of making something produces a more satisfactory result than another, some designs must be better than others. This book is about computer applications, the particular ways software can be put together and how it can be made better.

3

1.1   Design

What is a Designer?

The term 'designer' has become a devalued phrase often connected with over-priced goods and exclusive labels. Everything man-made is designed by somebody and the process is the same whether you are known or unknown. In the earlier part of the twentieth century the term 'designer' stood for something a bit more honourable. At that time a designer was somebody with new, modern ideas who was intent on making better products more economically.

The process of design is a series of decisions. The position of an object, the use of a technique, color, style, material; all must be chosen. We are all designers in one way or another. Setting out the objects on a desk requires small decisions. Planning the order of a day's activity involves making choices. The result of making these kinds of decisions is a plan or a design. However, a distinction should be made between designing for ourselves and designing for other people. Designing for other people involves responsibility; a responsibility to understand the needs of the person and to provide the best solution. If you are making a decision for another person, it has to be the choice that is best for them.

What is Applications Design?

The computer is a general-purpose machine. It is designed to read a list of instructions and carry them out. This is useful because a lot of activities fit into a procedure where one task is carried out after another. If an activity can be defined as a series of small tasks, computer technology can be applied to it. So an 'application' in this sense is an activity that has been computerized. Application software defines the instructions needed to achieve this.

An applications designer is the person who creates the software that defines the computer form of an activity. The designers of an application can decide what it will do and how it will do it. The scheme they produce will dictate how well the application does what it does.

1.2   Why Design is Important

The design of the chair you are sitting in determines whether you are comfortable or not. Perhaps you are not sitting to read this. It is the design of your environment that rules whether there is a seat for you. The design of this page, the characters on it and the way these words are put together, decides whether you will find them easy to read and understand. Design is in every part of the physical world and has a profound effect on the lives of people.

A designer is making decisions on behalf of other people. Therefore design is a form of government. Designers may feel their work has little significance in the world as a whole. But if it is intended for other people to use, it will be a part of their lives.

Attitudes to Design

Most people believe they are good designers even if they would never call themselves one. People know what they like and they know when something is designed poorly. It can be said that the design ability is a characteristic of the human race, as language and intelligence are. This can result in design issues causing conflicts, where one person's opinion doesn't match anothers. A forceful personality can dominate the design process. But who is to say that one opinion is more valid than another? The design process should be a democratic one, where all opinions of merit are heard.

As everyone uses their own design skills from time to time, design is not a skill they value highly in other people. Perhaps they feel that design is an instinct, not a skill that can be learned. This attitude often leads to complacency in the design of new products. Rather than seek professional help, the work is given to somebody who isn't busy. In this climate, it is not surprising if the designer who possesses a formal design training is the exception rather than the rule. While we can all be designers, design is not an instinct but a learned skill and as such can be improved by training.

How Computers Affect Lives

The computer is arguably Man's greatest key technology. New applications for this machine are being created daily. The remarkable thing about a computer is not what it does, but the number of things it can do it to. Will there be a single aspect of life that remains unaltered by computers?

Did the inventors of computers ever think about the changes to life that their creations would make? If they did, they probably hoped that the computer would enhance life, taking the drudgery out of everyday tasks. It seems now that the computer is reshaping, rather than enhancing, creating new things to do, making old things irrelevant. Going to the library, shopping, watching a film and working are things that can now be done without leaving the house. The situation will gradually develop where more and more activities can be localized.

The spread of computer technology into everyday life can be a process that is painless or painful. To the majority of people, computers are still new and they find them difficult and confusing to use. Far from making life easier, for these people, computers make life harder and consequently they resist using them. However, computers are no longer a side issue. People are getting less choice about whether they use a computer or not. Customers expect to have 'information at their fingertips'; they expect letters with no spelling mistakes and all the other advantages that computers can bring. So if people have to use a computer, the way it works has a direct impact on the quality of their lives.

Some people believe there are dark commercial forces at work, who will force everyone to use technologies they create. No one is forced to use a car, a television or a telephone, yet these things play an important part in modern life. If these technologies were as inaccessible as some computer software, life would be much harder than it already is.

1.3   Technology in Perspective

Everyday Systems

Everyday life involves moving from one procedure to another. We go to the bank, to the supermarket, the restaurant and at each place encounter a new system: queue here, pick this up there, go to counter three and fill in the right form. The users of these systems are assumed to have an understanding of them.

When somebody knows how the system works they have no trouble, but when the system is new to them, they can easily make mistakes and the result is that they are unable to finish what they set out to do. Some systems are easier to learn and use than others. This depends on the person designing the system.

Consider different types of restaurant. Some you go in and sit down where you like; others you wait to be shown where to sit. Fast food restaurants use a different system: you get your food then look for somewhere to sit. Each new restaurant that you try means learning a new system.

There are ways of helping people new to a system: instruction leaflets, notices, attendants and information clerks. People often learn a new system in the company of more experienced people, such as going to a new restaurant with someone who has been before.

What We Can Learn from Old Technology

A man walks into his office one morning. He has a shiny black eye. His colleague asks him if he walked into a door and the man says, 'Yes, I did, actually.' The excuse may be an old one but it is still plausible. People accidentally walk into doors every day.

Doors have been around for thousands of years. They are one of our oldest technologies and yet they still cause us problems. Doors still stick; they still slam in the wind; they open differently to the way you expect them to open; people get locked in and shut out; fingers get trapped; locks jam; bolts freeze and hinges squeak. If we cannot get this basic technology right, what chance do we have with computer software?

To answer that, let's look at a technology that has only been around for about a century – automobile technology. Considering how complex a machine an automobile is and how inefficient, it is remarkable how well the technology works. Providing it is well maintained, a car will transport a person from one place to another, at any time of day. It would be interesting to look at the dramatic effect car technology has had on the world. However, the relevant point is that anyone can use this technology with a little training. Once trained to operate one car, a person can operate any of a whole range of cars. If we transported a driver forward in time, from 1910 to the present day, that driver would have little problem adapting to a modern car. Many of the basic controls would be familiar.

This is where the design of the car differs from computer software. In a car, the complexity of the technology is concealed from the driver. To drive the car and get wherever desired, all the driver has to deal with is a standard set of controls. Compare this to computer software. Each new application introduces a new bag of technology; new concepts; new ways of doing things; new controls, each needing to be learned by the user.

Today's software designers tend to focus too tightly on technology. The technology is shown off like a chromed engine block and exhaust pipes, rather than hidden under the bodywork. Perhaps the development of technology is considered to be progress, but in truth, it is improvements in design that create progress and it is technology that enables improvements in design.

With the possible exception of computer games for young children, new software is getting more difficult to use when perhaps it should be getting easier. With each new facility that becomes standard, an extra layer of concepts is introduced, an extra layer of complexity added.

It is easy to see where this trend toward complexity will lead. There is already a technical elite responsible for creating applications. The current trend must lead to the birth of another group; a class of specialist users skilled at using the applications.

1.4   The Designer's Responsibility

Modern life grows complex, and one cause is technology. By considering the way things can be done, a designer can harness technology and make a positive impact on people's lives. Computer software is in control of much of the world's technology, so it is with software design that much of the responsibility to improve life must lie. Currently the trend in computer applications is to make systems that are more complex and require more knowledge to use. Designers have a choice, they can continue on this path or they can make applications easier to use.

Where there are cars, there are roads, and where there is software, there is design. Just as roads dictate where you can drive, the software designer dictates how a user will run a software product. The software equivalent of the traffic jam, exhaust pollution and the motor way pile-up are, no doubt, all challenges to be overcome. One by-product of the increased number of computers in our lives is the increased need for software authors and designers. The tools needed to write software are now commonly available, but the skills required to design it are not.

2

How to Start
the Design

The nearest equivalent to product design is planning a
long journey. You can, after all, just pick up your
passport, pack your credit card and walk out into the night.
This romantic vision probably wouldn't be something to
contemplate with your children in tow. So let's assume that
you have the responsibility of planning a trip.

Many routes will work, some will be quicker, some will be
cheaper. Some routes use well-trodden paths; some are over
uncharted terrain. Some journeys may make it clearer how
to get to other places in the future. Some routes can be
chosen that are independent of each other, but use linking
transport.

If the design process is a journey, it is not a journey through
an empty landscape. This chapter looks at where the design
will fit into the world.

2.1   How the Outside World Affects Design

If a planned software application has a commercial value, then project cost control has to be considered. This implies measurable progress towards a set of measurable goals. The revenues from sales of a product are expected to exceed its production cost.

If a product is to be released onto a mass market, then its stability is all important: once it is released it is too late to fix any bugs. This requires a program designed with a stable base that can be carefully extended with continuous testing. Program bugs appear roughly in proportion to the speed of development.

With these considerations, it can be seen that software production is much like farming. Although the business projections are straightforward, at the end of the day you are working at the pace the animals are happy with.

So before the design process proper kicks off, make sure you are aware of how the product that comes from that process will be used. Below is a closer look at some typical product aims, and the design aspects associated with them.

Mass Market and Profit

Software applications are sold like other consumer products. For a product to be as profitable as possible, it needs to be completed within budget, and respond to any important user demands that may emerge during production. The design needs to allow for many people to work on different areas at the same time, and take advantage of pre-written code. This implies a modular approach with the design concentrating on making the modules hang together.

Mass Market Cornerstone

The market for software is immature. Consumers need introducing to the new ideas that software brings. The cornerstone tag applies to most initial commercial products. If a company hopes to thrive with a new piece of software, it has to establish the market. It is important that the product is trustworthy and stable; thus effort focuses on the bug testing 'beta' cycle. The design must incorporate a stable base with gentle evolution. It isn't quite so important that the first release is exactly what users want, as long as the product is sound and shows off its unique selling point.

Internal Productivity Tool

Many large institutions write their own applications specific to their business. Software that isn't intended for the mass market does not need to be quite so user friendly. It can afford to use the jargon associated with the user's business as seminars and in-house training can help users get to know the product better. It is important to respond quickly to the needs of the users, who define the parameters of the application's usefulness.

Fixed Installation

Some software is included as an integral part of a system. Software associated with bank cash machines, vending machines and other hardware such as video tape recorders is not specifically chosen by the user. Neither is it competing directly with other products. This category also includes one-off systems for controlling plant, perhaps a power station for example. Software that is intended to work on a single type of machine, that the user is not in control of, has a massive advantage for the designer: if it works on one machine it works on all machines. It may be that software is written for literally one single installation.

2.2　Finding Out About Standards and Using Them

A standard is usually a specification laid down by either a company, a group of companies, or a standards organisation such as the International Standards Organisation (ISO). The purpose of a standard is to allow third parties to produce products that work with existing products. Not all standards begin life in the same way. Standards are sometimes published in the deliberate desire to create a market, as in the case of video recorders, CD players and anything that requires interchangeable media. Sometimes standards evolve by accident. One company gives their product the ability to use the data files of another company's product. Other companies' products follow that lead and the file format becomes a standard.

Slightly different from standards are conventions. A convention is not as formal as a standard. There may never be a published specification but it becomes accepted practice to include certain items or do something a certain way.

A commercial product may need to fit into a niche where a standard prevails. It is astounding how many programs end up being out of date as soon as they are released, simply because the designer thought that a certain idea wasn't going to catch on, or was too hard to implement.

The fastest moving market fads are normally those 'on the edge' of technology, such as PC applications and games. When the market for word processors was being fought over, the main weapon of the large companies was to expand the definition of what a word processor is. They did this by including a spelling checker and thesaurus. This has now become the convention.

How do conventions develop? Conventions evolve over time. A new application introduces a new technique or idea. Other developers borrow the idea. Users then begin to expect the idea to be implemented in all the new software they buy. And before you know it, there is a convention. If a convention is formally recognised by all developers it becomes a standard.

The number of hardware standards and conventions that must be handled is proportional to the range of hardware your application supports during its expected lifetime. The current standards must be supported as well as any that may be coming up. The designer must be constantly on the look out for ideas that have become conventions and ensure that they are included in their design.

It may be misleading to say the designer must always look to support future trends. This implies that only state-of-the-art equipment needs to be supported. The percentage of the target audience using such equipment may be small. Writing applications for the lucky few, with top of the range mega-fast machines, is a bit like designing clothes for super models when most of your clients are overweight.

The target machine is the machine the application is to run on. It is important to know what speed the processor of this machine is running at, and if or when it may be upgraded. Display screens support various video standards, so it is best to know what the current supportable resolutions are, or what video cards are commonly available for your target machine. Communications and modems are dependent on the speed of data transfer. Again, you need to know what the current and future rates are if you are developing an application that talks to other computers. There is a large range of printing devices that support a varying number of fonts. And again it is important to know what developments are taking place in printer technology. The usual way to find out about these standards is through the trade and specialist magazines that are commonly available.

If you are writing for an Application Program Interface (API), then you don't need to worry about this. Your work is translated via drivers that support an individual user's hardware. However, there is now another problem: you are no longer in control of exactly how the application appears.

2.3 Design in Focus

The design process is about making decisions and choices between alternatives. It is important to step back occasionally and take an objective look at what is happening. This enables the designer to see the decisions that must be made, see the context in which the design is being developed, and recognize the stages that the process has reached.

The Design Process Recognized

In the development of every computer application there is a watershed. This is the point at which work is begun on material that will end up in the final product. It divides development into two parts: before work begins and after work has started. This point can be reached two minutes after the idea of the application was first thought of, or two years.

There are a few stages to go through before the watershed is reached. The first stage is research. Research is the expansion of the designer's knowledge and experience, principally in the area of all computer applications but also about the intended application specifically.

Concept is the first important stage of a design, the point where the goal is set; the ultimate objective; the final destination of the journey. It may come before, during, or after the research stage. The basic concept behind an application can be lost or changed during development. This always leads to a poor result. If a team is involved in the design, the concept must be clear to all. This may involve discussion or writing the concept down clearly. If different people have different ideas about the concept, the project will travel in different directions.

Hot on the heels of the concept stage comes the visualization stage. Work done at this stage is often used as the basis for judgement of both project and designer, although it may not be as important as most people think. Visualization is the process of creating an image of something that does not yet exist, in this case a piece of software. The image may be only in the programmer's mind; it may be a sketch on the back of an envelope, a two-hundred-page document or a non-functional mock-up. However, a picture of the final product must exist somewhere and, again where a team is involved, it is helpful if it can be examined and discussed. An architect draws plans; a car designer builds a model. Applications designers draw a few squares on a piece of paper and say, 'trust me, I know what I'm doing.' The most important aspect of the visualization stage is the communication of ideas. Chapter 3 in this section deals with visualization in more detail.

Finally, before work commences, there is a stage of assembling tools and materials. Most developers have the basic tools they will need, but do they have the specialist ones that take the hard labour out of the job? Of course this stage may happen after work commences – but that isn't design.

Beyond the watershed there are two more stages. The first is development. A certain amount of design is always done in development. There are minor decisions to be made whenever a piece of code is written. These may be due to unforeseen problems or because something was too insignificant to be part of the visualization. It is easy to fall into the trap that visualization is the end of the design job; a lot of design is done during development.

The last stage of design is the evaluation of the finished product. There are some things that just cannot be visualized, some problems that cannot be foreseen. Designers are not gods; they cannot predict every eventuality. The only way to view the design of some things is with hindsight. Sadly, this rarely happens before the release of a product and post-development evaluation is often done in response to the user's complaints.

Go Your Own Way or Follow the Crowd?

If a product exists that has an established way of doing something, some-body will always make a product that does it differently. There are various reasons for this: some good, some bad. A reason that is understandable but sad is the copyright issue. An application is designed to be different so that it does not infringe the copyright of another product. This is change for the sake of change and not change for the sake of improvement. Good ideas may be lost and the user, moving from one piece of software to another, will be confused by the inconsistencies. It is right that people should have their good ideas protected, but such protection can create distortions, forcing development along routes that are not in the user's best interests. How far would the car industry progress if General Motors purposely avoided using the same control layout as Ford? Despite the fierce warnings and carefully worded small print on many products, companies are often less protective of their ideas than they seem. An appli-cation designer wanting to use another company's concept in their own design should try contacting them. Who knows what they will say? The company may be willing to make a licensing deal or allow use with an acknowledgement.

A better reason for doing something differently is to fix a problem. Computer software is an evolving thing. There will always be a better way of doing something. On the other hand, who is to say what is better. A designer must be sure that a change is definitely for the better before implementing it. In the evolving software world, designers want to make their mark, they want to do something new, pushing back the frontiers a little. This sometimes leads them to reject an established technique simply because it is established. These people reject ideas because they are 'not invented here.' It is worth noting in passing that many designers are icon-oclastic. This may or may not make them good designers.

There is merit in doing the existing thing but doing it better. Better may mean faster, it may mean doing it in a clearer way or with more facilities. The original product may be flawed; it may have a glaring design fault that is easily fixed with a more modern interface. Certainly in the games industry there have been many examples of products that do not techni-cally improve on previous games, but are tuned for a wider audience. Good examples are the console games: Super Mario and Sonic the Hedgehog. Although many more advanced and innovative products were available, when these games came out, Sonic and Mario were more 'playable' due to well-thought-out design being applied to existing tech-niques.

Future Proofing Your Design

Designing software for easy maintenance

It is fairly safe to assume that a new piece of software will not be the last word spoken on that application. There will always be new developments and new platforms that will change the demands of the user. Designers must expect modifications to be made to an application in the future. To this end, the designer must anticipate – not the changes themselves – but the way the changes may be achieved.

The usual reason to update an existing design is to rewrite the interface, probably because it wasn't well thought out in the first place, or the intended use has been expanded, or the application is running in a new operating environment. It may originally have run on a mainframe computer but now must run on a personal computer, for example.

When the time comes to update the application there are two possibili-ties: the first is that the design will be extended using the core routines of the original code. The second is that the new program will be written from scratch, but will work in a similar way, or be compatible with the original.

Extending the original program from existing code will depend on the structure. If the original code was not written with this in mind, it may be almost impossible to separate the useful code from the redundant. If this is to be done successfully the original must use a modular system. It is common to use 'drivers.' These are programs that form a bridge between an application and the hardware it runs on. If the hardware is changed, new drivers can replace the old without having to change the original application. This can save time and prevent the introduction of bugs.

The design must go beyond the use of external drivers and have an internal structure that also reflects possible developments. This may mean breaking down the design into functions that could work independently of each other.

Here is an example: a word processor has a few basic functions: text input, text display, text editing, text formatting, printing, spell checking and perhaps a mail-merge facility. Out of these functions a few are constant: text input and text editing for example. The others may change as user requirements mature and devices such as high-definition screen displays and laser printers become more commonplace. By writing each function as a separate module, all working with common data, it is easy to upgrade a function without causing disruption to the whole program. It also allows third-party technology to be used. In this case the word processor might be upgraded to use True Type fonts or Postscript printing commands.

2.4   Spontaneous Programming

It cannot be denied that programming is a creative activity and sometimes the programmer has the need to 'just write something.' You may expect a book about design to insist on a thorough specification before you touch a keyboard. Indeed the bigger the project and the more people involved, the truer this is. However, it is not always necessary or desirable to have a full design worked out before code is written.

For a small group, getting started on the code before a formal design is complete, is unlikely to be the budget disaster that it would be for a large team. The enthusiasm generated by a small team – given creative freedom – can accelerate the speed of development, so motivation can be one reason for 'getting stuck in.' Time lost by reversing bad decisions may not be so great.

Formal designs can stifle creativity, preventing the best solutions to problems springing out of development. If an application contains a problem area it can often be beneficial to give a programmer the freedom to tackle the problem head on. It is not always possible to tell that an application has a problem area until work begins. Producing an early prototype can highlight any problems. It can also help define the vague ideas that are inevitable in the early stages of the design process.

Much of development goes into techniques rather than working code. Spontaneous programming allows techniques to be tried and developed. It also allows ambitious ideas to be tested for feasibility before inclusion in the main design.

Some strategies are not flexible. If the plan is to create a program in modules, each handled by separate programmers, then the methods of communication must be kept, otherwise the whole exercise is sunk.

Prototyping and building models is a tool common in other design disciplines. However, it hasn't found much favor in applications development. The software industry is the only place where you might expect to find the mistakes made on day one carried through to the final product.

2.5 Evaluation

Involving the users in the development process

Continual evaluation is an important part of the development process. There are three groups that should have the biggest say in the process of evaluating an application: the people who will have to produce it, the people who will have to use it and the people who hold the purse strings of development. Each group has their own requirements from the project and their evaluation should be confined to those areas. The development team should be evaluating the design to ensure that it is feasible technically; the users to ensure that it is what they want and works as they would expect it to. The purse-string holders should be evaluating the design to ensure it can be produced on time and on budget and that there is a need to produce it in the first place.

User evaluation is perhaps the most difficult part of the project's evaluation. This is because users are removed from the area of development, there is no routine communication with them and, when the developers do talk to them, the users may not be able to properly express either their criticisms or their requirements. Also the user is unlikely to be aware of the possibilities the computer offers. It is therefore up to the developers to actively seek the users feedback during the design and development process.

The developer should ask a potential user – someone outside the immediate development team – to try out the application at every stage where there is something of value to be learned. When there is something up and running, the best way of proceeding is to allow the user to try out the application without any help. If the designer observes the user they can quickly get an idea of where the application is confusing, where other problems occur and, importantly, how the user operates the program. Clearly, the value of this process will depend on the computer experience of the user and what they expect from the program, so it is best to try this with a range of people of differing skill levels.

A useful technique in evaluation is to video-tape the output from the computer or log it in some other way. This provides useful reference for the developer – they can see where the user hesitated, made mistakes, or stopped to make comments. The guinea pig may make a mistake only once. That has to be treated as a valuable piece of information vital to the development team. If the error is recorded, it isn't lost or overlooked. A video tape can also be viewed when asking the user later what they were thinking, or expecting, at a particular point while using the program.

In the games industry it is common for developers to employ games testers. These are usually young men with a passion and aptitude for playing games. It is their responsibility to find bugs in games and to test them from start to finish, ensuring that the games are completable. The ideal bug tester can never be found. The inexperienced tester can provide useful feedback about what is confusing or unclear about a game, but they often cannot express this in terms that the programmers find useful. The experienced bug tester has learnt how to communicate and to recognize what is a bug, but by the time they are able to do this, they know so much about games, they don't make the mistakes a novice would. This is the same for applications development in general. A continuous supply of uncontaminated guinea pigs is needed for testing.

What is alpha and beta testing?

It is now common practise for applications developers to release early versions of a program to a limited number of users for trials. Different companies use different terminology but this is usually called 'alpha' and 'beta' testing. The alpha test provides the user group with the opportunity to provide suggestions or 'wish lists.' These may or may not be incorporated into the final or 'beta' version. The beta test allows the program to be tested by the closed user group before its final release. The hope is that they will report any bugs before they appear in the published version.

Evaluation in software development is more advanced and formalized than it has ever been. However, it doesn't yet approach the same level as that used by the film industry or washing powder companies. While software remains as complex as it is, it would be difficult to take the same research approach as other consumer product industries.

2.6 Designing within the Project Environment

Design is no longer the sole product of a single designer. The design process is merely one part of a project. 'The design' now appears, in fact, to be something abstracted from 'the project.' In truth, design is likely to be done by committee because there is too much at stake: the product must satisfy the trends of the marketing men, the budget of management, the concerns of the technical support team as well as the wanderlust of the programmers.

Most projects that go wrong start to go wrong from day one. Usually it is because there is a misunderstanding about the direction the project should be going in, caused by a lack of communication between those involved. This can result in much of the design process revolving around a basic flaw within the project. It is important that the original vision of the program is maintained throughout development so that side issues and red herrings do not obscure the basic design.

3

Tools For the Job

Software development is still in its infancy, and is still one of the few creative processes where the outcome is not apparent once the input is finished. The need to compile source code – i.e. turn computer instructions into something that can be 'run' – is perhaps the equivalent of forcing a literary author to write in a foreign language they are not fluent in and later re-translating the text, producing the final work.

There is an increasing number of tools that allow the developer to directly design a program's interface, but very few that do anything to help produce the internal mechanics.

3.1   The Development Platform

In the general case, an application will need to run on one or several target machines or platforms. The term 'platform' is a term for a basic system of a particular type. Of course, the target platform and the development platform may be the same, as is often the case for a PC application.

The target platform can be viewed as a machine with a processor and an operating system. The application is software that works through the operating system, manipulating the processor and making it do something. The target system usually has output and input devices that can be used to create an interface.

The development platform also has a processor, an operating system and various input and output devices, but their main use is to help facilitate development of the application. It is quite common that the development system itself may be under development, which is a reminder that the software industry is still just a shiny sand-castle.

When designing for a well-established platform, the programmer may have a large amount of existing or 'legacy' code that can be used for the new application. Experimentation should also be easier. When using an unstable or untested development platform, the bulk of the work must be on simple code with a known outcome, as experimentation is risky when errors may come from the code or from the platform.

3.2   Development Tools

Software Development Kit

A Software Development Kit (SDK) is usually designed by hardware manufacturers or operating system producers to enable a program to make direct use of facilities. Within the kit is likely to be an Application Program Interface (API). This is a library of pre-built routines that help the programmer by providing some of the standard functions. The programmer can expect to find either code that is directly usable – and can be accessed by the program – or example code which can be copied and customized to the required purpose.

There may be a specialized language, or functions may be built around an existing language such as 'C' or 'C++.' The kit may provide tools for editing and debugging such languages – although this is rare. Usually the best that can be expected is a utility program to convert data from an existing tool, to data that can be used by the system.

Although an SDK can be invaluable to the programmer learning a new system, invariably the kit falls short of expectations. Much time and effort can go into getting examples to work properly. It seems to be one of Murphy's Laws that any library routine provided works in a way alien to any practice the programmer has met before. Also library routines rarely cover the ground you hope they will, leaving one or two major problems to be solved. And usually the reason for the function's omission is that the SDK's developers didn't know how to do it either.

Low Level

At the heart of every computer is a microprocessor. This chip understands a limited set of primitive instructions known as machine code. Programs in machine code can be created with a software tool called an assembler. Assembly language is referred to as a low-level language because it comes at the bottom of a hierarchy of language levels. Compilers for other languages are written in assembly language. So it doesn't matter what computer language is used to create a program; at the lowest level the processor is executing machine code. Does it then matter what language is used to create an application?

A program may be written solely in a higher level language – like 'C' or BASIC – solely in machine code or in a hybrid combination of the two. The designer must decide what parts – if any – of the application need to be written in a low-level language. The factors that will influence this decision are these:

- The size of the code created.
- The speed of the code created.
- The time taken in developing the code.
- Any requirements to alter the code in the future.
- The ability of the tools available to produce the required result.

Let us look at these factors in more detail. First, the size of the code created. An application has to fit into the memory capacity of the machine it runs on. Also, some media are restricted in storage space such as: games cartridges; 'smart-cards' and internal firmware that must fit the capacity of a chip. Assembler written code is minimalist, containing only the code essential to the application. The output of a high-level language compiler, however, may contain code for commands supported by the language but

Choosing the appropriate development language

Which programming language? Factors that affect the decision

not used by the application. Therefore if code size is an issue, assembler should be the chosen development language.

Manipulating or searching large amounts of data, doing complex arithmetic calculations, handling input and output in real time and animating graphics, all require a large chunk of the processor's capacity. If the processor cannot keep up with demand the result will be delays, pauses and slow screen displays, all characteristic of heavy processor use. Some languages produce faster programs than others. 'C' compilers are generally accepted as producing code that executes quicker than – for example – equivalent BASIC code.

Higher-level languages do not produce as efficient code as assemblers can, but they have other advantages. In comparison, high level-languages are easier to learn and use than assembler which requires specialist, experienced, programmers. It is much faster to develop an application in a high-level language; many standard functions can be accessed with a single command. In assembly language, equivalent functions would need several pages of code, plus the knowledge to write it. Writing a program to achieve a simple task in assembler can take a long time.

At one time all arcade style computer games were written in assembler to gain the advantages of speed and space efficiency. As processor speeds have quickened, it has become possible for games developers to use fast high-level languages like 'C'. The majority of today's games are either written entirely in assembler, or in 'C' with assembler routines to produce fast graphic displays.

The trend in games is toward ever more realistic three-dimensional graphics. Code to produce this type of graphics is not easy to write in assembler. This is because the geometry calculations, needed to make the image, require the use of floating point arithmetic. In assembler it is easy to use integer math but floating point is difficult. There are techniques for getting around this problem but they are cumbersome compared to using the mathematical functions of 'C'.

Faster processors have allowed games developers to use off the shelf 'C' language libraries to generate their graphics. Games – like other applications – are getting more complex to develop. The code for a game used to be the work of a single programmer but now a game is more likely to be a combination of several people's work. In that environment, the economic cost of developing in assembler will eventually get too large and it will cease to be the main tool for games development.

The primitive instructions of assembly language do not produce code that is 'readable.' That is to say, a programmer returning to a piece of code, previously written – perhaps by another programmer – will find difficulty in immediately grasping the true function of the code. This is less of a problem in high-level languages where much of the code is written in English statements and easily followed structures. For this reason, it is easier to 'maintain' – adapt or debug – high-level language code than assembler. This reason, above all others, is the major advantage of higher-level language development.

Application Generators

An option for some designers is to use an application generator. These are similar to programming languages but contain facilities to create specific applications. BASIC and 'C' may contain commands that allow file handling and searching to be done. However, a lot of programming skill is still required to create a database application from either of these languages. A database application generator provides everything that is needed to build a database program from just a few commands. There are many generators available: from the creation of multimedia presentations to integrated business systems and indeed games.

Figure 1
Europress Software's
Klik'n'Play. An
application
generator for
producing games

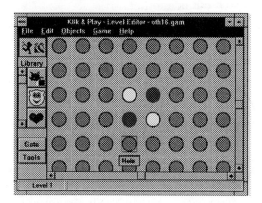

Further Development Tools

There are a large number of tools associated with software development, apart from the code generator and code maintenance tools.

(i) Painting and drawing tools

Tools for editing icons and bitmaps are gaining more and more importance as graphic interfaces advance. Three useful functions of a paint package are: editing bitmaps at a pixel level, resizing a bitmap and manipulating the color palette.

(ii) Word-processing tools

The code itself is text, though the code generator may come with its own special editor that can work with the program language's syntax. Any text that appears in the application along with documentation and some type of data, can be generated with this tool.

(iii) Transfer and compression tools

These tools enable code to be moved around, to other programmers or other locations.

Programs that are available via an electronic forum or the Internet are usually compressed to save downloading time. Bitmaps and other graphic data may be compressed to save storage space.

(iv) File format conversion tools

Tools don't often do everything you need. So different tools have to be used for different tasks. This causes problems when the tools save data in different file formats. A conversion tool may take in data in one format and save it out in another.

(v) Custom built tools

It is sometimes necessary to write a custom built tool to create data for an application. Another reason might be to convert or automatically edit data from one format to another.

Prototyping

An important stage in the design of a new building is the point at which the architect's plan is used to create a model. With a model, two things can be achieved. The first is that the architect can see the design in the context of the surrounding buildings or landscape. The second is that the design is turned into a form that is readable by people unable to read architectural plans.

Software prototyping can achieve the same two things. A prototype can be used to test the design, try out techniques and refine the interface. The other aspect is that it can be shown to the users for approval at an early stage and amended if necessary.

A prototype should be quick and cheap to develop. It is becoming a common practice to build prototypes of Windows applications in Visual

BASIC before moving to costly development in 'C' or 'C++'. The prototype does not have to be well written or built to carry a full load of data. It merely needs to demonstrate how the application functions and highlight areas of weakness in the design. Performance and cosmetic presentation are not an issue with a prototype. Wherever possible, library routines and previously existing code should be used.

The faster a prototype is developed, the less impressive it has to be. The people it is shown to - users or managers - will not expect a finished product in so little time. In other branches of design, it is considered a bad idea to present something finished looking to a client, when showing it for the first time. This is because the client feels that they have had no say in the design and that it has been presented as a fait accompli. If it is true to say that a quickly developed protoype does not need to be impressive, then the inverse is also true. Something that has taken a long time to produce will produce a negative impression if rough and unfinished in appearance.

One negative aspect of prototyping software is that because it exists and can be demonstrated, managers may think development is further advanced than it really is.

Even if no prototype is produced, a similar problem occurs: software departments are pressed to demonstrate programs during development. Code written hurriedly, cobbled together for a demo, is often badly written. Allowing insufficient time to replace this code, before preparing for the next demo, is one way to guarantee a poor application.

3.3   Finding and Using Tools

Tools themselves are normally small self-contained programs that are not too hard to write for small teams or even single programmers. As a result there will be an increasing number available but this, in turn, will make them more difficult to find. What tools to use and what tools to develop are questions that should be based on what tools are already out there, waiting to be picked up. The result of insufficient research is re-inventing the wheel.

Tools are also beginning to decrease specialization. Just as man developed into a tool user, developers must be ready to use any tool at hand rather than sticking to just one tried and tested favourite. The cost of this multiplicity of tools, however, is lack of compatibility. It may occasionally be necessary to use a third tool to bridge the gap between data produced by two others.

4

The Design Specification

There are many things that are set down on paper only as proof of their own existence. In theory, by the time you have written a design specification everybody involved already understands what will happen next. Everyone not involved will just leave it to you anyway.

Nevertheless, a complete specification is the only formal expression of a design and provides a lighthouse from which you can later steer by. It can also form the basis of a defence when things go wrong.

The first stage of
the design
specification

4.1   Technical Brief

Before a full specification is written, a short brief or 'Tech Spec.' needs to be compiled that outlines what is to be done. Large amounts of the process are likely to remain fluid, which is why it is important to define the containment areas: things that don't change and impose limits. This brief is the equivalent of the one page synopsis that an author may give to a publisher, or the 'treatment' used to summarize a storyline in the film industry. The job of the brief is as much to say what will not be done as much as what is being attempted. The brief may also be presented to new or contract programmers to help them decide schedules.

Involving the
users in the
design process

4.2   Starting Dialogue

A commercial product can either be design led or market led. For a market led product, the early dialogue must start with the users, or a controlled group of users.

A design led product introduces new ideas that break the mold in some way, beyond the user's expectations.

Think about the fast food industry. Did it come about because a large number of people said they were looking for a place they could buy prepared food to walk away with? Or did it come about because companies such as McDonalds thought that people were looking for such an outlet?

Technical dialogue starts when a brief first appears. It is fairly important to keep a Chinese wall between market/design issues and program/development issues.

It is in the nature of a good programmer to make suggestions that reduce his or her load. These are necessary, but can wreck a design if they are aired too early on. Similarly, non-programmers tend to have little idea of the time needed to add 'just one more small feature' and this attitude can ruin deadlines.

To create useful feedback on a design, you have to allow people to talk freely about what they would like to see. Electronic forums such as those found on Compuserve or Delphi are excellent places for these discussions. They allow any members of the team to comment at any time no matter where they are. They encourage sensible discussion due to the ability to read past points and build on them. Also the written discussion can be used as reference in future. Time often dims the reasoning behind some decision made. It may be that some people are more open when they can type what they want in privacy, as opposed to face to face.

4.3   The Full Specification

Visualizing the Design

Before the development process starts it is necessary to create an image of the final product. For a programmer working on their own with no one to answer to, this may only need to be a mental picture, or a quick scrawl on the back of an envelope to act as a reminder. A designer with a group of skeptical users, or a boardroom, to persuade will need a more detailed and convincing image of what they have in mind. Most projects depend on the designer's ability to put across the output of their imagination to another person.

There is more than one way to express a software concept. Here are four methods to use:

Methods for presenting design ideas

- Write a description – (figure 2.1).
- Create a model or prototype software – (figure 2.2).
- Illustrate the design with a series of static screens – (figure 2.3).
- Produce an illustrated document – a cross between a flow chart and a comic book – (figure 2.4).

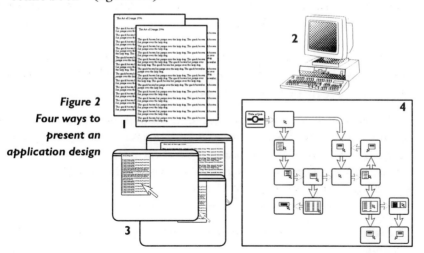

Figure 2
Four ways to present an application design

It probably does not matter which method is used, provided it expresses the concept clearly and in enough depth. However, some methods are more time consuming than others and for this reason it is best to limit each technique to the specific parts of the design where they are most useful.

**The second stage
of the design
specification**

Writing a Specification

Writing a specification is like producing any other piece of work; it must address the audience it is being written for. So the first question to ask is, for whose benefit is the specification being written? There are three possible audiences: the people who will be using the product, the people who will be developing the product and the people who are paying for the product to be developed.

There is little point in filling the specification with detailed technical issues if it is to be read by non-technical people. Likewise, the issues that interest the financiers of a project may not be relevant to the function of the application. Therefore it is wise to separate technical issues from other issues.

**How to structure a
design
specification**

How does the designer begin writing a specification? The best way of structuring a specification is to first provide a summary or short overview of the entire application. It should explain the function or what the program is intended to do for the user. The original brief can be used as reference for this. This section should be written plainly, cover the various functions and not assume too much technical knowledge from the reader. If any jargon has been invented to describe new concepts, these concepts should be described here. The overview is the introduction to the product. It exists so that anyone reading it will immediately grasp what the product is for and broadly how it is used.

The overview section can now be used as a skeleton on which to place the flesh of detailed description. The structure of the specification should reflect the structure of the application, so the description starts with the screen that the user sees on first loading the program. Each function is described in turn as if the software were being used. This forms a picture of the software that can be described as an 'interface specification.'

Of course not all the program is visible to the user. Various programming techniques and methods may need to be specified. It is best to keep this separate in a 'technical specification.' What the program does and how it does it are two different issues. If there is cause to change either the interface design or the technical design later on, those changes can be more easily achieved if only one area is examined at a time.

To summarize, the complete specification should have three main sections:

- Overview
- Detailed interface design
- Technical specification

In addition, any tables or conventions should be included in appendixes at the back. These may include a list of keyboard commands or specify the format of data files to be used by the program, for example.

Once complete, the specification can be referred to by the development team as they start to develop the application. Any changes or additions that arise out of the development process should be documented in the specification, so that it develops in parallel to the application. If this isn't done the specification will get out of date and lose both credibility and relevance – and therefore authority – as changes occur.

Completion of the Design Specification

At some point, the design dialogue will start to expand to areas that are best left to a further revision or release of the product. When this happens the design is probably ready.

The development cycle itself ends when there are insufficient problems being thrown up by testers to continue development. The design specification is complete when an initial model of the system has been shown to function properly in some basic state.

4.4   On Time, On Schedule

Software development is notorious for broken deadlines and slipping schedules. Why should this be the case?

The success of a software application usually depends on its being innovative. If new technology is being developed, who can say how long development will take? This is perhaps mitigation for some slips in schedule. However, much software uses well-tried technology and is still delivered late.

Certain factors affect the length of a project: the motivation of the developers; the pressure applied by management; the ability of the developers; and the problems encountered by them. Each will affect the day-to-day progress made.

The designers influence over the progress of a project

Designers have an important role to play during a project. They have a direct role in the difficulties encountered by the developers; poor design and lack of forethought will allow the developers to wander up blind alleys, spending time solving problems that should not have happened. The designer is also in a unique position to monitor progress. With close knowledge of the design, they can check that programmers are not drifting too far from the plan. It is in the nature of some programmers to spend extra time on the aspects of the program they are more interested in. This can lead to other parts being neglected and time being lost.

The designer also has influence over other factors. Poor design leadership and frequent changes in the direction of the project will demotivate the development team. It is difficult to labour enthusiastically on something if you know your hard work may be discarded at the whim of a designer.

A designer who is aware of the abilities of the development team can tailor the design to suit. Complicated but impressive techniques can be discarded in favour of simpler ones.

A factor that should be the responsibility of the designer is: how ambitious the design is. Most projects fail to meet their deadlines because the development team has underestimated the amount of work involved and over-estimated the speed at which it will be done. Designers can help prevent this situation by keeping their designs simple, monitoring progress and pointing out features that are non-essential and can be dropped from the schedule.

4.5   Specification and Design

While most companies have now defined for themselves exactly what a technical specification should entail, there hasn't been enough history of program development to verify what is right and wrong for a project of any given size. This inevitably leads to using the methods of incremental progress or repetition as the only safe route to a successful project. As man hours of projects increase, it will be more important that the technical specification refers to a control hierarchy – i.e. who is in charge of developing what code, and who is reliant on that code to work. This mirrors the way object oriented code is internally structured.

We have discussed the designer as communicator, and the designer as politician. In fact a good design team will have a mix of communicators, politicians, experienced developers as well as young enthusiasts. These skills may be spread out among many, or shared by a few individuals.

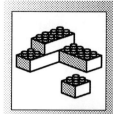

Section II

Designed to Use

Putting an application together is a bit like building a house or a car; various methods and techniques are used to make the different parts. The following chapters introduce some of the basic methods available to the application designer and outline the reasons why they might be used.

1

Computer Literate versus The Rest

We start by looking at the focus for interaction: the user. It is surprisingly simple to forget that a program is written for others to use. Before an interface can be designed for your application, consider who will use it. The program's audience can be defined as a set of users, whose profile we will examine in different ways.

1.1   Computer Literacy

Intuitive versus Hands-on

There is a pair of traits that any general audience can be split by: intuitive and 'hands-on.' Intuitive people build large abstract models or worlds in their minds which to them are as real as reality. Hands-on people are practical and prefer empirical knowledge. They don't truly understand anything until they have had their hands on it. The whole concept of programming is, of course, intuitive. Hands-on people are not necessarily wary of computers but put a premium on interaction with people and real things.

Graphical User Interfaces (GUIs) are developed with hands-on people in mind. Often when you find someone claiming the superiority of a Command Line Interface (CLI), you can bet that person is intuitive. For the intuitive audience, the very nature of computing is interesting and it can be beneficial to emphasize the computer nature of the application. The hands-on have no interest in the process by which they retrieve the information they need. More to the point, they may not be aware of it either.

Designing for different audiences

Analyzing User Needs

There is no argument for making applications generally usable – an application must be usable to those who need to use it! Let us imagine two applications and their respective audiences. The first is a simple data conversion tool written for a small group of colleagues. The second is a multimedia viewer – installed in an art museum – used to get background information on paintings being displayed.

Let us use two criteria upon which to examine these examples:

• Does the audience understand computing?
• Is the audience sympathetic to your application?

The first audience may already be used to using other productivity tools for their work and already using a range of software. This would imply that the developer of the interface should concentrate on efficient forms of input. As the audience will probably know the designer, they are able to appreciate that the application exists as a modifiable program. This means that feedback is possible and the program may be improved. Any errors that cause the program to crash can be reported back to those responsible.

The second audience needs to be resolved down to its lowest common denominator, as we are in no position to make assumptions about museum visitors with regard to software. We cannot assume the audience is computer literate, nor necessarily aware that they are using a program or even – in some cases – a computer. The interface needs to be transparent; a concept we will return to in chapter 5. There must be no reference at all to any computer related terms. The graphic style and presentation must be consistent with other areas of the exhibition.

Here are some further criteria to use on the intended audience:

- Will the audience be working with the application continuously, or just now and again?

- Will the audience be able to relate their previous experience to the application?

- Is the productivity of the user an issue?

What is Computer Literacy?

Computer literacy is a phrase that describes a user's personal knowledge of computing. The section of the population that has the highest level of computer literacy is the under thirties. Since the 1980s computers have been common in schools. This has given most children the opportunity to gain some computer experience. The total number of people who can use a computer is increasing but there is still a large body of people who know nothing about them.

There are many fundamental concepts that a person picks up on the way to being computer literate: for example, the concept that the computer holds information in its memory only as long as power is supplied to the machine; the concept that the machine cannot be 'broken' by pressing the wrong button. Without this basic knowledge, the uninitiated often cannot complete the task they are attempting on the computer. For example, software that requires typed input will only continue when the user presses the Enter key. The knowledge that the computer always needs this cue comes from experience. This is such a common function of applications, that designers do not feel it is necessary to remind the user to press Enter. The assumption is made that the user understands what they need to do. Perhaps another way of defining computer literacy is: the user's ability to fill in information not provided by the software.

Designers find it useful to be able to leave out some information and rely on the user's intelligence, intuition and experience to bridge the gap. This is perfectly acceptable where conventions and technical terms that are widely understood are used. To use an analogy; when writing to the bank manager it should not be necessary to include an explanation of what is meant by 'mortgage agreement.'

The designer can do a number of things to reduce the level of knowledge required to use an application. The obvious thing to do is provide step-by-step help to lead the user through. This is not always practical. Most applications are too complex to be handled this way. So broader measures are needed. The two basic things the designer can do are: restrict mistakes and provide information.

Restricting mistakes can be achieved by cutting down, disabling and concealing options from the user. For example, options in a word processor – to apply spell checking or text formatting – can be concealed until the user has typed in some text. This prevents the user from activating a function that has no data to work on and would therefore do nothing.

Providing information – the second measure – includes providing feedback to an action and offering help. Feedback lets the user know they have achieved something or that there is a result from their last action. It can be as simple as printing a message such as: 'your file has been saved,' or making a beep sound to indicate that a key has been pressed.

Offering help includes explaining: what to do, what is happening and why. Chapter 11 explains how to include help in an application.

Reduce the level of computer literacy required to use an application;

• By giving step-by-step guidance if possible.
• By preventing the user from making mistakes.
• By providing feedback.
• By providing explanation.

Designing for the First Time User

Every user is a first time user (or new user) when they begin using an application. How quickly they become familiar with the application, and reach the point where they are using the program productively, depends on: their computer-literacy, how closely the interface resembles something they are already familiar with and how easy the interface is to use. However, the application's designer can help the 'getting to grips' process along by including certain features.

Some programs include special help screens that appear when the program is first started. These sometimes appear only once and are then permanently disabled or, more likely, the user is offered the option of switching them off.

It is useful to remember that menu options and icons start off as closed doors to the new user. Until they open those doors they do not know what to expect. It is therefore useful to provide explanation before things happen rather than during. An example of this kind of help might be a status bar that displays the function of a button when the mouse pointer is moved over it.

For a new user, the function of an icon is concealed

The earlier points made about designing for less computer literate users apply to designing for first time users too. Both cases have to deal with the problem of bridging the gaps in the user's knowledge of the application. The important points from above are: allowing access to only the parts of the program that are of immediate use, and providing explanation. It is especially important to provide explanation for concepts that will be new to the user.

It should be possible to switch off any feature that is intended to specifically help a new user and which might irritate, or get in the way of, an experienced user. The interface for a first time user should be like scaffolding: a temporary structure.

An interface designed for the first time user should be a temporary structure

1.2 Using Metaphors

A metaphor is a representational model used to help define a task. In its literary sense, a metaphor helps the reader to see an object or situation in another light by use of apt alternative description. An interface uses a metaphor to lock the user into a predefined way of thinking that will help the user understand the task more readily.

What is a metaphor?

An Example Metaphor

It is possible in some computing environments to make simple calculations in the Command Line Interface (CLI):

```
>?15+4
>19
>?20*5
>100
```

where the question mark means 'print.' While this is straightforward, the user is given no guide to limitations, available functions, etc. In a GUI operating system, this simple facility is often given to the user via a pocket calculator metaphor. The user sees a simple calculator on screen, and can use the pointer to operate the buttons and thereby mimic the operation of a calculator.

Metaphors allow a benign illusion to be created. In the above case, the user accepts that they are now 'using' a 'pocket calculator.' This form of play acting guides the user and the application into actions and behaviour that are well controlled.

In the CLI, the outcome of:

```
>?20+5*4/6-2
```

will clearly depend on which operations take precedence; the user is given no indication of how the sum will be resolved. With the calculator metaphor however, the current value can be seen as the digits and operands are entered. This is a facet of any calculator:

Enter	Display reads:	
20	20	
+	20	
5	5	
×	25	
4	4	
÷	100	(So 25 x 4 has been resolved)
6	6	
–	16.666666	(So the result of 100/6 has been resolved)
2	2	
=	14.666666	

It would not be obvious – using a CLI – how to represent square root, raising to a power and any other function that hasn't a symbol on a keyboard. And even then, the CLI does not promise to respond.

The metaphor does depend on the user being familiar with a calculator and its symbols. And necessarily, the metaphor limits operations to those of the calculator it is representing. A metaphor usually steals a familiar interface from elsewhere, and it is important that it is an interface that is well understood.

Metaphor Considerations

In the previous example it would be foolish to create the calculator metaphor and then make the calculator operate in a non-standard way. It is important that if a metaphor is used it is maintained as completely as possible. For this reason it is essential to choose the right metaphor and to use it consistently.

How to choose a metaphor

When choosing a metaphor consider: is it universally understood; is it based on a concept that is common knowledge to the intended user; is it dependent on the user's knowledge of another technology or skills? For example, a metaphor based on 'ringing up the price' on an old cash register might not be understood by somebody who has only seen the modern equivalent. Is it ambiguous? Does it map well to the application? For example, a jukebox would not be a good metaphor applied to a music playing program that played one piece of music and then stopped. The jukebox metaphor implies the option to set up a multiple selection that plays one after another.

More Metaphor Examples

There are now many metaphors used in applications. Here are a few of the commonest ones based on everyday office items or equipment:

The file: probably the earliest and commonest computer metaphor. A file is a place to store data of a varying quantity. It can be stored and then retrieved later. A computer file can contain only one item and it must be of a certain type; something known only to the computer literate.

The desktop: representing an office desk. Many different tasks are performed on the same work surface. Documents are moved around and processed. Is this a real metaphor? Did anyone ever use the term 'desktop' before computers were common?

The notepad: a useful place to scribble notes for reference later. Most notepads don't disappear when their power supply is removed, or when something else is written over them.

The trashcan: a place to put unwanted documents and files for disposal. Discarded papers can be retrieved from the trashcan. This is not always the case with deleted computer files unless some special management is done. This confusion has led to the use of an incinerator metaphor as an alternative. The re-cycle symbol is sometimes used, which causes a similar problem.

The cardfile: a simple database modelled on a card index filing system.

And the Moral of the Story is...

When to use metaphors

Metaphors are ideal for non-computer literates, and are fine for others too. They help to define tasks that might otherwise be too diffuse or abstract;

however, the use of a metaphor can imply that the application works in a way that it does not, illustrated in the examples above.

Metaphors do not necessarily provide the most efficient way of using the application. Most interfaces can be seen as layers between the system and the user. When too many layers are applied, the application slows down and, as a by-product of growing complexity, more bugs can be produced.

1.3　Designing for the Expert User

Even those who know nothing about computers will become familiar with a program they use continuously. It is important that the designer considers what happens after an application has been used for a while. When a program is run for the first time, the interface must guide and help. Later, guidance may be redundant; getting in the way and slowing down the user. The designer must consider the needs of the person who has made the transition from first-time user to experienced user.

Expert User Myth

A useful trait for us is that we are all able to learn. Humans can learn a range of new skills – with a little effort – as long as they bear some relevance to their lives. With the exception of the video recorder, the abundance of technology around us is firmly under our control. Things that appear daunting at first soon lose their mystery with familiarity.

An average user may take a few days to be comfortable with an application that they may go on to use for years. Certainly trying to remember inappropriate keystrokes or meaningless icons won't help, and if nothing friendly appears then it is harder still to gain a foothold. Nevertheless, given time, people can get to use just about anything. So is it correct to spend a large amount of time honing an interface to work well with the first-time user? How long does a first-time user spend being a first-time user?

Once familiarity is gained, the fog lifts and most further functions become obvious or straightforward. Essentially, the user follows the same track as the designer intended. The learning process starts as an oscillation between panic and understanding that flattens out with time. The user does not come into a tunnel on one side as a 'beginner' and out the other as an 'expert.' When did you last see an ad for an expert car; how about a beginner's car? Once you have spent your time learning to use an automobile – and have passed a driving test – you are effectively an expert.

You are already using all the car's major functions. Did you require a beginner's telephone to make your first calls? Do you consider yourself now an expert telephonist?

Unless your application will only ever be dipped into by uncertain users, you must not write an interface for a transient species. An expert user is really a position at infinity that no one reaches, and the term means the user 'has stopped learning.' At this point, your application will have outlived its usefulness. You must help all newcomers to get to grips with your application, but the main thrust of interface design is to help a competent user get the most out of the program.

All users will gain a level of expertise with an application they use regularly

- Do not write an interface for 'the beginner,' as it is a temporary state.

- Make sure learning is easy, and that a competent user gets the most out of the program.

Even Experts Need Help

Something that designers forget is that some functions will be used only rarely, even by somebody using the program continuously. These functions may be very complex, performing a specific – but essential – task. Even an expert user would welcome additional help in using these features. An example of this would be: a secretary using a word processor. Although the secretary uses the application all the time – to write letters to individuals – when asked to send a flyer to all customers, additional help would be needed to use the mail-merge facility.

These extra features tend to be late additions in the development of the program. Often they are not implemented in a way consistent with the rest of the interface and are poorly documented in the manual. The irony is that the more complex the feature of the program, the less information is communicated.

1.4 Computer Parlance

Computing is full of jargon that makes it difficult for less computer literate users. Even when they are given information, they don't know what it means.

In some cases jargon is a necessary evil. Computing contains many concepts that have no direct worldly parallel. It is essential to be able to name and refer to these new concepts. It's good fun as well.

In some cases an often used word begins to lose its everyday meaning and thus no longer causes confusion. A good example is 'RAM.' This is an acronym for random access memory but the word random is a misnomer; nothing in a computer system operates randomly. However, the term RAM is now firmly understood as: transient memory, used to store running programs and their data and has transcended its acronym origin. As a concept holding word, these three letters do a lot of work. Other examples of this are: WIMP and GUI (pronounced 'gooey)'.

Computer parlance words can be split into three groups: (1) Terms that are only supposed to have meaning for the application. (2) Terms that are only supposed to have meaning in the computing environment running the program (3) Drift terms that are dangerous and are re-used in different applications. Here are some examples of each:

Example application specific terms:

Pane – a special type of window.

Polyline – graphic function.

Spike – temporarily store data.

Stacking – layering concept for graphic objects.

Scribblemode – special mode of operation

Computer environment terms:

File, Directory, Open, Close – Usually understood as operating system terms.

Space – Generalized to mean either 'hard disk' or 'memory'

Edit – Sometimes used to mean 'change, replace' or 'write.'

Window – Can mean buffer, viewport, frame, display and is interchangeable with all these.

Object – Because of object oriented programming, this word is heavily overworked. Within an application it often refers to user defined entities.

View – Can refer to the applications user preferences, or to a change in the way a physical model is represented.

Drift terms:

Display – could be a computer screen, an option to show information, or the output from an application.

Format – could be a process applied to disks, the layout of a document, a particular type of game or a game for a particular machine.

Paradigm – er, yes.

The designer should watch out for similar terms and ensure that their meanings are communicated through the program. If the application has a help system with an alphabetic index, application specific terms should be listed. Also listed should be any other terms that the user may not have come across before or familiar terms used in an unusual context.

Technical Terms Need Explanation

As computers bring specialist technology into the reach of more people, the use of technical jargon becomes more widespread. Desktop publishing (DTP) has brought typesetting to the masses. Although the technology bears little relation to the old printing craft, users are expected to learn typesetting terms like kerning and point sizing. Should new terms be invented? The answer is probably no. To printers – updating to new technology – new terms would be meaningless. Having begun by using the old terms, it would make no sense to suddenly change to new ones. Over time, the old terms will have less relevance and be replaced by new terms invented as DTP evolves. This is fine provided the new terms are explained.

1.5 Case Studies

In the following case studies the level of required computer literacy will be assessed for three applications.

Case Study 1: Semi-Specialist User – a Paint Package

Paint packages are used to generate or modify computer images for a variety of purposes. The audience spectrum starts from anyone, at one end, to specialist graphic designers at the other. Therefore the paint package should be simple to use but incorporate advanced features for the expert user. As non-specialist users will be using the package, all the technical terms and concepts related to graphic design should be explained within the program.

Designing interfaces for a range of users

The design of the application is approached from the point of view of two people: the casual user and the graphic designer. The casual user will need a minimum number of features to achieve the results they require. These might be: the ability to change the drawing color; the ability to draw simple shapes like circles and squares; and so on. These features should be presented in an intuitive and convenient interface. The advanced features that might be included in a paint package – such as stencilling, palette mixing and so on – should be hidden or kept away from the basic features of the package. These features should be designed for the convenience of the experienced user who may emerge from the first-time user.

Case Study 2: Any User – a Word Processor

A word processor is a general purpose tool for creating written documents; useful to anyone who produces written words. The audience will range from a casual user, with little computer literacy, to a specialist using the program continuously.

Every word processor is used for a different purpose. This tends to lead designers into packing the program with features that will attract different, specific groups of customers. The result is that only a small percentage of the features of a word processor are utilized by an individual. Most of the features are ignored or not understood by the operator.

The designer's approach should be similar to the paint package above. The basic operations must be intuitive and convenient. The specialist functions of the package should be kept away from the general functions. Either by including them in a separate menu, or by using some other kind of 'gateway' to access them. One route might be to access advanced features by clicking the right mouse button over existing icons – although this is not recommended. The important point is that the specialist and advanced features should be separated and marked 'advanced' so that the user is in no doubt that these are unnecessary to the basic function of the program.

Consideration should be made of how often the user may wish to access a function. Some packages allow the inclusion of special characters to represent scientific, trade mark and copyright, symbols. These may not be useful to all users but a patent agent – for example – might be including them with every other word. A cumbersome method of accessing this function would impair the productivity of the agent. However, it is important to distinguish between functions; analyzing and estimating how often they will be used. Some word processing packages make the mistake of treating all functions as the same, offering the same amount of help for a complex function – used rarely – as for a simple function used often.

Case Study 3: The Specialist User – CAD Package

A Computer Aided Design (CAD) program enables a user to produce the technical drawings used by architects and engineers. The audience for a CAD package can reasonably be expected to understand the process of technical drawing; the various terms used and to use the application frequently, if not continuously.

For the designer, the emphasis in an application for a specialist user is going to lie in the area of productivity. Therefore including a large number of features and options is preferable to making the application easy to use. The designer has no responsibility to make the program usable by the inexperienced. However, this is not an excuse for a disorganized design approach or the creation of an unusable interface.

The basic functions: the tools to create lines, circles and symbols – and to manipulate the view point of the drawing – should be easy to get at. Less frequently used functions – perhaps to print the drawing or merge in the data from another program – should be kept separate. The key is to analyze the user's activity and promote the most used functions. Again, infrequently needed functions should provide more information and be made easier to use.

Case Study 4: Any User – an Automated Bank Teller (Hole in the Wall)

The Automated Teller Machine (ATM) allows the customer 24 hour access to cash from their bank account. Banks cannot assume their customers are computer literate. The software interface between the customer and the cash dispensing hardware has to be easy for everyone to use.

Figure 3 The familiar ATM

It isn't acceptable to have the cash dispenser disabled by a customer walking away in the middle of a transaction. Therefore any point where the customer needs to enter data has to be protected. This is done by the use of 'time-outs'. If the customer hasn't entered valid data in an allotted time, the ATM will cancel the transaction and reset for a new customer.

The users most likely to have difficulties using an ATM are: new users, elderly users and those who have difficulty reading or problems with their

Experienced users can become first time users again, when faced with revised software

Using feedback

vision. New users can include people who have been using the ATM for years, suddenly confronted with a revised version of the software.

Experienced users do not bother to read displayed messages, they recognize patterns and memorize procedures. Some people forget their four-figure Personal Identification Number (PIN) but learn the pattern of the number keys pressed. Sometimes a problem occurs, such as the machine running out of cash. A one line message is usually displayed and then the machine resets for the next customer. The experienced user won't expect to see a message at this point, won't read it and will be distressed when the cash fails to appear. In a regularly used application, when something exceptional happens, it is vital the user is alerted by something that grabs the attention. An audible warning is ideal.

Elderly users may have difficulty because they are slow to respond to the machine. Messages such as 'Type in the amount of cash required and press the Enter key' do not explain what an Enter key is or where to find it. While the elderly user is looking for their glasses, the machine times-out and resets.

An ATM can present problems to someone who is a poor reader. Often they understand money and can recognize numbers, but long-winded explanations and complex procedures can baffle them. It would be ideal if the ATM customer could see the various denomination notes and pick as many as they wanted by pressing on the touch sensitive screen. A good compromise is to give the user a choice of useful amounts; each one displayed on screen alongside a key set in the panel. This is the method that ATMs now seem to favour.

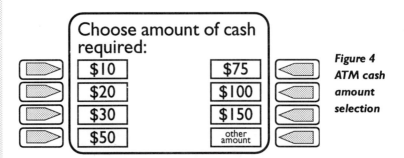

Figure 4
ATM cash
amount
selection

Current ATMs make no concessions for blind or visually impaired people. It would be a simple matter to include keys with Braille and an option for messages to be spoken. An ATM that talked the customer through the transaction might be generally useful.

A: These user-friendly interfaces just get in the way. They should be banned. If you can't read a manual you shouldn't be allowed on the computer. Bring back WordStar! If you wanted to cut and paste, it was a simple set of key presses. Typists could do the whole lot without taking their fingers off the keyboard. Now everybody has to crawl along in the slow lane with the simple folk. It makes me so angry...

D: Now that isn't fair. A menu interface may not always be efficient but even for the so called expert user it's relaxing. Have you noticed that it's far easier to watch TV when you're tired than read a book? Same point. I don't always want efficient! Sometimes I want to switch off and use a GUI.

A: GUIs are for zombies? Yeah, I can relate to that. What worries me is that GUIs are increasingly being used for critical applications like controlling nuclear power stations and dispatching ambulances. To use a GUI you don't need your brain in to make something happen. One wrong click and boom! Chernobyl II.

D: Until we get speech-based interfaces, GUIs must serve as the interface of choice. While I think you are being a little unfair, I do sometimes wonder if people have been taken out of the loop too quickly. I mean, are we treating everyone as if they deserve no better? The user is still given no way of expressing concepts other than 'File this' and 'Print out that.' Simple things like 'am I obviously doing something silly,' can't be asked because the software isn't listening. The task-centric approach is surely too rigid.

A: I think that's dangerous ground. Where would it all end? Would you tolerate the computer criticizing your work? No, the computer should just be a tool and you need proper training to use tools. You don't buy a hammer and expect it to show you how to nail up a fence.

D: Oh I agree about the tool part, except that if a hammer cost a hundred times more, I might start expecting it to avoid hitting me on the thumb at the very least.

1.6 Playing to the Audience

The application's audience seems like a fairly obvious issue, yet many interface problems stem from forgetting who the user is. Some of the basic points about the audience were outlined in this chapter. A few themes that surfaced such as metaphor, transparency, feedback and computer literacy will be returned to as they are all vital elements to programming for inter-activity.

A basic approach to application design is to consider what a program will do and how it will do it. A better approach is to also consider who will use the program, what they want to do with it and the best way of using what they already know, to help them understand it.

2

GUI *versus* Text

There is a wide variety of techniques available to the interface designer. In this chapter we are going to take a look at the difference between text based interfaces and graphical user interfaces.

2.1   The Story So Far...

Graphic User Interfaces (GUIs) are considered to be the state of the art in interface design. Windows, icons and pulldown menus are their hallmark. These are recently developed techniques. So how did we reach this point in the evolution of the interface?

Back in the computing dark ages, when a single computer filled a large room, it would serve multiple users at remote locations. Each operator had a Teletype terminal connected to the system. They typed in a line of text and the computer replied by printing on to paper. If the person mistyped, the whole command had to be re-entered. This was a major disadvantage.

Lucky users had a visual display unit (VDU). VDUs were used in the same way as a Teletype terminal except that messages were displayed on a screen instead of printed on paper. At first the screen emulated the roll of Teletype paper, scrolling each time a message was displayed. The disadvantage, that the user could no longer refer to previous output, was quickly solved. A static screen display was used and only those lines that needed updating were changed. As there was no print head, to indicate where the next character would be printed, the cursor was invented to show this. The lives of many trees were saved by the VDU and users gained the ability to edit their mistyped commands.

Two basic interface techniques were in use in these early days; the command line and the menu. Command lines had the advantage of being flexible, permitting the use of parameters to expand the range of possible commands. They had the disadvantage that they provided little information to the untutored user. Menus had the opposite attributes, providing lots of information at the expense of flexibility.

Mass production of microprocessors enabled the development of personal computers. Suddenly the user had exclusive use of the machines processing power. The machine could respond immediately to input. Menus now had a pointer or highlight bar, which could be moved up and down to select an item, rather than pressing the key that corresponded to the option. This was the beginning of using screen position as input information – a basic GUI technique.

Memory chips became cheaper and space could be found to store memory hungry bitmap graphics. Computers now had graphics capability. The reduction in costs also meant that specialist computers for playing games could be produced. These games machines, found in amusement arcades and homes, only had simple input devices with which to select options. Games were for children and therefore had to be simple and intuitive. The graphic user interface was born.

Soon a revolution occurred. Developers at computer manufacturer Rank Xerox unveiled a new operating system that depended on graphics. An essential ingredient of this was the mouse, a device for pointing to parts of the screen. The intention was to use a desktop analogy, combined with pulldown menus and graphic icons. They wanted to make computing more intuitive and to free the user from the tyranny of the keyboard. The term WIMP became associated with this, standing for windows, icons, menus and pointers.

That early WIMP environment has developed into the modern GUI. It has become accepted that this is the most intuitive interface available. The principles and assumptions on which today's GUIs are based have yet to be challenged.

What is GUI as Opposed to Text?

To appreciate the differences between a GUI and a text interface let us take a look at computer programs. A computer program is, in simple terms, a path. From the main path lead smaller paths to the tasks that the program performs. The user chooses which of the paths will be taken by the computer as the program runs. It is the job of the interface to interpret input from the user and tell the computer which to take.

An interface can use text to describe the optional paths that can be taken. If a menu system is being used, a list of possible options is displayed on the screen. Each option has an associated key, character or number. The computer then interprets the next key pressed as the order to take a path. In a command line system a whole line of text is taken in by the computer. It checks the string of characters against a list of commands until it finds a match. It then chooses the corresponding path.

In a GUI the optional paths of a program are represented by graphical devices. Graphics can be an icon or small picture, a button shape with or without text on it, or simply an area of the screen defined by a box. The graphics represent options or concepts relating to the computer's operating system. These can be: files, disk drives, directories and printers, for example.

To issue a command to the computer, the user moves a screen pointer, or cursor, to the screen position of the graphic and presses a key or mouse button. The computer interprets the screen position as the choice of path.

Using graphics interactively

A more sophisticated GUI will provide a greater number of paths by interpreting input in different ways. Mouse buttons can be clicked once, twice in quick succession, or held down while the mouse is moved. Each of these operations can be interpreted to mean different things.

There are benefits in the wide variety of ways graphics communicate information to the user. For example, a common computer operation is to move a file from one directory to another. This is something that happens unseen inside the computer. A GUI might perform this operation by asking the user to drag an icon, representing the file, from inside a box portraying the directory. Moving the file's icon physically across the screen, to leave it in a different directory box, is a graphical way of showing how the computer functions. It is much easier to see that the file has been copied from its first location to the new directory. This is a way of providing the user with a ready made mental picture of what is happening. In a text system the user is left to invent their own concept of what is going on.

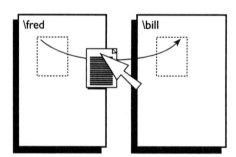

Figure 5
Representing a file
moving operation
using
a graphic image

The information a GUI conveys is visio-spatial. That means that it can be physically seen and that it provides information according to an objects position relative to other objects. In contrast, the file moving operation in a text-based command line system would be something like:

```
MOVE <source file spec.> <target file spec.>
```

The GUI has the advantage that the operation can be easily understood by the user and can provide visible feed-back that it has been successfully completed. However, this is only useful if the user understands the operation in the first place.

Where We are Today

The acceptance of GUIs was delayed by the low processor speed and poor graphics facilities of early mass market machines. Also, an uncertainty about standards stopped some software publishers from converting their existing programs. As the speed of modern machines began to increase, so has the use of GUIs in programs. In the future, machines will have more processors dedicated solely to screen performance and the facilities available to the designer will be much greater.

A modern GUI usually has an implementation of a WIMP interface using a mouse for a pointing device. The screen can be organized into different sized windows, whose function can vary. The development of standard interface controls has helped users familiarize themselves with different applications more quickly.

The designer can use the features offered by the GUI with a library of routines made available from a common programming language such as 'C.' Although the programmer often has to adjust to a hardware independent style of writing, after the learning curve has been climbed, usable products are quite straightforward to create and maintain.

2.2 Weighing Text Against the GUI

Why Text is Still Good

Although the GUI has become very popular, text interfaces still have a lot to offer. The ability to display text is considered a fundamental function of a computer. So most computers can output text. It would be unusual for a computer designer to make text output difficult for the programmer. It follows that printing text on screen is easy to do and doesn't absorb much of the processing power available to the program.

It is quicker and easier to develop programs where text forms the basis of the interface. And text is something that is always available to the programmer. Creating text to be displayed, and positioning it on screen is less work than creating the equivalent graphics would be. Text-based programs often run faster than graphics based and therefore respond more swiftly to the user's input.

As all general-purpose computers cater for text, but may use different systems to display graphics, it is easier to translate a text based program from one computer to another.

There is a natural assumption that a GUI is easier to use than a text based interface. One argument is the accepted fact that diagrams aid understanding. This book, for example, contains many for that reason. However it is not always the case that a GUI is easier to use than a text interface.

Users new to computing often make better progress with a simple command line rather than with a point and click interface. This is because the user domain – the area in which the user has control over the computer – is limited by the user's knowledge. Unfamiliar commands are effectively hidden. In contrast, the user domain of a GUI is almost unlimited and this permits the user to easily stumble into unfamiliar territory. The CLI usually returns to the familiar prompt if something goes wrong. The GUI, on the other hand, is deliberately structured not to do this to maintain continuity. Another reason is that the user is likely to be able to read instructions. They may find written instructions easier to understand than the same information presented as computer graphics, particularly if they have not had much experience with computers. An interface for a non-computer literate user is one case where text can be a better solution than a GUI.

Certainly, all GUIs must contain text explaining what is happening and what should be done next. The way the text is written and presented will make a big difference to how easy the interface is to use. As a final illustration that text is still important, it is worth remembering that all GUIs come with a manual and all help screens use text.

Text Limitations that GUI Improves On

Programs that use graphics have the advantage of being visually interesting. This makes them seem more interesting to use in general. Most users realize that it takes extra effort to produce a graphics-based interface and therefore perceive them as having greater value.

When displaying the status of something, it is easiest to read a graphic representation. On a speedometer or other type of gauge the information is given by the position of a pointer. It would be harder to read the same information in text. Spatial concepts that involve size, capacity, position or anything quantifiable can be better illustrated by graphics.

Using icons

Text can quickly fill up screen space. Also, if it is not displayed in its correct orientation it becomes illegible. A GUI can get around this by using buttons or icons that can be packed tightly together in any direction. Graphics also have the advantage that they are not language specific. A text interface can only be used by someone who understands the language.

• Do use graphics to show quantities and states.

• Do use buttons when space is limited

But Sooner or Later You Have to Use Text

On their own, neither text nor graphics can communicate all the information the user needs. Used in the wrong place, they can each create an interface that is confusing or unusable. Text cannot provide the instant feedback that graphics provide and graphics are tied to visio-spatial concepts. Only in combination can they produce a good interface.

Take, for example, a designer developing a GUI. The GUI has two buttons; screen areas that can be clicked on with the mouse pointer. The buttons alter the speed of some process, one to make it go faster and the other slower. To communicate the purpose of the buttons, the designer uses an analogy; a picture of a hare on one button, a picture of a tortoise on the other. If the user has heard the fable of the Hare and the Tortoise, all is well. Perhaps the user is an Eskimo or a South American native and doesn't know this story. To such users, the pictures are of unfamiliar animals. Suddenly the designer is not communicating a concept but testing the user's general knowledge and ability to figure out the connection between the pictures.

Figure 6 Buttons based on the Hare and Tortoise fable.

It would be better to use text on the buttons: one button saying 'faster' the other 'slower.' Although the Eskimo and South American may not be able to read the text, there is the possibility of translation without loss of meaning.

Interfaces that provide cryptic clues, as if playing a game of charades, are primarily testing the user's intelligence, not communicating a message.

2.3 Choosing a Text or Graphics-based Interface

So What is Needed?

Interface designers must work out the needs of their program before considering the interface. It is very likely that they may wish to improve

Choosing the correct metaphor for an icon

Graphics based on cultural icons are not universally readable

a program later; at which point they will appreciate a good initial decision. A new interface technology that becomes available could improve the program. Knowledge of the program will enable the designer to quickly assess the benefit of the technology.

Whatever they end up doing, all programs are just manipulations of data that somehow get into the computer and may have to come out. This is where the designer starts.

First, at the conceptual level, what type of input is to be expected? The designer will find this far easier to think about by ignoring what they know about computing. If a handwriting analysis program was to be written, for example, it would need to somehow input sample handwriting. This could be implemented by either using a graphic tablet and pen to create a suitable sample, or by reading in an existing one using a scanner. Virtual reality data gloves could be considered as a possible candidate.

However it comes in, the sample will have to be translated for the internal format of the program to work on. But the internal format should not be a factor in choosing the interface. In this example, the program may need to break up the writing into short lines or vectors. The vectors indicate the angle the writing is at and how hard the writer is pressing.

How are results to be displayed? Surely it would be nice to display the example on screen, outlining graphologically significant areas. A GUI would probably help this aspect of the program, as the user could click on areas of the handwriting seen on screen and ask about what they conveyed.

Here are some examples of different input interfaces:

Application	Input type	Input Interface
Graphology	Handwriting sample	Scan in an existing sample
Word processor	Text document	Type letters in through the keyboard
Driving simulator	Steering	Move joy-stick to represent direction
Paint program	Lines, strokes, scribble	Mouse or graphics tablet
Chess game	Piece moves	Drag and drop pieces via mouse

Most applications will seek input straight from the keyboard or from previously created files. Output is normally limited to the screen, further files and possibly a printer. This often leads designers to the conclusion that for standard applications it is unnecessary to start from basics when thinking about the interface.

- When designing an interface, start from the conceptual level.
- The interface to an application interprets the users input and presents corresponding output and feedback.
- The internal workings of a program should function independently of the interface.

2.4　Case Studies

The following studies demonstrate how different interfaces can change the user's perspective of the same program.

Case Study 1: Word Processor in Text Screen – Word Processor in GUI

The word processor extends the functions of the typewriter. The basic input interface is the same, the output being available on VDU as well as just paper. However, the extra facilities of a word processor must be accessed without conflicting with the typing interface.

The keyboard is both the typewriter and the interface for entering commands. This is a typical dual role or context change problem. It's solved by extra keys that can be used in conjunction with letter keys to issue commands. Thus typing 'B' will enter the character 'B' into the text being written. But by typing 'Alt' and 'B' the user can issue the command 'make the following text appear in bold print.' A mouse pointer used to select icons can eliminate this context change, by having all processing commands available without recourse to the keyboard. But not all users like to stop typing in order to pick up a mouse.

One very important aspect of a word processor's operation is that its display keeps up with the user's speed of typing, to maintain the typewriter metaphor. Text screens have no problem here, but only recently have low end computers run GUIs quickly enough to be acceptable.

A graphic screen can present text as it would appear on a printer, whatever the typeface. This is referred to as What You See Is What You Get (WYSIWYG). Even better, text can be woven with pictures to produce a full document.

The feedback of the full presentation of the text, to the writer, may not always be beneficial. Writing is often done in note form, with the user just typing in unfinished ideas. In this context, screen presentation becomes unimportant. The extra processing involved can reduce the performance of the software making it sluggish to respond to the user. This is why many users still prefer text screen editors for originating text.

Word processors are now expected to be able to cut and paste text from one place to another. In some software the cut passage disappears into an invisible buffer. This can be very disconcerting for the user. It leads to frustration when the passage is accidentally overwritten by the next cut. An ideal GUI could use a pointer to select, cut the passage and drag it to its new destination. This visio-spatial task is unrelated to the contents of the passage and is free to work entirely on a graphics level.

Perhaps it is a surprise that a clearly textual subject would work on a graphical level at all. This highlights the need to separate input concept and interface from the internal workings of the application. Similarly feedback to user response is also a key factor to interface design.

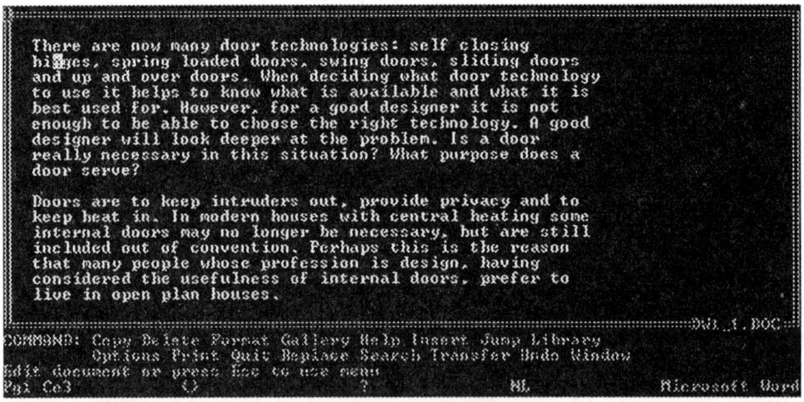

Figure 7 Microsoft's – text based – Word for DOS

GUI based word processors provide real advantages in terms of visual feed-back. The user can see exactly what a document will look like before it is printed out and this at least saves wasted paper. In terms of productivity, the text based word processor has advantages also. Which is better, GUI or text? As time passes, the answer must surely be GUI. Even if we all stop using paper and start exchanging documents electronically, there will still be the need to include pictures and use the various effects available in print. However, until the problem of performance is fully addressed by developers, and they realise that the needs of a keyboard operator conflict with use of a mouse, the text interface based word processor will still be a useful tool.

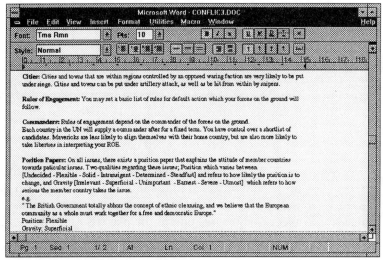

Figure 8 Microsoft's Word for Windows

Case Study 2: Text Adventure – Graphic Adventure

An adventure game usually consists of a fantasy land, which the player must explore. The player controls a character within the land. The player's character can manipulate various objects to help him proceed in his quest. The interface problem is that of translating the player's desires into the right character's actions.

The first adventures were driven by text data. The player entered text commands and the program described the current location and result of actions with text messages. A typical location description would be:

```
You are in a small room.
There is a closed door to your North.
There is a gold bar on the ground.
```

The adventures physical world would describe a set of locations, each with a set of links to other locations. The links were normally described as compass directions to the player. In the example above, the location the player is in has a link to another location described as 'North'. This unusual method of movement is used to avoid worrying about the player's orientation.

Along with the locations, the adventure also contains data representing objects that are scattered around. In the example, an object with the name 'gold bar' is situated on the ground. To interact with this world, the player enters a command:

        Pick up gold bar

The program then has to translate this English command into an internal description. This process, known as parsing, provides the designer with a wealth of problems. Some can be hinted at by the size of the English language, the illogical idioms of everyday language as well as the much loved English characteristic of one word having two meanings.

A decent parser will have no problem with the above example. The phrase 'pick up' would be found in the internal dictionary and the noun 'gold bar' found in the list of object names. The program would then transfer the object from its location to the player's list of possessions.

The problem with the text entry interface is that the player is expected to use a limited set of commands from the infinite variety available and yet express all his intentions clearly. This means the parser has the job of filtering out invalid or ambiguous input. Consider the following:

        Pick up the feather

        Close the door

        Eat the gold bar

        Leave the room with the bar

        Leave the gold bar alone

The first two commands will be parsed easily enough, but they are impossible actions – the door is already closed and no feather is present. The third command tests the accuracy of the data description of the real world. The fourth command is ambiguous: does the player wish to use the gold bar in some way to help leave the room, or just pick it up and then go? The last command does nothing but could be picked up by the parser as a command to go somewhere. All of these commands are perfectly legitimate text statements, which the interface has no way of keeping out.

Using graphics interactively

A graphic interface represents the scene in an entirely visual manner. The room is drawn. A gold bar is clearly drawn sitting on the floor. A door can be seen to the north of the room. There may be a text description to add atmosphere, but the scene is otherwise displayed fully in graphics, limited only by the colours and screen resolution available to the computer and artist.

The graphic interface translates actions based on the position of the pointer on the screen. Only allowable actions may be selected, based on the object the player has pointed to or highlighted. Some common actions may be presented separately from the drawn scene. These may be represented as icons or text, and may be selected to help form a command.

Clicking on the picture of the door will enable a list of actions available to be tried. The program may just default to opening the door. Similarly, clicking on the gold bar would enable the player to interact further with it, depending on the data description of the gold bar and objects the player already has. In this case, the gold bar would probably be transferred to the player's possession.

Most of the problems with text parsing disappear with a graphic interface. The player cannot interact with an object not represented on screen, and his actions are limited to a set of common actions. Of these, some may be made unavailable when an object is selected. On clicking on the picture of the gold bar, an icon representing eating could be temporarily removed.

A negative aspect of this approach is that solutions become immediately visible. The enjoyment factor of an adventure game is experimentation with your surroundings. The available actions are made obvious by the way the interface works and thus reveal information that should be discovered. For example, with a text interface the command:

```
Kneel down and pray
```

could be used near a statue of a deity. It may not occur to the player to try it, but when they do and something unexpected happens, the player should feel very satisfied. The interface has done its job without – literally – giving the game away.

This cannot happen using the graphic interface. When the player clicks on the statue, the option to pray must be given if the player is allowed to try it. Thus the player doesn't have to think of it for himself.

In this way a graphic adventure is often reduced to a touch and learn session, which is a testament to the power of the interface to subvert the designer's original intention. It also illustrates the graphic interface's ability to make things obvious.

D: Text adventures? Glad to see the back of them. All that fiddly entry 'Go north, Get shovel' etc. Make one typo or use a word not in the dictionary and the game responded 'I don't understand Go nortg' or 'I don't understand travel north.' Now you just click on a shovel and Indy picks it up on screen. What have we lost?

A: Depth, flexibility perhaps? With the old Infocom adventures you could type 'Pick up all but the shovel' and the program understood exactly what you meant. That's a very intelligent interface that's been thrown away. Programs didn't need a lot of fancy graphics. Can't people use their imaginations?

D: You're right about the 'get all' of course. What's happened is that the text instruction has an intuitive plural: The player thinks 'I need everything here' and simply writes 'get everything here'. But no such graphical plural exists. The collective drag selection which works for a set of neatly stacked icons, in a Windows file box, fails here because the things to collect are not all drawn square and are unlikely to be all standing in a row. So there's a conflict between the real world representation of the shovel, gold etc. in the game world, and the need for the player to communicate to the program that he wishes to gather them all up.

A: So if graphical adventures have less to offer than text, how have they taken over?

D: Because what they do offer is a pleasing visual response, as well as more of a feeling of interaction. They can also 'cheat' and use arcade elements to bolster the action.

A: Yes, that does make a game more interesting. However, it's the puzzles that really appeal to adventure players.

D: Of course some clues are now visual, like a painting on the wall or a complicated piece of machinery which needs fixing. As is usual, if the game uses the graphic side effectively, then no comparison can easily be sought in text.

A: I guess it's down to the skill of the designer. I still feel it's easier to put atmosphere into a text game. A few creepy descriptions and the players imagination does the rest. Its hard to do that with graphics and make them communicate their purpose as well.

Case Study 3: Text Spreadsheet – Graphics Spreadsheet.

Computer applications often mimic an activity that has previously been a manual activity. Word processing mimics typewriting. A paint program mimics sketching and painting. The spreadsheet mimics the rows and columns of a financial ledger, automating the calculation of sums and totals.

The spreadsheet is usually used as a financial tool, to ask 'what if' questions on sets of related numerical data. A sheet is a grid of cells, each cell shows the value of the current equation it has been asked to compute, or just the value it currently represents. For instance, a multiplication table could be constructed

```
Cell:
value or equation
A1:         B1:         C1:         D1:
       1          2           3           4
A2:         B2:         C2:         D2:
       2        B1*A2      C1*A2       D1*A2
A3:         B3:         C3:         D3:
       3        B1*A3      C1*A3       D1*A3
```

This would show:

```
A1:         B1:         C1:         D1:
       1          2           3           4
A2:         B2:         C2:         D2:
       2          4           6           8
A3:         B3:         C3:         D3:
       3          6           9          12
```

As each cell has a unique address based on its tabular position, access to cells by just typing 'A2' or 'Z3' is possible. The keyboard cursor can be used to move from one cell to another.

A cell holds two pieces of information: what it currently represents, and an equation that probably relates it to the contents of other cells. This is not a natural concept to grasp, there is no equivalent device that allows two things to occupy the same place in the way they appear to in the spreadsheet, so the interface is often tricky. Usually a highlighted cell will show its related equation away from the grid so as not to confuse the user.

The most obvious improvement when the system has a GUI is access to the cells themselves. This can be done in a more direct manner than before. But this is to be expected, because a spreadsheet is a tabular construction that requires visual logic to comprehend. On closer inspection we note that the *contents* of the cell have been abstracted; the positions of the cells are more important than the content.

This may appear strange, as the program's job is seemingly based on the manipulation of the cell's contents, but in fact a GUI gives the program an extra presentational dimension that it didn't previously have. After the 'what if' questions have been asked, the user can turn the tabulated information into charts or graphs because the internal representation of the information can easily be translated into another graphical form.

There is more than a sneaking suspicion that the better presentation helps the user to feel more comfortable with the figures – he has control of how they look, but not what they are. 'OK,' says the user, 'so the figures may show a loss but at least I can make them look neat for the boss.' This trivializing of the principle of a program is a common feature of GUI representations and must be taken into account by the designer. The user is given the discretion to 'fiddle about' and possibly distance himself from the information in front of him.

Case Study 4: A Typo Correction Program

In this chapter the relative merits of text based interfaces and GUIs have been introduced. The following example shows how a designer would analyze an application. The next chapter will reveal the designer's choice of interface and explain why he chose it.

The project:

A typographical or 'typo' correction program.

Purpose of program:

A simple utility to spot a set of known typing and spelling errors in a text and correct them, e.g. teh -> the, necesary -> necessary, etc.

What is the conceptual input?

The utility works on text. The examples are associated matching pairs of words.

What happens internally?

The utility would process a text file, search for the typos and replace them with the corresponding corrections. The result is a corrected file. The typo examples are stored as pairs in a simple database.

What interface?

The user needs to be able to select a file, and this is best done by presenting a list of existing files present in the current workspace. The user may also want to just quote a filename or file specification, and the existence of the chosen file or files needs to be verified.

The user also needs to choose a name for the target file. If the target file exists – or is the source file – the user must be warned that a file will be overwritten.

The user needs to be able to enter or edit typo/correction pairs. The user should be presented with a list of pairs already present, and be able to select a pair and edit it, or add another pair.

How would improvements affect the interface?

In some instances, it might be useful to 'turn off' a pair. This is needed when what would normally be a typo is, in a temporary context, a legitimate spelling. The interface needs to be able to show which pairs will be used and which not, as well as to switch them on or off.

2.5   What are the Other Alternatives

As screens get larger, and processors get faster, the GUI can only improve in quality. On screen text will diminish simply because it is easier to make graphics look better. This is equivalent to stating that the quality of airline food will improve because there is very little else that can be improved to entice customers from one airline to another.

At some point in the not too distant future this entire chapter could be re-written as GUI versus Speech Interface, with the GUI taking the inferior position. What matters, however, is not the world of computing, but the world outside. It matters that drivers respond to coloured traffic lights, or that important messages must be written for confirmation. A court of law works with verbal testimony, a novel is read on the page. The interface is, after all, meant to complement or mimic existing mediums of communication.

3

The Fundamentals of Input

This chapter deals with the activity of getting human information to the computer in a form that it can manipulate. This activity has few parallels and so has been given its own name: input. Although input can come from many sources, most information comes directly from a human or indirectly via a translation device like a modem.

3.1   Input: It's Not All Keyboards and Mice

Computer controlled devices have many forms of input, usually reflecting how we see their use at the time. The earliest machines were seen as large calculating engines, so the only input required were the sums whose answers were sought. The interaction was that between a great Zen master and his curious acolyte. Questions or simple programs were described on punch cards or tape. That a card with holes in is completely divorced from usual human communication simply underlined the awe and alien nature of the electronic brain.

As computers became smaller and more commonplace, a greater number of human operators were needed. The relationship between man and machine became more familiar, and so did the communication. Low level languages enabled operators to enter data and simple programs through terminals and keypads. It is easy to see that a secretary with a typewriter and an operator with a terminal may have been considered similar types of workers.

There is a huge variety of possible input devices. As the use of personal computers has widened, only a small number of devices have been adopted and not always the best for the job. The QWERTY keyboard is not recognized as being efficient. It is based on a design intended to slow down the typist – to prevent them typing so fast the mechanical keys jammed together. Six-key keyboards were introduced as an alternative but have not gained general acceptance. Specialist machines use graphic tablets, touch sensitive screens and light pens, all of which offer a lot but are fairly expensive. Business standardization has killed many input variants.

Meanwhile computers were developed to collect input through other sensory devices such as temperature and pressure detectors – even limited sight – without the need for humans to spoonfeed them.

Arcade games used many different input devices to enhance the experience. The game 'Missile Command' was one of the first to use the concept of a screen cursor, which was controlled with a trackball. The player chose positions on the screen that became targets for missiles. William's 'Defender' preferred to give the player a lever and five buttons to control a fast space ship. This made it fairly hard to master, but didn't appear to give the player any less enjoyment, even if the most common cause of player death was pressing the wrong button. Atari's 'Battlezone' simulated the control of a tank by using two levers that each controlled a caterpillar track.

At the Lowest Level

For the designer it is useful to understand how input works. Input is the point at which the computer listens to the human user. If it is badly done, the computer may mishear the user or the user may not be able to express what they want from the machine. All software contains some input and it is important to be able to make the best use of the information the user provides. Computer game designers have long appreciated the relationship between good input and good software. Faced with simulating complex activities like flying an aeroplane or performing a pole vault, they have found many original and imaginative ways of getting that input, often from very limited input devices like keyboards and joysticks. So how do they do it?

At the lowest level, the computer can only understand one kind of message: whether a switch in an electrical circuit is open or closed. All forms of input, no matter how complex the information at the human end, are broken down to this computer-digestible form.

How the computer reads information from the outside world

There are a few basic techniques that form the building blocks for all input. These are:

- Reading more than one circuit at a time.

- Counting the number of times a circuit is switched.

- Measuring the length of time between the circuit switching from one state to the other and back again.

- Performing a function some-time after the circuit is switched, unless the circuit reverts to its previous state.

- Using the state of one switch to change the context in which another switch is used

The building blocks of input

Making Switches Fit the Real World

Humans can process a rich source of input; all five senses are needed to display intelligent behaviour and survive. The first communication stumbling block between humans and machines is the vast difference in our sensory apparatus. Computers only contact with the real world is via the switch, but fortunately mechanics can be used to extend this unpromising start. The following are the main computer input devices.

The Button and the Key

A physical input device has three main axes in three-dimensional space to move in, but remember the hidden axis, time. The button is the crudest input device of all, being a simple switch with a mechanism to break the circuit after it is released. The computer doesn't keep a constant watch on the state of a circuit but looks at intervals. The position of a switch may be read many times a second. Thus the input of a button may be seen as a stream of ticker tape, with each mark or gap representing the switch state at the moment it is read.

By reading the ticker tape, a computer can recognize the distinctive pattern of a 'hit' – the action of quickly pressing and releasing the button – a 'double click' or holding the button down.

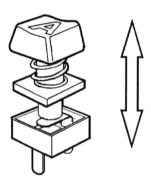

Figure 9
The key switch is the commonest form of switch found connected to a computer. The arrows are a reminder of the amount of information that can be gleaned from a simple switch

The Joystick

The classic arcade game device, the digital joystick, usually has a set of four switches at the compass points of the stick, any two of which can be closed at one time, allowing for eight states to be read. A fire button (or two) appears at the tip of the stick, or on the base. The joystick can be used to describe any point on a plane because the stick moves along orthogonal axes.

The joystick was fashioned to look like an aircraft joystick whose controls are mechanically linked to the rudders in the wings. However, a digital joystick has far less freedom than a graduated mechanical one. An analogue joystick, which converts movement into changes in current, is often used with flight simulator type games. Ironically new fly-by-wire aircraft no longer have any direct mechanical connections and operate like a flight simulator interface.

With the button, we saw the example of gestures that increased the communication options available. The 'waggle', the movement of a digital joystick quickly from one extent to the opposite, was one method to translate the player's aggressive energy into the game, with often negative consequences for the joystick.

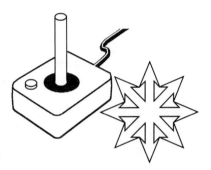

Figure 10 The digital joystick usually returns a byte of information. Each bit represents the state of one of the four directional switches with additional bits devoted to fire buttons. Certain combinations of bits – where the switches are on opposite sides of the axis – should be impossible

The Mouse

The mouse converts the movement of a ball into digital information. It is the best way to describe a point on a plane, and is usually used to drive the pointer on a WIMP interface.

The mouse electronics measure the speed and direction of rotation of the mouse ball in the x and y axis. A slotted wheel is rotated between a light and a light detecting switch as the mouse is dragged. Each time the switch is activated, the count is increased by one; a use of the second building block from the list above. This measurement is scaled, translating the movement over the work surface into movement of the screen pointer. This is the equivalent of power steering in a car, as a small movement from the mouse is scaled up to a larger one for the pointer.

When a mouse is double clicked, it uses the technique of counting switch states allied with the concept of measuring the time between changes. This combination results in a unique signal to the computer, a signal that has a different meaning to a single click, or the button being held down and the mouse moved to drag an item across the screen. In the latter case

Figure 11
A two-button mouse.

the mouse button is used to change the context of the rest of the input from the mouse. All three instructions are indicated with the single switch of the mouse button. The mouse button itself is not a complex mechanism; however, the schemes of input associated with it are.

3.2 Input Design

Mouse Fundamentals

The mouse is a device that is intended to create a physical relationship between the position of the user's hand and a screen pointer. It translates movement in the real world into data the computer can understand. This 'point and click' device is currently the best interpreter of human intentions.

Mouse input methods

There are three main ways that the mouse is used:

- Clicking a button over a particular screen area to activate a function.

- Double clicking on a screen area, to activate a function in a different context.

- Clicking on a displayed item, holding down the button and dragging the item to another part of the screen.

However, there are many other ways the mouse may be used, with or without an onscreen pointer.

Mouse Pointers – Rules to Remember when Designing Mouse-driven Interfaces

There are several points the designer should consider:

The most important is that a good mouse interface does not break the relationship between the mouse on the desk and the pointer on the screen.

How to use the mouse to access functions by clicking on icons

Double clicking is not a natural action and is not used in any other man—machine interface. In the real world it is unusual to find something that will only work the second time it is activated. As a double click can be used as well as a single click on an icon, there is the possibility that the double click functions will go unnoticed by the user. This has the effect of concealing options, something that can be used to advantage in some interfaces but will cause problems in others. Double clicking should only be used in an interface intended for experienced, computer literate users.

A mouse can have one, two or three buttons on it. Only one button is really necessary.

On mice with two or more buttons, it is usual to use the left button as the button to activate main functions, as this is nearest to the index finger for a right handed person. Use the other button to cancel selections.

Do not use different buttons to change the context of the function being activated. This creates an unfriendly interface. For example, a paint program where the left button accessed functions to draw on one screen while the right button drew on another, would be very confusing to use.

Don't create an application where it is necessary to pick up the mouse and move it to increase the range of the pointer. This is a problem that occurs when the mouse is tied to the size of the displayable area instead of the screen size. The mouse physically moves only 20 – 50 mm over the desk, when moving the screen pointer from one side of the screen to the other. Making the screen scroll only when the mouse is moved requires the user to increase this amount. It is possible to scale mouse movements. Mouse mats are around 200 mm across. If the screen pointer can't be moved across the screen by a mouse moving within this range, the scale is wrong.

Don't reset the mouse position. Some applications reset the mouse position after exiting from a dialogue. This is a break in the desk – screen relationship and must not be done.

Don't use the mouse buttons as a toggle for a function related to the mouse pointer. For example, in paint programs the mouse pointer is used as the brush. There are two ways of doing this. The first is to only paint when the mouse button is held down. The second is to click the mouse button and paint continuously until the button is clicked again. The second method appears to have the advantage of needing less effort to keep the button held down. However, the first method is closer to the real activity of painting than the second. The artist spends more time moving the brush over the canvas than with the brush in contact with it.

A primary function of the mouse is to allow the user to select a function by clicking on a part of the screen. Ideally the area that is clickable should have a border to define it. It is common to display text on a menu bar with no defining clickable area. This is acceptable but is sometimes carried into dialogue boxes where it is not acceptable. Some interfaces highlight the clickable area when the mouse pointer is moved over it. This lets the user see they have the pointer in the right place. When the mouse is clicked, it is essential that feedback is provided to show that something has happened. This can be an audio and/or visual indicator.

How to create feedback to mouse activity

Keyboard Fundamentals

A keyboard is a matrix of crossed wires that make contact when a key presses them down, closing the contact. A signal corresponding to the key, or key combination pressed, is sent to the processor. Usually keys such as Alt, Shift, and Ctrl can be used in combination with alphanumeric keys to produce extra commands. This means that a program can accept typewriter like text entry as well as other commands through the same device.

As the central processor may be too busy to act on key presses as they come in, the identifying code for the key press, known as the key token, is sent to a buffer or waiting area within the system's memory. When the processor is ready, the key token is read.

This implies that the computer may not be able to keep up with typed input, and in some cases this is true. If the processor is giving all its attention to input, there should be no problem, but if the keyboard input is only processed occasionally, an application can slow down. In an application in which the user is allowed free text entry, it is important that the typewriter metaphor is maintained and that text instantly appears on the screen.

When a user presses down on a key, the hit must not produce more than one instance of the key's intended function. The program must wait till the user releases the key before accepting further input. This is referred to as debounce and is essential for a keyboard driven application. After a certain time, some applications assume that the user wishes to repeat the key, in which case the debounce rule is not applied. This can be seen in some command line interfaces. With older computers these things were handled by software but modern machines now include electronics that handle debounce and key repeat.

Keyboard Don'ts

Button combinations are tricky to use, and should only be used when no other method can be found, or the function is a rarely used one. In preference use function keys or 'stacked control keys'. For example, pressing the Alt key puts the input into a different mode where the next key opens up a menu. PCs can be reset by the combination Ctrl, Alt and Del which is intended to be difficult to press with one hand. The most prominent keys on QWERTY are spacebar and enter key, so they shouldn't be the default input for unrecoverable operations such as exits or deletions. In these cases, the user should have a little difficulty.

It is important to remember that the topology of a keyboard is not always fixed from one machine to another, so one should not make assumptions about the positions of special keys on a keyboard. If necessary, a reprogrammable keyboard interface should be considered.

Size and Vectors

Information to describe things can come in two parts: 'what is it and how much of it is there?' When a mouse starts moving it has a velocity, a variable which comes in two parts: a direction and speed. Humans becoming emotional may express themselves via the 'how much' part of a control. The obvious example is playing a video game, getting excited and wrenching the joystick about. In some cases the extra information can and should be ignored, but in others it is inherent to the input.

Consider converting the control of a steering wheel to an alternative input device. A steering wheel only has two directions of rotation, but it is important to relay the speed of rotation as well as the position of the wheel. Small changes in either direction can be made quickly, though large ones cannot. If numbers were placed around the wheel, one could in theory represent the steering wheel with a set of radio buttons – only one down at a time.

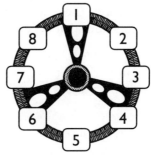

Figure 12
A notional push
button interface
representing a
steering wheel

Consider simulating turning the wheel from position 2 to 5, either smoothly, or in a quick jerk. This can be represented via buttons in the way the buttons 2 through 5 are pressed, but is very difficult to accomplish. Similarly it is simple to press 7 then 3 in rapid succession, an action that cannot be achieved by turning the wheel.

Input Ergonomics

A badly designed computer interface can cause physical injury to its human user. At one end of the scale is the game that gives a player blisters and cramped fingers from using the joystick. At the other end of the scale is the word processor that gives its user Repetitive Strain Injury (RSI). It is the designer's responsibility to ensure that they have done everything they can to minimize the risks to the user.

RSI, as suffered by keyboard operators, is damage caused to the wrist tendons that connect muscles in the forearm to the fingers. The damage is caused by over-use of the fingers to make the small repetitive movements associated with typing. The software is one factor in many that may lead to somebody acquiring this crippling condition. However, the software designer can play a part in preventing the problem.

Repetitive strain causes permanent damage to the victim. Temporary pain and discomfort can be caused by any application. Over-use of a mouse can cause cramp, lead to pins and needles in the hand or 'mouse claw.' Also it can be argued: where stress is considered harmful, software that is frustrating or stress inducing is also harmful.

How to design a healthier interface

Here are some tips to minimise physical injury to the user:

Try to minimize keystrokes to those just needed for text. Things that may increase the keystrokes are: hot keys and extra functions on control keys, interfaces that require multiple key presses to move cursors or make selections. There is no way of avoiding some form of keypress to activate a function. The only measures that can be taken are to reduce the number of functions that need to be accessed and to make them easy to access.

It is possible to monitor the amount of key presses and button clicks that occur during a time period. Offer the option to warn the user they are overdoing things but do not force them to stop or force the information on them.

GUI based word processors and DTP packages sometimes require the text cursor to be placed in the gap between two characters – a gap two pixels wide. This requires manual dexterity roughly equal to placing a pea onto the end of a drinking straw.

Where an interface is implemented on a 640 pixel wide screen, the mouse moves physically 50 mm to move the cursor across it. This means that to move the pointer one pixel, the mouse must be moved 0.07 mm; less than the width of a pin. There are many applications that call for pixel accurate positioning using the mouse – CAD, paint programs, WP and DTP applications, for example – to pick up a small black square or handle. Good designers should not create applications that require this. They should always use the keyboard, or a magnification mode, to position an object or cursor when precision is needed.

Where a function is in constant use, to change modes or use a particular tool for example, do not use small icons. The more often the function is used, the bigger the icon should be. Small icons require fine control of the mouse. The user will grip the mouse extra hard to achieve the fine control, causing straining and cramps. The user that clicks on an icon and misses will become frustrated and stressed, using even more effort to control the mouse. Mistakes have to be corrected, doubling the amount of strain on the user.

Choosing the size of icons

Use grids and 'snap-to' systems to make pointer positioning easier for the user. Fine control of the mouse is not required to move the pointer to a grid position; mouse movement is effectively scaled up.

Don't create applications that require continuous mouse clicks, let the user 'paint' by holding down the button.

Beware of creating applications that require a lot of click and drag. In fact, try to avoid click and drag as much as possible. Holding down the mouse button and moving the mouse at the same time causes discomfort and is prone to errors. Allow the user to recover from an error if they release the button accidentally while dragging the mouse.

If there is only one logical thing the user can do next, do it for them. Don't make the user take unnecessary steps like closing a lot of windows after activating a function.

3.4 The Potential for the Immediate Future

We now see the computer as a tool, and we are not so interested in laboriously typing in data as letting it release us from the rigors of work.

Primitive voice input works well, but the vocabulary recognised and computer intelligence to interpret the words heard is very limited. Voice input would be a useful advance helping to do away with the cumbersome graphic interfaces of today. However, the user would still need to phrase commands in a way computers understand. Much of human communication is done in a coded way. 'I feel thirsty,' is really saying 'can I have a drink.' Also non-verbal body language plays a large part in human communication. Too much background noise means that a voice input device has to be very sensitive to the speaker but not to someone speaking to him. A basic 'personal' level voice recognition system for simple commands is already available. This is still prone to background interference but has enough intelligence to recognize one user's voice from another.

Handwriting recognition is probably not all that useful as most people who need to can still type. Also, as computer use grows, handwriting skills will be replaced by keyboard skills. Until translation errors are on a par with typing mistakes, handwriting recognition is not a particularly useful form of input. What matters is the possibility of being able to write without recourse to a bulky keyboard.

The movie industry is beginning to use 'body-suits,' a development of the virtual reality data-glove. These are computer input devices that translate an actor's movements into information the computer can understand. This information has been used to animate computer generated cartoons and remotely controlled monsters.

Image recognition is an area with huge potential. Already there are systems that can read car number plates from the roadside. Optical character recognition is well advanced but our interest is in direct human to computer interfaces. Is it possible that a computer may be able to lip read competently before voice recognition is fully workable? Perhaps being able to read sign language is another possible image processing route to communication.

Computers will eventually be able to translate and manipulate all types of information. It can only be a matter of time before computers are able to completely emulate humans in terms of intelligence and their physical senses. When that happens, we will be able to communicate with them as we communicate with each other.

3.5   Case Studies

Case Study 1: Notional One-button Interface

Complex input devices offer the interface designer a lot of freedom. As an exercise in appreciation of this freedom, consider operating a machine with just one button, key or switch. For the purposes of this exercise we'll assume the switch is of the joystick or mouse variety – that switches on when pressed and off when released.

The machine to be controlled is a car. It could be: a simulated car in a game, a toy car with a remote control on a wire, or a real car with adapted controls. The basic things that a car can do are: go, stop, steer left and steer right. How can four separate functions be requested by a single switch?

This is a relatively easy problem to solve using the building blocks of input. It has already been explained how three different functions are indicated with a single mouse button. This approach simply needs to be adapted for four functions. Here is one possible way of doing it:

Function	Control
Steer left	One press
Steer right	Two presses in quick succession
Speed up	A single, long press
Slow down	Three or more in quick succession

Note the 'brakes' function is activated by three or more presses. This brings the vehicle to a halt if the user panics and just hammers the button.

Another way of controlling the car would be to display the functions as a list and rotate a pointer so that only one function was current at one time. One press could advance the pointer with a double press in quick succession to indicate: 'that function is required.'

Of course it is totally impractical to operate a complex machine, in real time, using a single button. However, there are a number of interfaces that rely on one or two buttons to operate them. Line printers and digital watches may use a small number of buttons in different modes.

Close study of the one-button car example will highlight the practicalities of low level input design. It is quite difficult to differentiate one function from another. The computer tells which function is being requested, not by being told directly, but by eliminating the possibilities.

Control of the car would consist of getting started and then using the left and right steering controls to alter direction. It is assumed that if the wheels were steering the car to the left, the right steering control would bring the wheels to the 'straight-on' position and then over to the right. The interface could be made much easier to use by having the steering return to the central position automatically. This kind of 'intelligence' can reduce the amount of input the user needs to make.

A: What's the worst game control you ever saw?

D: Zaxxon was pretty appalling. Controlling a ship that was moving in isometric 3D with a joystick on the wrong plane was daft. Most other bad interfaces are perfectly usable after an uphill struggle, but they mar the game.

A: I never liked the sports games where you had to waggle the joystick. It always meant your playing ability depended on the type of joystick you owned. And the other games I hated were the ones where you had to use the keys A, Z, O and P as cursors. I could never get to the point where I pressed the correct key unconsciously. So I always had to think about which key to press and think about moving the finger poised over that key.

D: Any home computer game that used a set of keys that couldn't be reprogrammed was always fatal. It's odd though how the flavour of the game is sewn up in the interface, almost as much as the ease of play. But when you think about it, that's not so surprising, its the input and subsequent feedback that involve a player, not interactive presentation of the game – however pretty.

A: That's true. One of the worst games I ever played had the best interface I've come across. The game was to get a small jumping insect out of a set of caverns infested with bats. The only controls were jump left or jump right keys on the keyboard. The clever part was that while your finger was on the key, an 'energy bar' was drawn up on the screen. When the bar reached the required power you released the key and the bug jumped. You quickly became used to the amount of time needed for a certain height jump. And could release it accurately by allowing the key to flick up under the power of the spring beneath. The overall effect was to produce an interface that emulated something resembling the spring loaded plunger on a pinball machine, using only a simple switch.

Case Study 2: A Sliding Square Puzzle

This is a computer implementation of a children's puzzle. The puzzle is a picture cut into squares and placed in a frame. One square is missing and all the squares are jumbled. The idea is to unjumble the squares by sliding them up, down, left or right into the space of the missing piece.

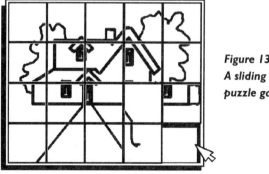

Figure 13
A sliding square
puzzle game

The problem is simply to recreate the sliding activity of the real puzzle in the virtual world of the computer. Let us consider three possible methods of input; the keyboard, the joystick and the mouse.

There are three basic activities involved. Selecting a piece to move, selecting the direction to move the piece in and telling the piece to move.

The keyboard version is implemented using the cursor keys. These control a 'puzzle cursor' that specifically highlights a piece of puzzle, only moving inside the puzzle frame. There is no point in having the cursor free floating, it can only indicate the puzzle pieces. The user can move the cursor left, right, up and down, only restrained by the sides of the frame. It would also be possible to have diagonal moves by reading key-presses from more than one cursor key.

To move a piece, the user would press another key, shift or perhaps the space bar. This would indicate that the cursor key presses should be used in a different context. The direction of the cursor keys now indicates the direction to move the selected piece.

A different method could use the shift key a different way. It could be used on its own to select the piece and change the input mode. The difference is that the user could release the shift key and the piece would still be selected. Then the next cursor movement would be taken as the direction and command to move the piece. However, if the user chose to move a different piece after selecting, there would need to be a deselection command. This could also be done with the shift key.

Both methods could be combined in one interface. This is done simply by checking whether the cursors keys are down when the shift key is pressed.

The joystick interface would be similar to the keyboard. The joystick directions would replace the cursor keys and the fire button the shift/select key.

A mouse interface would be entirely different. A very simple interface would allow the user to select any of the movable pieces with the free floating mouse pointer. Clicking on the empty square would then indicate that the piece should be moved to the new position.

A more elegant method would be one that is closer to the real activity being simulated. This could be done by clicking on the piece to be moved and dragging it in to the space. Ideally it shouldn't be necessary to drag the piece all the way. A click followed by dragging in the right direction should be enough to make the complete move. If the piece were nicely animated and there was some audio feedback this would create quite a realistic feel to the interface.

Note how the two approaches of input efficiency and task simulation produce quite different interfaces.

3.6 The Death of the Keyboard?

The keyboard still dominates the personal computer, but with other computer utilities, such as the ATM, game or information console it is replaced by more appropriate devices. While it is possible to replace a mechanical keyboard with some form of liquid crystal touch tablet that can replicate a keyboard when necessary, until speech recognition is usable, the QWERTY keyboard is still needed for text input. Surprisingly, other cultures that do not share the twenty six letter Roman character set have not seriously attempted to replace it, they have learned English instead.

So the keyboard remains, seemingly a remnant from the typewriter, but still the main form of communication with software. Indeed the success of word processing software threatens handwriting skills, as education establishments increasingly accept written assignments from students straight from the printer. The keyboard thus ensures its own survival.

4

WIMP *and* Controls

In the design of computer interfaces the Graphic User Interface (GUI) is the single most important 'grand consensus'. The latest forms of GUI commonly include windows, icons, menus and pointers and these are usually referred to as WIMP interfaces. Although this type of interface has become a desirable trademark of user-friendly, high-quality software, care must be taken to realize why this is and whether any other approach may be equally valid.

4.1   How to Spot a WIMP

The classic WIMP environment has a menu bar at the top of the screen, from which menus may be 'pulled down' or 'pop-up'. It has one or more sizable windows in which text or icons appear and a pointer that can be positioned to 'select' items. The pointer is usually an arrow-shaped symbol that can be moved around the screen under the control of a one or two-button mouse. These are the basic components but others may be present, including button bars, alert or 'dialogue' boxes and sliders.

There are many operating systems that use a WIMP environment of one kind or another.

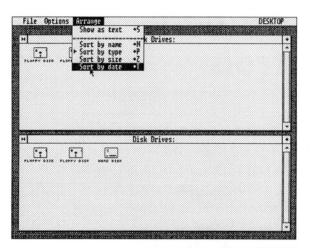

Figure 14
Digital Research's
GEM operating
system

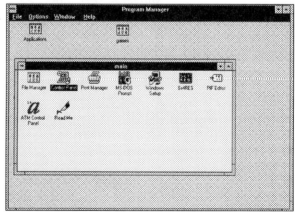

Figure 15
Microsoft's Windows
operating system

It is not always necessary to use the facilities of an operating system to produce a WIMP environment. Many applications use their own WIMP interface. Here are two examples of applications that use their own WIMP environment:

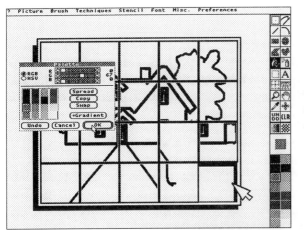

Figure 16
Electronic Arts' Deluxe
Paint

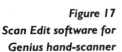

Figure 17
Scan Edit software for
Genius hand-scanner

Analyzing the WIMP Environment

The premise of WIMP is to provide a consistent 'face' or 'front-end' to many apparently different programs, therefore easing the learning process. For instance, the first entry on most menu bars is the option 'File'. The user can safely expect this menu to contain the 'save' and 'open' options for handling the applications data files. There may also be a useful looking 'Help' option.

It is assumed that programmers can reduce design time by creating a generic skeleton program containing the parts common to all applications. They are not required to write the code to produce the various graphics, as these come ready to use. As long as programmers put the pieces together in the prescribed way, the eventual result is a WIMP application. The program should just be a set of functions that act on available data.

This user-centred approach to application design works very well for some programs, particularly those in which graphically represented data is being manipulated. The simple board game Reversi – known also as Othello – is a good example. The size of the board can be changed by the player and the game itself is played by placing counters on a grid. The player just points to the square he wants to move into, and a counter is drawn in.

The success of a WIMP application rests on whether the skills needed to use it are in fact familiar. It is more likely that an application will be produced for a WIMP interface if it is already similar to an existing WIMP program. This is because GUI programs are often designed in modular form and different programs created from similar building blocks. The interface is built up in the same way. In fact, the interface becomes the driving force behind the program.

It could be argued that WIMP has slowed down the evolution of software design. As application designers become more aware that users have standard requirements, they spend less time creating appropriate new interfaces. Then again, there are now more programs available that are readily usable. At least this awareness guarantees that an application has a standard interface.

4.2   The Mechanics of WIMP

A WIMP environment is made up from a number of components which interact to present information, data and user options. There are several different WIMP environments, each implemented in slightly different ways by their authors. In this section the functions of the most common components are explored.

Using graphics interactively

Windows

In a WIMP environment the window represents a work area. A window will contain an application or data such as a document or picture. Windows can be opened or closed, resized and moved around the screen or within a larger window.

Running an application in a WIMP environment will open a window that represents that task. Closing the window shuts an application down or quits the application. If the window represents a datafile, the file is closed or abandoned.

Resizing allows more than one application or datafile to be shown on screen at a time. Movement allows multiple windows to be arranged in a handy layout.

When designing something that will appear in a window, designers must consider what will happen if the window is resized. They must choose between maintaining the ratio of height to width or allow the image shown in the expanded window to be scaled to fit the new shape. For example, a circle remains round but gets bigger or smaller or it is stretched or squashed like a rubber ball. Another possibility is to make no changes to the scale of the windows contents, simply to use the window as a 'keyhole' onto the image.

The interface designer may face a greater number of problems when using windows. As the user has control over the shape and size of the window, the interface itself is changeable.

Windows are useful to display data and to represent 'holding areas' where some item may be stored. If there is no data to be displayed, and no items to be manipulated, there is no need to use a window.

The ability to contain an application or data inside a window, change the windows size and move it around the screen, is not in itself useful. It is only useful in the context where multiple applications need to be running at the same time. Or where two files need to be open at the same time. If this is irrelevant to the application, the designer should consider whether the extra effort of using a window is justified. Of course, as windows are integral to WIMP, designers may find they have no choice in the matter.

Sliders

Windows may be scaled to show only part of an image, for example: the top half of a page of text. If there is more image than can be shown inside the window it will usually have 'sliders' or 'scroll bars'. These are selectable areas that scroll the image under the window. This type of slider is often used in other applications where there is a value that the user can alter. Examples would be a sound utility where the volume could be adjusted, or a game where the user could select a time limit or skill level.

There does not seem to be a standard way to implement sliders. When the user clicks on different parts of the slider, different things happen in different applications. This clearly undermines the 'global consensus' of the WIMP environment and it causes the user to fight with the interface. For example, moving the slider by 'click and drag' in some applications causes the displayed area to scroll immediately, while in others the display is not updated until the slider button is released. Clearly the immediate scroll is dependent on the processor speed of the machine and the programmer's ability. Standardisation collides head-on with technical limitations.

The design of some sliders is fundamentally flawed. With the slider shown below, the user is able to click in the area either side of the central button.

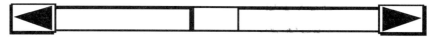

Figure 18 The WIMP environment's slider allows a value to be adjusted or a semi-hidden display to be scrolled

This moves the button one increment in that direction. If the button passes the point the user has clicked, the direction of movement reverses. Users will be looking at the window to see whether the area they require is visible. They may click again without looking at the position of the button. They would be shown the previous area instead of the next area, which may cause confusion.

This problem is usually solved by preventing the button from passing the point that has been clicked. However, the resulting half move of the image can be as irritating to users as being shown the previous image. This is especially true when the image is part of a large document split into pages and the program displays pages separately. This problem can be solved by providing more information within the slider's graphics, as some WIMP environments do.

Sliders provide a visual cue for the user, that the state of something can be changed by degree. They are therefore best used in situations where this is not obvious or where a visual indication of position is better than some other indication.

Using sliders

Where it is technically possible, sliders should show an immediate response on the display. Flawed or not, sliders presented as standard should use the standard implementation. Sliders presented in an original way may not have to follow the standard but should operate intuitively. If there is a choice to be made in the design, an option is to simulate the workings of a real world device. For example, the sliding volume controls of a hifi. These do not move around of their own volition and would be disconcerting if they did. Sliders are not one of the better WIMP concepts and their implementation should be considered carefully.

Icons

In the context of a WIMP environment, an icon is a small pictogram that represents and opens an application, or starts a function. It can be clicked-on to start the application or function. This is the purest form of icon but the icon concept has been stolen and adapted to work in many different contexts.

The value of an icon is that it is easily recognized. A user can spot an icon by its shape, color and screen position and associate it with the task they wish to carry out. Many designers make the mistake of believing that the purpose of an icon is to convey information about its function – to tell the user what it does. But the purpose of an icon is to act as a visual reminder – to remind the user what it does.

On its own, an icon is unable to explain its own function unless it conforms to some widely known standard – an internationally known chemical hazard symbol, for example. An icon for a new function requires an explanation in text, provided by some form of context sensitive help.

An icon can be of any unique symbol. The fact that icons have pictures, aids the user in associating an icon with a function – a picture creates stronger associations than an abstract symbol. Symbols, pictures and text used within an icon should be included for the purpose of making the icon easily distinguishable from other icons and to help the user remember what the icon does.

Icons appear in many forms. Here are four categories that icons can fall into: There is the metaphor icon, e.g. the pencil that accesses the drawing function; the modified alphabetic character icon, where an initial is used in association with another object or symbol. This could be a T together with a cross-hairs to indicate 'Target,' or a 'U' with a line underneath to represent 'Underline.' Also there is the abstract icon, where the designer has been unable to come up with a symbol to adequately express the

Figure 19
Four icons from
each of the main
categories:
metaphor,
modified
alphabetic,
abstract and
explanatory
diagram

concept behind the function. This often results in the use of a checker board, over-lapping squares, crossed double-ended arrows and other primitive symbols. The final category is the explanatory diagram icon that attempts to show the function of the icon with a diagram of what it does.

It is not a good idea to use icons for applications where the user is new to the software. It is very difficult to express an idea, or concept, with a single picture in such a way that the user can make an immediate association. The use of metaphors can express concepts, but only in cases where it is a direct parallel to what is happening. For example, the pencil icon leads to a function where the user draws on screen with the mouse pointer.

Icons are best used in applications that will be used regularly and at which the user is expected to become an 'expert user.' Icons provide a short cut to functions that would otherwise need to be selected from menus or some other laborious method. Icon design is perhaps less critical than some imagine. Users quickly associate a symbol with a function, no matter what the symbol is, so long as it is unique.

Icons work well when they are seen in the context of other icons. By placing an icon among related icons, an association can be built up that clarifies its function. This is useful for an icon that would be ambiguous when seen on its own. For this reason it is good to use non-functional graphics – or indeed text – around functional icons. For example, a block of icons could be set aside and titled 'drawing functions' or 'file functions.' The user then does not need to know the purpose of the individual icons but can remember the function in the context of the title.

It is important to avoid icon confusion; similar colors and symbols in the same areas, tend to hinder, rather than aid instant recognition. If two symbols are similar, such as a pen and a brush in a paint package, it is better not to orient them in the same way.

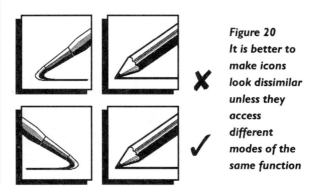

Figure 20
It is better to make icons look dissimilar unless they access different modes of the same function

Figure 21
Avoid icons that
set up the wrong
associations in the
user's mind

Some icons convey the wrong associations. For example, an icon containing a hammer may be associated with the letter T if it is shown upright.

Icons can use symbols, that are universally understood, for common functions. This aids the user by allowing them to recycle the knowledge gained from using other applications. Obviously, standard symbols must only be used for standard functions.

Icons and the first
time user

The purpose of an icon is to act as a landmark for experienced users. A new user will not know what an icon does until they activate it for the first time. Later, they will only remember what the icon does if they made a clear association between the function and the picture on the icon.

Menus

How to use menus

A menu bar provides a list of options that are assumed to be of interest to the user. Menus use English words to define a further list of available commands. In some cases a menu bar is fixed upon the top line of the application, remaining in position while the program runs. Here, it is always available to the user and eradicates the need to learn new keystrokes or command words.

The length of a menu word on a menu bar defines the amount of space available for clicking-on to select it. Thus very long or very short words are to be avoided. In some cases a menu bar can run onto two lines, but this is clearly very untidy and should be avoided.

A menu bar can also appear vertically in a stack, and instead of being in a fixed position can pop-up on demand. One advantage of this is to call up a menu stack that is relevant to the time and place that it's called.

The term 'menu' of course refers to the choices offered in a restaurant. The culinary menu is split into a group of headings under which the dishes served are listed. The number of entries under any heading may vary from two or three to a dozen. Some dishes may not be available.

When a WIMP menu choice is invoked, a sub-menu is called which offers a list of commands thought to be represented by the heading. This is in the form of a 'pop-up' list of commands, listed vertically in a stack. In some implementations this pop-up menu remains in place, obscuring the screen until an option is picked, or until the menu is cancelled by clicking on another part of the screen. The alternative taken by other WIMP systems is to force the user to keep his finger on the mouse button to keep the pop-up menu visible.

A pop-up menu may then invoke another pop-up menu but this is rare and rightly so. Sometimes an option will be in the form of a flag or two-way tick. It can be fairly difficult to tell whether an option has been actually selected, unless there is some immediate evidence, as the menu disappears instantly. Options that cause another pop-up menu or dialogue box to appear are usually denoted by ellipsis after the word on the menu.

An interesting design feature is the grayed-out option. This represents an option that for some reason is not currently available. Conversely, it tells the user that a certain option may become available later on. This is the one good reason for not removing the option altogether. It should be noted that if a list remains constant in length, the user can become familiar with the positions that the options occupy – another reason to use graying instead of removal. Menus that remove items not available can cause great confusion. The user is forced to hunt through all the menus in search of the function that is missing, eventually wondering whether they just imagined the program had that function in the first place.

The comparison of a WIMP menu and restaurant menu may imply that the menu is being used as a metaphor. Unfortunately this logic breaks down very quickly. If I go into a restaurant I have never visited, I know that I can find 'salmon cakes' under 'fish dishes'. If I don't know what tirama-su is, at least finding it under 'desserts' narrows the field.

Figure 22 A proper menu bar with food on it!

This is because the titles in restaurant menus are usually non-overlapping sets. Very few dishes could appear in more than one place. If we draw a Venn diagram to represent the five menu titles: Starters, Fish, Meat, Vegetables, Dessert, we would find very few overlapping areas. We know that sometimes small versions of the main course may appear in Starters.

Taking a word processor as an example, we see the following menu bar options:

File	Edit	View	Insert
Format	Utilities	Macro	Window

Where would you look for the following?

(1)   Search for instances of a certain word.

(2)   Print the document

(3)   Spell check the document

(4)   View a different document

It is unlikely that anyone could be certain which menu bar heading contained the needed function. This is because the headings do not form recognizable discrete sets. Care must be taken to create meaningful categories; the designer should not be too ashamed of defining a miscellaneous category if some options really do not fit in.

A menu is a particularly good way for the user to access functions and utilities that are not required constantly in the application. The user may well notice the option's existence well before it is needed. Menus are not a good way to display modes or switchable states within an application, e.g. whether a snap grid is in use in a graphics package – as the option's state needs to be continually visible to the user. This is what button bars are for.

Alert Boxes and Dialogue Boxes

The alert box informs users that something has happened or is about to happen. A box is displayed in the centre of the screen with the message printed inside it. The program is usually halted and will not continue until a key is pressed or a button clicked to make the box go away. The more complex brother of the alert box is the dialogue box. The dialogue asks for a decision from the user. It may have two or more buttons that can be clicked, or an area for inputting a string of text. It may be as simple as a box that asks 'Are you sure?' And gives the options: yes or no. It may be as complex as a file selector. This shows: the list of files available, with the option to select one or change the directory; an area to enter a file name; and the options to continue or cancel.

How to use alert and dialogue boxes

It is common to provide a default option that is activated when the user presses the Return key. The default should always be the safest option: to cancel, to not make changes, to not lose data.

There are two types of dialogue box used in current WIMP environments. The more common type halts the program until the user responds to its demand. This type is sometimes referred to as modal. The name of the type of dialogue box less often used is the modeless box. This is displayed and allows the user to alter some option or parameter of the application. However, it does not disappear after a selection is made. It remains active while the program runs. This is useful in applications such as word processing: where the user has control over the type style of the text being entered it has the advantage of giving a constant display of the currently selected type. Modeless dialogue boxes are ideal for frequently repeated functions that require a parameter such as text or a range or numbers.

Dialogue boxes are useful devices. In a clear way, they present information and decisions the user can make. However, if asking the user to make a decision that affects their data, the dialogue box must provide information about the consequences of the choice. For example, a dialogue box displayed for a global search and replace function should warn that it may be difficult to reverse the operation. If a spell checker offers the option to check the whole document, following a check of a high-lighted word, it should warn the user that this will result in the loss of their current position in the document, if a spelling error is found. On the same point, the button that initiates a function from a dialogue box is often marked 'OK.' It is better if this button says what the function will do. For example it should say, 'print document,' 'save file' or whatever the function does.

Use alert boxes for one off messages to the user. Use dialogue boxes to provide additional options after the main option has been selected from the menu. Use dialogue boxes to enter minor data like text for file names, passwords and titles.

Button Bars

How to use buttons

Many applications, that use a mouse as the input device, feature button bars. This is an area of the screen where additional functions are accessed by clicking on an icon. Unlike the irregular shapes used for applications icons on the desktop, buttons are usually represented as a square. Some WIMPs show the buttons pressed in to indicate they are activated, while others may simply highlight them. Buttons sometimes select a function and sometimes switch or toggle something between two states. A further variety is called the 'radio button'. This is a button that when activated, de-activates another button.

Arrow buttons are sometimes used to control a value. One button increases a value while another decreases it. This is a useful way of adjusting a value without forcing the user to abandon the mouse and use the keyboard.

Button bars are useful for providing quick access to a program's functions or the option to change frequently used settings. It is because they are so accessible that care must be taken not to assign critical functions to them. 'Turn music on/off', is an appropriate function to assign to a button. 'Format hard disk' is not.

4.3 Designing for the WIMP Environment

Designing for a WIMP environment imposes a number of restraints on the designer. Therefore, it is worth a few minutes thought to decide whether a GUI is the right type of interface for the application. Having decided that the application does require a WIMP interface, it is worth a few minutes more thought to analyze the functions of the program and how the various WIMP components can be used to represent them.

Do You Need a WIMP Environment?

The WIMP environment can be used as an interface for most applications. However, it provides many facilities that may be surplus, irrelevant or even incompatible to some applications. The designer must decide.

WIMP interfaces are good at working with other programs. They have facilities to move easily from one to another without losing data or settings. They are good at providing a consistent interface across a range of applications. So a suite of programs could all operate in a similar way. This also saves development effort.

WIMP interfaces are good for manipulating data of a graphical nature. They present information in a clear and consistent way. Complex applications can be presented to the user in easily digested chunks. They are good for applications that require dynamic changing of user functions, something useful to applications of a creative or exploratory nature.

Programs that are best suited to the WIMP environment are user driven – the user chooses when to apply functions using the tools available.

However, there are good reasons to not use a WIMP interface for certain applications. There is a large overhead in both operating speed and complexity with graphical interfaces. This would normally rule out the use of a WIMP for a real time application. Where the display of information and response to it is critical, the interface would interrupt the flow of data and hamper input. Some applications require a rigid, single path structure. A WIMP interface is not appropriate for this.

For applications where the primary input device is not a mouse, the normal implementation of the WIMP environment is useless. As soon as the user takes their hand off the mouse, the benefit of the mouse driven interface disappears.

The Good GUI Guide

Here are a few useful tips specifically for the WIMP interface designer.

Be consistent with other applications that use the same environment. Follow the conventions and join the 'grand consensus.' Otherwise why are you using it?

Consistency with other applications is useful because it increases the amount that is familiar to the user and decreases the amount to learn.

Use a menu bar with a small number of meaningful categories. Keep the number of options under each menu option limited to no more than the limit of human short term memory, i.e. about seven or eight. If this isn't possible, you either need to trim down functions or seek alternative structures.

There are a couple of ways of dividing functions into categories. They can be lumped together by type – for example, all the file operations placed under the heading File. Or they can be lumped together by context – for example, a variety of options that all operate on highlighted text. The first method is the current convention and should be used for common – already existing – functions. The second can be used as an alternative method of dividing up new functions that have no established conventional place in the menus.

Naming functions on menus

When naming functions use a combination of short descriptive words that create an association in the users mind. To use the examples from the section on menus above:

Function	Suggested name
(1) Search for instances of a certain word	Find word
(2) Print the document	Print out
(3) Spell check the document	Spell check
(4) View a different document	View new doc

Avoid using similar sounding function names under separate headings. It is easier to remember a unique item than one that is similar to another.

Create as few windows and dialogue boxes as possible and remove one before overlaying another. Overlapping elements look fussy, visually cluttered, and can confuse the user.

Using buttons and icons

Use buttons for two state options and modes. Use buttons for frequently used functions, particularly those to do with manipulating the display of data.

Make sure icons are clear and simple. If they cannot be simple, make them distinctive.

Give consideration to the 'input focus': that point of the screen the user is looking at. Don't dislocate a button, slider, icon or clickable area, from the function or data it affects.

When positioning menu items and buttons remember that users do things unconsciously and sometimes misclick the mouse. Items that have opposite meanings should be separated to avoid disasters. An example would be: avoid placing save file just above or below open file in a menu.

How to position buttons

Always put the button that cancels an operation in a consistent position. This is one way of making the user's unconscious automatic behaviour work to advantage. Buttons that should be in the same position consistently are those that cancel an operation without loss of data. This is so that if the user clicks without thinking, they will not do any harm. A consistent position for the cancel button may not be appropriate at the end of a long procedure to set up a function – printing a document for example. Cancelling unconsciously and thus losing all the time taken in going through the procedure would be frustrating for the user. This may conflict with being consistent with other applications. The rule is to use consistency to work for the user's benefit, it is only necessary to be consistent where it has a specific purpose.

Don't make all aspects of 'open' and 'save file' boxes alike. Always title them to avoid confusion and preferably alter the position of the button that makes the operation proceed. This will help prevent the user absent-mindedly loading or saving a file over their data.

Use one-option alert boxes to confirm that an operation or function has been carried out when there is no other indication that it has.

And Don't Forget the Keyboard

When designing for a WIMP environment the keyboard's significance tends to be played down, except where text entry is necessary. However, many applications have keyboard equivalent keystrokes. Where a multiple keystroke can represent a menu selection, this is known as an accelerator or hot-key. Hot-keys are essential for functions that may be accessed continually or at regular intervals. Hot-keys are intended to minimize the amount of clicking and menu selection required and thus reduce the amount of time and effort used. They have the advantage of allowing the user to keep their fingers on the keyboard. While hot-keys are generally a good thing that benefit the user's productivity, they can also contribute to problems with RSI. See the previous chapter.

Some people prefer not to use a mouse or may not have one connected when they need to use the program. Remember to include accelerators and hot keys to access the menus and functions. Also use the cursor keys to move scrollable areas, or to move the cursor around text and data areas.

D: When I first saw Windows 2.0 on the PC, it was completely hopeless. By the time version 3.0 came out Microsoft had borrowed the Mac's interface to form the Windows we all know and love. But the main aim of Windows is not to improve the user's life, it is to help Microsoft take over the world.

A: Hey, don't knock it. Wasn't it God who said: 'the WIMPs shall inherit the Earth?' Isn't it to everyone's benefit that there should be a standard method of interacting with the computer? After all there are many common interfaces between man and machine: cars, telephones, bicycles for example.

D: That's perfectly true, although most of these have evolved to some extent, and certainly not via one company alone. But your examples lay bare the strength of established interfaces. Any of the machines you mentioned, once their interfaces have been learned, can be used anywhere in the world (bar externally forced local variations).

Is the WIMP interface the simplest and most bare bones basic state that the computer interface can reach? I think WIMP as we often see it may be the equivalent of a hydrogen-powered car, two pretty tin cans connected with wire, or the penny farthing. Examples of their type, but not necessarily defining examples.

A: WIMP isn't intended to be 'bare bones.' It proclaims itself as the latest high technology. 'Look how many features I've got,' it says. So as a universal interface maybe it's doomed to failure.

To my mind, WIMPs don't provide the right kind of link between man and machine. Cars, bikes, phones; once their interface is learnt they can be used entirely unconsciously. Shouldn't we, as interface designers, be trying to create the software equivalent of the steering wheel? An intuitive mechanical link between the user's intention and the state of the machine. Certainly the mouse achieves this, but the rest...?

D: Yes, you could be right there. The mouse is the strongest part of WIMP, the rest is probably transient and subject to presentational fashion. Have you seen my pink plastic telephone?

A: No, but I've seen telephones in all shapes and sizes. And they all work the same way up to a point. The basic functions are the same but any additional features are individual to the model. I can foresee problems over the next couple of decades when the domestic telephone's functions will include video and data communications. Will designers be tempted to go for a sophisticated interface like a WIMP or will they keep the old handset and keypad?

4.4   Case Studies

If we could all draw, it would not follow that we would all be as able as Leonardo da Vinci. Similarly, ready-made GUI pieces do not turn themselves into well designed applications. It is necessary to be critically aware of needs and basic points all through the design process. As design goals may vary, an argument used to veto one idea can sometimes be used to support another. Putting oneself in the shoes of the user certainly helps cut through apparent contradictions.

Case Study 1: Search and Replace in a Menu

While working with text, it is common to search for the occurrence of a word or phrase, perhaps to alter it or replace it.

One design option would be to include an appropriate pop-up menu:

> Find..
> Replace..
> Find again

Each of the first two options could bring up a dialogue box to allow text entry of the search word, and text for the replacement word for the second option. Other search conditions such as direction of search, case sensitivity, and whether the word is part or whole would also be asked for in the dialogue. After the first case has been found, the user may select 'Find again' to continue searching for matches through the document.

This, however, is not a particularly good design. The 'Find again' may be used many times in quick succession and is thus inappropriate as a menu item. The search dialogue box is a sub-set of the replace dialogue box, and could be called from the same menu command. At the moment, three lines of pop-up menu are taken by this function.

A better implementation used by some developers is to use just one menu item 'Search/Replace' to invoke a single dialogue box. This box has text entry for both search and replacement words, with a check box to designate whether a straight 'search' or 'search and replace' is required, as well as the further options previously described. When the user has finished, a small modeless box containing only the search/replace text and a button marked 'again' appears. The user may move the box to an appropriate place and click on the 'again' button to search through the text.

This assumes that the user does not wish to run a search and a search-with-replace concurrently and this seems reasonable. It is also wise to point out that modeless dialogue boxes may interfere with other functions, as the box remains until the user shuts it down. As usual, design must be done as a whole, not in parts.

Case Study 2: The Filebox

Files exist on most systems as a string of characters followed by a suffix that further describes them. For most applications, files are created to store data. Many applications force the user to associate their data or work with a Disk Operating System (DOS) filename. In this sense, the user and the computer are 'meeting each other half-way' the advantage being: the filename is always a discrete and – usually – application independent entity that the DOS understands. However, files are not always easy for the user to find and manipulate.

The filebox has become the standard way for a user to search for and retrieve files and is a good example of the WIMP interface at work. First a list of files is alphabetically sorted and represented as a list of names. The directory from which the files come may be determined either by the application or by the directory from which the application was started. The application may filter for certain files by suffix; there is no point showing the user files that have no meaning in the context of the program. The resulting list is displayed in a window and scrolled, if necessary, to reveal all the items. The user can now treat the files like names in an address book. By clicking on a name, the user can select it as the active name. The user can then choose to open the file, or at any time cancel the operation.

Early interfaces could only handle a single text choice entry, which allowed the possibility of spelling errors. Just producing a list isn't enough, however. It is the scrolling to check each entry, without limiting the window size, that makes the filebox so good. By allowing the user to see the file and click directly on the words, a very positive connection is made, reducing errors and making life easier. At any point the user can push the cancel button – that is always visible – to return the application to its former state.

Case Study 3: Drawing a Circle

A fully featured drawing package allows the user to draw shapes that can later be altered. We look at the simple task of drawing a circle in a WIMP application.

Unbelievably, this seemingly simple task is not consistent in all packages. The first problem is that a circle is only a special case of an ellipse – one whose foci meet at a common centre. When a user defines an ellipse dynamically, they pull the shape out from the starting point, defining two extremes:

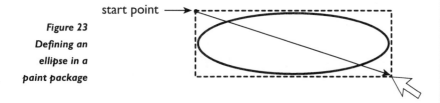

start point

Figure 23

Defining an

ellipse in a

paint package

Thus an ellipse is fitted inside a rectangular box formed with one corner as the start position, and the opposite corner as the current cursor position. In this sense, a circle is treated as an ellipse that happens to fit into a square, and is referred to as being 'constrained.'

A circle may need to be described from its centre, as opposed to its edges. For instance, to draw a third circle to fit in between a pair of concentric circles, you need to draw it from the common centre.

Most packages allow the user to select a circle drawing tool, which allows ellipses to be drawn in the fashion described above. To use the circle constraint, a key must be pressed while using the mouse. Another key is pressed down to draw the circle from a central position, thus the user may end up with a finger on the Shift key, one finger on the Alt key and a finger on a pointer button as the shape is dragged out. Obviously this is a little awkward, but worse, it requires a further source of information to remind the user of the keys required.

Instead of the single ellipse tool, the tool could have four facets, described by a set of zoom out icons:

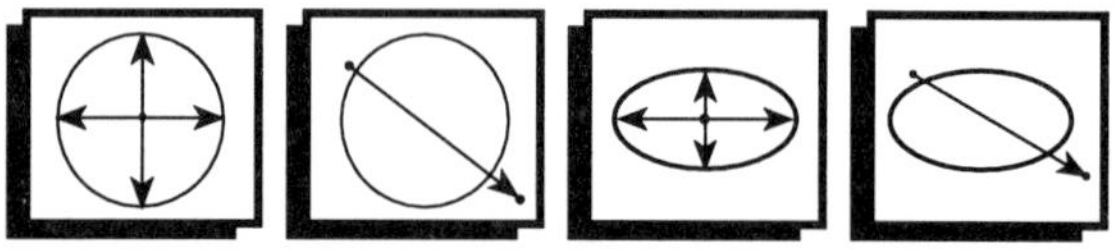

Figure 24
Icons that describe four
different aspects of a
circle drawing function

This differentiates between the ellipse and a circle, and how they are centred.

4.5 Choosing a GUI

The popularity of window type interfaces has led to the terms GUI and WIMP being somewhat interchangeable. A GUI does not have to be a WIMP application and there are many applications such as interactive TV and video information systems that prove this.

When designing an interface, think about how it should ideally look. Then think how it would look under one of the proprietary graphical interfaces popular on your target machine. By separating the two in this manner, you can see what may be lost from the ideal case, against the gains of using the proprietary option.

5

Context Switching

It is important to provide the user with clues when context
is changed in a program. To do that, the designer needs to
recognize a context change and to understand the
techniques that can be used to illustrate the change.

5.1   What is Context Switching?

While talking, we have several ways of changing the context of communication. Raising tone – in English – means we are asking a question. A slight dip is used to indicate an imperative, or an order. There are further clues in body language.

In conversation we are usually aware when the subject has changed. Misunderstandings and talking 'at cross purposes' occur when one person has missed the cue for the subject change. This is used to good effect in situation comedy but in an application program it's not so funny.

In software, the conversation is one sided. The user tells the program what to do and the program tells the user what it is doing. The user can say 'I want to change the conversation' but it is always the computer that makes the change by saying: 'Okay, now we're talking about.'

5.2   Types of Context Change

It is usually the user who initiates a major mode change, but other context changes are made by the software. There are identifiable types of context change and different ways of introducing them.

Transitions

The commonest type of context change is the transition. This happens when the program moves from one major mode to another. Some functions will remain the same while others may be deactivated or perform differently. The main task may be broken into different activities each represented by a mode. An example would be a database program where entering data and searching for it were different modes.

In film and video, the transition between one context and another may be punctuated with a special effect such as fading the screen, sliding one image over another or panning out from an extreme close-up. In speech, such transitions are prefaced with stock phrases such as: 'I've been meaning to tell you,' ' you know what,' ' and another thing' and 'Hey!' These devices help the audience prepare themselves for reception of information in a new context.

Interludes

Although most context changes are switches between one state and another state, some changes are temporary and brief. These are interludes in the main task.

A conversation between people may be halted for a moment to perform a sub-task such as asking: 'Do you want milk and sugar?' A TV program is stopped to show a commercial break. The main activity is interrupted to perform another task.

Of the two types of interlude, the first is not specifically called by the user. It is imposed by the program. A dialogue box, which may stop all other operation, will return the user to where they were before the necessary information was displayed.

The second type of interlude is user controlled, where a sub function is activated from the main program. This change is only temporary and it is probable that only one function works in this context. An example might be the 'print document' function of a word processor.

Hidden

The hidden context change is one where there is no apparent change of mode, but the function of the program has changed significantly. For example: there is a great deal of difference between a word processor with no data loaded and one that has text entered. With no text entered, many of the functions cannot work: printing, saving and formatting cannot be done without raw material to work with. Many word processors check for alterations to documents and change the operation when text is entered. When this happens, the context has changed although the user may be unaware of its happening.

5.3 Modes

A mode is a particular form of operation that dictates how some of the standard tools and functions will operate.

Reverse gear in a car can be said to be a different mode of operation. The car's controls will still work while the car is in reverse, but have different effects with respect to the forward gears. The accelerator now moves the car backwards. Steering to the left now turns the car so it faces further right. Looking out of the front window will no longer help with avoiding obstacles. However, the heating controls will be unaffected. It is usually non-trivial to put a car into reverse gear; there may be no indication on the dashboard that the car is no longer travelling forwards.

In software, modes are used to increase the range of options to the user and to differentiate between tasks. A paint program may use a number of different modes where the same basic controls produce different effects.

An integrated office package may use modes to differentiate between word processing, using the spreadsheet and so on.

A tape recorder has two distinct modes, playback and record. The play button needs to be pressed together with the record button to facilitate the change of mode. Rewind and fast forward will move the tape as expected in either mode, and stop – stops either operation. Usually a red light is used to indicate recording. This is important, as the user must be reminded that recording, unlike playing, can overwrite information that is already on the tape. The tape recorder example illustrates how a mode is changed in the real world. A software mode change should be as intuitive. The designer must ask:

What warning is the user given that the mode has changed? And do the controls still work in a logical manner? What feedback changes occur? Some software examples follow.

Snap Grid

Both painting and drawing packages often allow the artist to draw or drop shapes onto the vertices of a grid. Thus a rectangle dragged across the screen 'snaps' into position with its edges automatically aligned to the grid.

Clearly some drawing operations will be affected by the grid, and in different ways, while others will not. The perfect feedback indication, that a grid is in use, is to actually draw a faint grid in the background. When this isn't possible the next best thing is a bar button clearly visible, so the user can check if they are not sure of the package's behavior.

Draft View

Word processors with 'What You See Is What You Get' or WYSIWYG capability often allow the writer to work in a draft mode that is quicker – and sometimes easier – to read as it uses a standard font. Obviously the screen will appear different for each mode, but the writer should still be warned that certain operations will now behave differently, such as: italics, underlining and other changes to the typeface or page layout.

Game Overview Map

Flight simulators and war games often include a strategic overview map. This allows the player to plan their campaign, viewing the complete battlefield. The normal view will be a close up of the action. The display may change from abstract symbols representing a small scale to a realistic display that gives more detail. There may not be enough space to show all the information in the overview. This is a context change that is easily understood. It is similar to the activity of searching for a city in an atlas or a sentence in a book. The searcher scans the pages to the right one, then takes a closer look to see the detail. The overview map is also used in desktop publishing and word processors to show a small version of a page of text, without showing the actual text.

5.4 Context Related Techniques

A wide variety of techniques is used to provide the visual cues that indicate a context change. Here are some of the important ones:

Establishers

In film and video a sequence that tells a story is started with an establishing shot. For example, a gangster story may start off with a picture of the Chicago skyline with a caption that says 'Chicago 1928.' This allows the audience to understand the context in which they see the next shot: an old-fashioned car driving down a street. Without this clue, the audience might see a modern street and in that context, the age of the car would be unusual and significant.

How to illustrate a context change

An establisher can be as simple and unobtrusive as briefly highlighting a button, or area, when it is clicked. On the other hand, it could be a dialogue box that is displayed before a new mode is entered.

Pauses

A short pause before changing mode can provide a useful way of indicating a context change. On old, slow computers, it is sometimes possible to see the screen display being redrawn. The effect is not considered desirable and efforts have been made to eliminate it with faster hardware and software. However, the effect does perform a useful service. It allows the user time to assimilate what is happening and to keep pace with the computer. Humans expect mechanical things to take time to operate, we feel uncomfortable with things that operate faster than our nervous system can respond.

Context Specific Pointers

How to use graphic feedback to illustrate context

The usual WIMP application pointer is an arrow. However, many applications change the pointer shape depending on the context they are in, i.e. what the program will do if the user clicks now. This position dependent feedback is another useful exploration tool, as the user can 'scan' the screen and see how different objects affect the pointer. This in turn suggests what the object's use is. This process is used to good effect in graphic adventures.

There are various commonly used pointer shapes:

An 'I bar' for positioning a text cursor;

Cross hairs to mark a significant position for selection;

A circle to mark the point of rotation;

A no-entry sign to indicate that an operation is illegal in the current context;

A copy of an icon to show that it is being dragged.

The 'busy' symbol, which may be an hourglass, a 'ZZZ', a clock, a busy bee, etc. is used to indicate that the processor is too busy to receive input.

Figure 25 Three types of 'busy' pointers

Using feedback

This avoids the user receiving late feedback or, worse, failing to make their input because they made it when the computer wasn't listening or ready. And late feedback is of no use as it breaks the illusion of communication.

A range of context sensitive pointers can often be found in paint packages. For example: the fill area tool is often represented as a paint can or paint roller. When the mode is changed to line drawing, the pointer changes to a pencil. When the mode is changed to cutting out an area, the pointer changes to a pair of scissors. On the other hand, during any of these activities, the pointer can be moved over the tool bar. When this happens, the mode is changed to tool selection and the pointer changed to a simple arrow. This tells the user that the selected tool has no effect in this context.

Attracting Attention to Different Input

How to create feedback

Humans are able to search a page of text and pick out a number without reading every letter. This natural ability can be exploited by the designer.

Attention can be drawn to an item by making it stand out from the other items surrounding it.

It is not too difficult to work out what will attract a user's attention. Human senses are geared to primeval survival. Therefore the things that stand out from the environment are: movement, unexpected sound, colour and pattern. Therefore, the ways of attracting attention to a particular screen area are to use: animation, a colour that is unusual or meaningful like red, or a shape or symbol that is unique. It would be difficult to use sound on its own to indicate a screen position. However it has been used very effectively, especially in games, to indicate context changes. This is sometimes one or two beeps of varying pitch, or it could be a change in the background music to indicate that there is going to be a change in activity.

Using sound as feedback

5.5 Errors Caused by Context Switching

People can be confused, 'put off their stroke,' or forced into making errors by sudden context changes in software. Why does this happen?

When a person has been using a tool, machine, or computer software, for some-time they begin to operate it automatically. Repetition of a series of movements or actions becomes ingrained. This happens subconsciously, allowing the mind to concentrate on the required result, rather than making the hand or muscle movements. The person may not even realize they have learned to do this. A driver who is asked how to steer a car round a corner would probably say: 'I turn the wheel right and the car turns.' However, in the car they would turn the wheel to the left in anticipation of turning and then to the right. If they didn't do this, the rear wheels would cut the corner and perhaps hit the kerb. Somewhere, in the course of learning to drive, they have picked up the skills of steering and now they no longer have to think about how to do it. They just do it.

On the road, the likeliest cause of a road accident is a sudden change in context. A car pulls out of a turning, suddenly blocking the road that was clear. A sudden context change in software is not so serious. However, in software, context changes happen more often. Sometimes they are obvious – when a dialogue box pops up to obscure the screen – and sometimes they go unnoticed – when cursoring past an unseen control code that changes entered text to bold.

In video games, part of the challenge is to respond quickly to new situations. The skill lies in learning the necessary automatic movements to be able to respond quickly enough. The penalty for failure is to start again. Sometimes the danger is made obvious – with a monster appearing – and sometimes the danger is not obvious and must be discovered – the monster flashes green prior to exploding.

Applications can be as frustrating to use as computer games if the user is penalized for missing a context change. An application that provides no feedback at all has not told the user to change what they are doing. This will inevitably result in the user making an error. Using a common function – such as saving a file – will become automatic to the user. If the function displays a dialogue box that says:

Save this file. Are you sure?

the user will get used to clicking 'yes' without reading the text in the dialogue. One time in a thousand, the disk where the file is to be stored will be full. If, in this situation, the dialogue box says 'Disk full, do you want to abandon the file?' It can be almost guaranteed that the user will press 'yes' automatically.

Another example of how changing context can cause confusion to the user is the ATM or cashpoint machine mentioned in chapter 1 of this section. These machines enable the bank's customers to get cash quickly from their account. The procedure for doing this becomes an automatic, subconscious activity. It may be something like: Push in card, enter PIN number, select cash withdrawal, enter amount to be withdrawn, remove card, receive cash. A user of this system, who is operating it subconsciously, can easily be confused at several points. Changing the layout of the keypad, for entering the PIN number, is likely to cause the user to enter it incorrectly. Another problem would occur if the position of the keys did not match the pattern tapped out subconsciously. A more likely problem occurs when the machine is nearly out of cash. If the machine does not have enough money to fulfil the customer's request, it usually prints a message and cancels the operation. The subconscious user, not reading the message, is then dismayed that the operation seems to have proceeded normally but the money hasn't come out.

When actions become automatic it is easy to make errors. Usually the errors are caused by doing the right action in the wrong context. For example, a person saves over a file when they meant to cancel the operation. This is particularly true in graphic user interfaces, where an operation is based on physical positions and hand movements. The actions to save and cancel are both the same but they operate on different parts of the screen.

If errors can be caused by unnoticed context changes and also by the user doing something automatically and unconsciously, what can be done to prevent these errors? Strangely it is the context change that can solve the problem. The user has to be brought out of an oblivious working state into conscious realization. The way to do that is to show something new and unusual – something out of context.

To prevent errors, careful consideration must be given to where and how context changes will occur in an application. It is best to make one context look very different from another, using colour, screen layout or whatever else is effective. One alternative course of action is to reduce the number of context changes to a minimum and where they occur, make them as obvious as possible.

5.6 Losing Transparency

What is transparency?

The concept of transparency has been mentioned in previous chapters and refers to the degree to which the user is unaware of the machine as an intermediary. If a program exists to accomplish some sort of task – writing a letter, doing the accounts, destroying alien hordes, etc. – then a transparent interface is one that doesn't get in the way of that task. As a program may occasionally need to alter the relationship between the user and the task, we need to investigate what lies between the two.

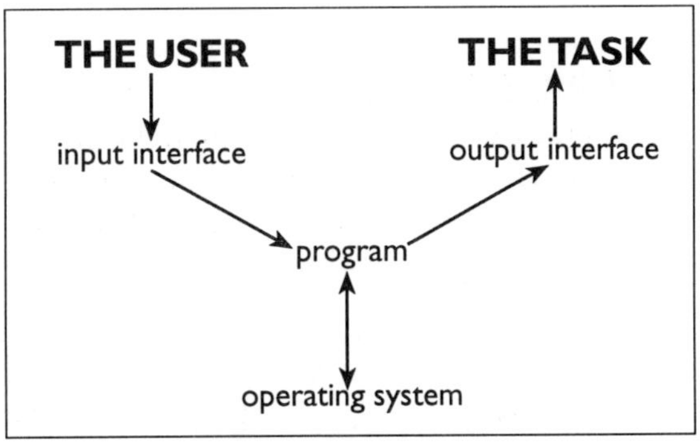

Figure 26
The relationship between program and user

THE USER	THE TASK
input interface	output interface
program	
operating system	

The ideal relationship between the program and the user is that of reserved butler, quietly going about his business, with his master neither knowing nor caring much about him. When the need arises, he gently informs his master that a visitor is at the door, or that dinner is being served.

There are several easily identified points at which the interface may need to break with a direct relationship with the task. It is at these points that transparency is most at risk.

Starting a Program

The entry point into a program is where the interface must first establish itself. In this respect, a WIMP interface started from within a WIMP environment has a natural advantage.

To continue a previously started task, program data may need to be reloaded. When retrieving a saved task, if the user is only presented with a list of data files he is forced to break the association with the task, and work with the operating system parlance. There are various ways to help maintain the user-task connection. Many role-playing type games ask players for descriptive strings rather than file names when the players wish to save their positions in the game. For example:

> 'Just before the Big Red door'
> 'Knee deep in Death'

These strings are then associated with the saved data files, and used as a reference to loading.

Drawing applications can present the user with a miniature view of the artwork that appears with the filename. An additional method is to give the users a list of the last files they were working with. This is very sensible as a user will no doubt be saving and loading the same files while working on a single task.

Stopping a Program

When a program is terminated, the relationship between the user and the task should be ended smoothly, if not logically. As a user expects to be able to shut a program down at will, the program cannot quite dictate the circumstances of shutdown.

Most modern games will fade out and return to the main screen from which the user can exit to the OS. This is a presentational issue, but it nevertheless retains the sense that the game world is real and continuous. If you dream of a telephone when it is really ringing by your bedside, a smooth transition is preferable to a harsh one.

Speed

The slow speed of the hardware can make some interfaces unusable, simply because the program is one step behind the user. The user is forced to take the speed of the interface into account, thus breaking the connection with the task. This is still one of the fundamental reasons for lack of transparency. One way to reduce this problem is not to ask the user for input while the processor is too busy to handle it. The use of busy pointers - as mentioned above - highlights this.

Too Small a Window

Another problem area arises when too much information needs to be handled and the screen is no longer big enough to show it. This happens at some point to nearly all applications and should be handled in sympathy with the task. As the screen size is unlikely to be relevant to the task in hand, the user should not be aware that the screen is a problem.

To present a continuous landscape, action games evolved the use of scrolling, which has the effect of a panning camera. Immediately the user understands that the game world is not limited to the screen, but the screen is a window onto the world.

Error Handling

When an error occurs, the user will of course be very aware that he is using a computer. Most household tools, after all, do not suffer from crashes. Most errors occurring through standard application use are caused by the program expecting something that it isn't given, such as the right floppy disk or a number below one hundred. To cause least break up between user and task, error messages and resulting options should be related as closely to the task as possible.

For example, here are two messages given for the same error:

> Error writing file to drive.
> There is insufficient room on the drive to save the document.

When it is couched as a problem with the document's size, users are at least able to see for themselves that, by discarding some text, they can salvage some of their work.

5.7   Other Issues

Keeping it Constant

Whatever does change in a program, it is wise to keep something constant, so the user has a perspective on the application as a whole. The title bar in a WIMP environment usually contains the title of the application program itself, while a constant reminder of the current mode can be placed on a lower bar in the program window. If a program can be characterized by a set of distinct modes, then it should always be possible to display a single message relating to it. For instance, some word processors can be in either 'Page', 'Outline' or 'Draft' modes.

Context Sensitive Help

One advantage of modes is that they can aid intelligent help utilities to work out what a user is stuck on. Help is context sensitive if it applies to what the user is doing when it is called for. For instance, help in a programmer's editor may give a description of the meaning of the last instruction that was written. Help itself will be discussed in detail later in Chapter 11.

5.8   Case Study: Getting a Position on a Map

Using graphics interactively

This example shows many of the context change issues at work.

A program needs a country as input, and the interface interrupts its normal screen to present a map of the world, the idea being for the user to select a country by clicking on its geographical position.

The user, not having worked with the current screen context before, needs to feel that he understands the controls. This is done via experimentation with the pointer and watching for feedback.

In summary the user needs to:

> 1) Establish possible options, i.e. legal domain,
> 2) Find the required selection,
> 3) Check for confirmation that the selection was taken.

In the context of the map these relate to:

> 1) Countries,
> 2) Positioning the cursor over a country,
> 3) Country flashes when clicked, display returns.

How to use feedback

Something on the screen whether it be on a caption bar or a help box should remind the user that the program is now waiting for a country to be selected. This prompt reminds the user of what is expected, useful if concentration has slipped.

The domain is in this case a country. So if the pointer is over the sea, the user must realize that this selection would not be acceptable. This can be indicated by a dormant or neutral pointer. There is no need to be negative by using a no entrance sign – for instance – as this is more often used to signify domain that is illegal in the given context, as opposed to impossible.

When the user moves over a country, the pointer should change to indicate that a selection is acceptable. The cue should be something positive such as a target, or a crosshair, etc. If it is within the scope of the program, the country could be graphically outlined, or filled in with a vivid color. This is more useful if multiple selections are possible.

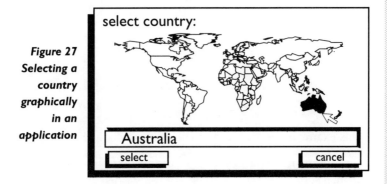

Figure 27
Selecting a
country
graphically
in an
application

To emphasize that the selection is recognized, the name of the country should appear in a separate selection box. This is especially useful if the map is too small for text to be superimposed on it. By this method the user can sweep the map and intuitively work out what and how to select legal input from the domain. The final selection can be done by a button on a box, or a double click over the graphic of the country. If done by double click, it is necessary that the focus is accurately over the selection. As an error could occur here, the best feedback would be to flash the country selected to visually confirm the selection.

5.9 Designing in Context

The work done by a program to help with context changes, such as loading and showing a different cursor, or re-drawing a portion of the screen usually requires a fair amount of hardware resources. As programs always seem to outstrip the resources available to them, there is pressure on designers not to spend more resources on an area seen as cosmetic.

Context changes in software cannot be avoided. It is in the nature of computers that they are reactive, changing the information they present, depending on what the user is doing. It is important to anticipate how a user may react to a given change in context and to ensure that the change is not overlooked. It is also important that the user understands the new situation after a context change has taken place. Therefore it is worth spending resources in this area.

6

Graphics, Animation and Screen Presentation

*I*t is said that: 'a picture is worth a thousand words.' This is *not always true. Pictures and text both communicate information. Many factors affect the value of the information communicated.*

6.1   Use of Graphics

An on-line shopping catalog intends to offer plants and flowers. The application's designer has the choice of using plain text or illustrations of the blooms available. Although the decision seems clear-cut, there may be other factors involved such as: the amount of data that can be transmitted, or the space available in the database for storing it. Whatever the difficulties, in this case, the benefits of graphics outweigh the disadvantages. A prosaic description of a flower, no matter how poetic or accurate, is never as good as a simple picture. The illustration of a flower can be a hand drawn botanical study, showing the shape of leaves, root systems and number of petals; it can be a photograph that shows a real plant. However, neither illustration would be any good without the catalog text giving information on growing conditions, seasons, and soil. The designer must analyze the information to be communicated and provide pictures where pictures offer better information than text is able to.

Three types of graphic images are used in computer applications: static, animated and interactive graphics. Static graphics are simply pictures, illustrations or charts displayed by the program. Animated graphics refer to images that appear to move on screen. Interactive graphics change dynamically with input entered into the computer.

Using graphics interactively

Graphics are good at communicating certain types of information. The plant catalog contains pictures of flowers. The information being provided is not just 'this is what the plant looks like.' It is also communicating: 'this is the color, this is the shape, this is the size.' All these elements are quantifiable. In many applications there is a need to communicate data that is in the form of quantities such as: time, disk space, distance, cost, or speed. It is much easier to assimilate this kind of information if it is shown in a graphical form. However, it is important to include a reference to show what the data is being measured against. For example: an application that takes a period of time to run has to tell the user how long it will take. It could do this simply by printing the percentage of the task completed on the screen. A better way is to show the percentage as a bar graph; where the length of the bar represents the amount of task left to do. However, the bar on its own is insufficient information. It has to be shown in relation to something that represents 100 per cent of the task.

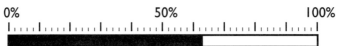

0%   50%   100%

Figure 28 How much is left to do can be seen at a glance using a bar graph like this. It is important to show the numbered scale or the graph seems meaningless.

Graphics can be used to draw attention to something. When there is a mass of information on display, it is difficult to pick out vital items camouflaged by the ordinary. Underlining, emboldening text or flashing a cursor make information stand out. This 'highlighting' is achieved by creating a contrast – in color, tone or movement – with the surrounding image. For example, with a multicolored moving image – perhaps a movie of a street scene – the best highlight would be something static drawn in a plain color. On the other hand, for a screen full of static text, the best highlight is a moving image in a color that contrasts with the text.

Drawing attention to something

An Overview of Bitmap Graphics

There is a piece of tapestry. It is three hundred and twenty stitches across by two hundred stitches down. The needle woman, who is making the tapestry from a kit, has 256 different magic threads. She is very pleased. The last tapestry she made, she could only use sixteen magic threads. The needle woman has just finished her design. She followed the instructions and used the different numbered threads to make the stitches. Now all she has to do is use the magic chart to color the stitches. She has a choice of two million different shades on the chart to apply to the 256 threads. Although the needle woman had made many magic tapestry kits, she was always intrigued that once she had sewn in the threads she didn't need to touch the tapestry. She could change all the colors of the threads by changing the left-over ones still in the box. 'There!' she said, holding the tapestry up to show her cat, 'I've made a lovely green sky and a nice maroon-colored beach.'

Clearly this is an analogy. The cloth represents the screen. Each stitch is a pixel. Each thread is a pixel value. The magic color chart is the list of available colors that the display will handle. The 256 different threads represent the palette of pixel values that can be displayed, each one of which can be set to any of the two million colors.

Screen displays explained

6.2 General Screen Presentation

A few general principles can be applied to create an aesthetically pleasing screen layout. The main factors that affect the visual appeal of a man-made object are balance, color and ornamentation. These can also apply to software screen designs.

Artists have always given a high priority to the composition of their work. The two things that affect composition are balance and focal point. With a photograph or painting, the artist's primary concern is to draw attention to something within the frame of the picture. The viewer's eye will rove

Creating aesthetically pleasing screen displays

across the image picking out bits of interest. The artist will use various tricks, such as converging lines, to lure the eye to the focal point of the picture. Beyond that, they will try to make the picture 'balanced' by carefully positioning the main features of the picture within the frame. The Renaissance painters discovered a rule to this positioning. The rule is to divide the frame into thirds, horizontally and vertically, then place the focal point of the picture at one of the four intersections. The two third, one third, proportions seem to have universal aesthetic appeal and can be found in the architecture of early civilisations.

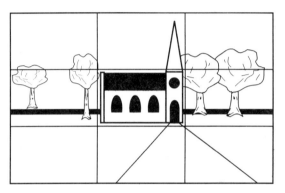

Figure 29
Which of the two pictures (Figures 29 and 30) do you find more aesthetically pleasing?

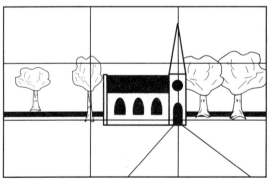

Figure 30

When single items are placed within the frame, placing it dead centre – as in figure 29 – creates a boring picture. This is because the eye is drawn naturally to the centre of the screen. Placing an item there doesn't give the eye anywhere to rove. It is the ability to move the eye around the picture, picking out new things, that makes one picture more interesting than another.

Balance can also be achieved by the orientation of an item. A figure standing at the edge of a frame facing inward toward the centre creates balance, while a figure in the same place looking out toward the edge would seem unsettling.

Figure 31 (left) Figure 32 (right). Which of the two pictures (Figures 31 and 32) do you find more aesthetically pleasing?

It is also unsettling to have things placed on the very edge of the frame.

Figure 33
So what are
they not
showing us?

When positioning something within a frame or when a margin is left around a frame, it appears better balanced to have a larger margin at the bottom than the top and sides.

 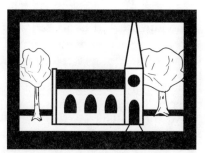

Figure 34 (left) and Figure 35 (right). The broader bottom margin of
Figure 35 produces a better balance than the even border around Figure 34

It may be better to place important information on the right hand side of the frame and not in the bottom left hand corner. Cinematographers consider the bottom left to be the weakest corner of the frame. By which they mean, the viewer's eye is not naturally drawn to it. In advertising, the right-hand page of a double page spread has the greater value, as it is thought the right-hand page commands the greatest attention.

Pictures of humans should not be scaled in a single axis. A local TV station has a regular weather report. In order to make their weather-girl fit the frame, they scale her along the y-axis making her taller and thinner. Unfortunately this has the effect of turning her into a caricature of herself complete with irritating, exaggerated movements. This is merely irritating in a weather report but would look ludicrous in drama.

With a mouse driven interface, it is difficult to set up an image using traditional composition, as the mouse pointer acts as the picture's focus

Is this relevant to software? The designer should be aware of how their audience will see the information presented on screen and appreciate how the eye is drawn to interesting items and led around an image. The aim should be to provide a focal point on screen. This can be a difficult thing to design for, particularly when using a mouse pointer. The pointer will act as the natural focal point, yet is mobile over the whole image. It is not necessary to compose a software screen like a Renaissance painting. However, it is useful to understand why some screens seem better laid out than others.

Color

Using color

When color is used, the designer must consider both the mundane requirements of the software, aesthetics and any associations the colors may set off in the user's mind.

Using color with icons

Red is considered a warm color, blue a cold color. In pictures, warm colors bring the image forward, while cool colors make them recede. In software this could be used to make an icon or button stand out by displaying them as red against a cool colored background.

Emotions are also associated with colors. Red can mean anger or danger. Green is associated with calm and tranquillity. Color is also used to denote gender: pink for girls, blue for boys.

Some color combinations can create further connections. Green and red suggest Christmas. Yellow and white can suggest fried eggs. Green and brown, the military.

Choosing colors can be a difficult process and relies heavily on personal preference. This is why a lot of software gives the user the ability to choose their own colors for an application. However, 'natural' colors such as stone greys and earth browns are generally acceptable to all. It is only when colors are 'loud' that they become unacceptable.

The designer can create an unpleasant effect by using too many contrasting colours. Each of the colors: red, yellow and blue has a contrasting or complementary color. This is a mixture of the other two colors. So for red it is green, blue it is orange and yellow, purple. These color combinations clash. If you want harmony in your image, avoid them. On the other hand, used with subtlety, small areas of contrast can lift an image and bring it to life.

Colors appear different when they contrast with other colors, so that a color displayed against a contrasting background, will appear different to the same color displayed against a non-contrasting background. This can be an important issue where color recognition is part of the application.

As well as considering color, the designer should consider tone and tonal contrast. It is the tone of colors that give what we see three dimensions. A box – painted the same color all over – would appear to be a colored blob without the changes in tone where edges created shadows.

To make one color stand out from another, it is not enough to use contrasting colors, there should also be a contrast in tone. For example, there could be a great deal of color contrast between a red and a green scarf. A black-and-white photo of the scarves would reveal that the two scarves were nearly identical in tone. It is very difficult for the eye to focus on two colors with high color contrast and low tonal contrast. This is why it is hard to read red text on a green background.

When designing a screen image, tonal information has as much importance – if not more importance – than color information. This becomes an issue when the palette of colors to be used in an application is limited. A good artist can produce interesting images with whatever colors are available, providing they have a good enough range of tones to work with.

When selecting a palette, the designer should aim to use a range of neutral colors, using darker tones to make less important information recede, lighter tones to bring important information forward and contrasting colors to bring attention to things.

General Artistic Considerations

The designer should always try to use a consistent style of presentation. This means sticking to a particular font, sticking to the same size graphic elements, such as buttons. If symbols – for example: arrow heads – are used they should all be of a similar style. If a relief effect is used to make buttons and dialogue boxes appear to be three dimensional, this should be used throughout the application. Consistency will give a professional, well-thought-out look to the software.

Screen layouts should never look squashed or cramped. Allow space between items on screen and use consistent spacing between graphic elements to give the layout a balanced appearance. Avoid making a screen look too cluttered.

Use ornamentation carefully. In the early days of software design there was no scope for adding non functional embellishments to software. However, graphic displays have improved to the point where it is now possible to include all the needed information and non functional graphics too. It has become commonplace to find information panels with highlights and shadow to make them look three-dimensional. In games it is usual to add ornamentation to displays based on the theme of the game. This is a trend that will undoubtedly continue in software for publication.

An important point to note is that a clear distinction must be made between what is functional and what is not. Games designers often make the mistake of including vital information in what appears to be a non-functional display. Sometimes they make the mistake in reverse and make a non-functional ornament look as if it ought to do something.

6.3 Static Graphics

Static graphics are the software equivalent of the book illustration or photographic slide. Static images can be generated in two ways. The first is to use graphics primitive commands, from the programming language being used, drawing the picture pixel by pixel. The image may be created by using lines, rectangles and circles, or by plotting pixels using tables of co-ordinates. The second method is to have the picture stored in a form that can be easily copied to screen memory. The original data may have been created by using graphics primitives or it may have been created with a tool such as a paint program or scanner. Storing and displaying images in this way is a much more efficient method than generating graphics as they are needed. It will also lead to more professional looking results.

Colors versus Resolution

With modern computers, the designer will often have a choice of screen display to use in an application. Usually the choice will be a trade off between the number of pixels and the number of colors that can be displayed. For example, the screen may be capable of displaying 16 colors at a resolution of 640 x 480 pixels or 256 colors at a resolution of 320 x 200 pixels. Both modes have strengths and weaknesses when applied to different applications. The low resolution of 320 x 200 is not suitable for displaying much text, allowing only forty characters across the width of the screen. With the higher-resolution mode, 16 colors are not enough to display photo-realistic color pictures. However, resolution and color choice can both be used to counteract these weaknesses.

Lack of colors in higher resolutions can be countered by using 'stippling.' This is a technique where two colors are checker-boarded together to create a mixture. A range of greys can be combined with the primary colors to extend the palette.

Monochrome can also be used. There is much less information in a monochrome screen as only the tone of the color is used and not the hue. So, for photo-realistic images in high resolutions, the designer can use black and white pictures very effectively.

In lower resolutions, drawn lines look more like a row of squares. This coarseness can be counteracted by the technique of anti-aliasing. Anti-aliasing involves blurring the margins of objects with mid-toned colors and this is when having a large number of colors available becomes useful. Many paint packages and image rendering tools will provide some form of anti-aliasing. However, artists can also achieve this effect manually.

Incorporating Images from Commercial Paint Packages

Displaying images in applications

The best way of generating images, such as company logos, icons and diagrams, is to produce them using a commercial paint package and then import them into the application. This can be done in two ways. It may be possible to include code that reads in the image as a data file from the paint package. This is often the most convenient for development, making it possible to alter pictures without affecting the application in any way. Graphics can therefore be produced independently of the program development. However, applications will often need graphics that are not straightforward rectangular images. Graphics may be required to create a part of a display panel or a button. In this situation it is usual to write a tool. This tool reads in an image file from the paint package and saves out graphics data in the required format. Packages being run from a common environment often share formats, thus allowing graphics to be freely added to other applications.

Reading Different File Formats

It is not a trivial task to read in data from a commercial paint package. File formats are proprietary information and may not be freely available, although many of the popular ones are well documented. Image files often use compression schemes and this can make them complex to read. Most developers tend to find an image format they understand and stick with it. They will then use one of the many conversion programs available to convert from other formats to their pet format. Another approach is to use a 'snapshot' program that saves out a displayed image file when a hot key is pressed. These utilities do not care what software is being used, but will save out whatever is in screen memory in their own format. In this way a variety of paint packages can be used to create specific graphics for an application.

Reverse Engineering and Run Length Encoding

The most popular compression method used in image files is called 'run length encoding'. The compression algorithm is based on the assumption that the image will contain areas of a single color. Compression is achieved by counting contiguous bytes of screen memory that are the same. The original byte is stored followed by a count. Any single occurrences are stored normally.

Displaying images created by off-the-shelf applications

A programmer may wish to display an image produced by a commercial paint package within their own application. To do this it is necessary to understand the layout of the file. Image files usually contain a header where information is stored about the height and width of the image; the palette colors it uses and other miscellaneous information, such as the screen mode it was created in. If no documentation is available, it may be necessary to discover the header layout and compression format by experimentation. The programmer may do this by using a tool that allows examination of individual bytes of the image file. By comparing two image files, one blank and one identical – except that the first pixel has been set – the programmer may discover the place in the file where the first pixel is stored. By changing the palette colors only, they may be able to determine the position and format of the palette information in the file. Determining the compression scheme may not be so easy, particularly with the more modern formats, but many applications save out in one of the older formats for just this purpose.

Digitized and Scanned Images

Getting high-quality static pictures onto a computer screen can be achieved in three ways. The first is to painstakingly draw them, pixel by pixel, using a paint package. The second is to use a three-dimensional scene-rendering tool. The third, to use digitized images, is much quicker. Several different input devices are able to generate digital images. These are: hand scanners, page scanners, still digital cameras and analogue-to-digital boards, which convert a video signal to a digital picture. All can produce results that are adequate for most applications. Here are some guidelines that should be considered:

Digitizing is basically a copying or duplicating process. And as with all copying processes, the quality of the digitized image will depend on how good the original was. The highest-quality and the lowest-quality pictures can be obtained from video. Using a video camera pointed at a still image or a still video camera, it is possible to set the lighting conditions and the size of the image to the optimum position. This is more difficult or may be impossible with scanners. Images can be grabbed from video tape or disk. This generally does not result in high quality pictures. A picture that may seem sharp when viewed as a video will look fuzzy when frozen as a single frame.

Retouching

Few images digitize perfectly. Sometimes the image is so blurred by the digitization process that the original information has been lost. In these cases it is possible that the image will need to be edited using a paint package. This must be undertaken carefully, as hand drawn graphics look different to digitized graphics. Badly edited sections of the image will stand out like a clown's nose. Cutting and duplicating parts of the image can produce better results. It is a good idea to 'clean up' the picture by editing out stray pixels. The digitizing process can amplify minor details. These detract from the focal point of the image.

Few images are entirely suitable for digitizing. The loss of resolution can transform an excellent photograph into a joke. For example, a tree clearly seen in the background of an original image can be transformed into a giant green alien splodge when digitized. The best course of action is to get rid of it completely. Cutting a clear section of the sky line and pasting it over the offending tree often does the trick.

Scanners may pick up some details of a picture and not others. By adjusting the controls it may be possible to pick up those missing details, but often the original ones will be lost. This is a frustrating situation. A solution is to scan several images and combine the best parts of each using a good paint package.

The Best Use of Digitized Images

Games designers have been quick to utilize digitized images. They use them to provide visual interest whenever there is an interlude in the play of a game. Static images are costly, because of the amount of time they take to produce, so when there has been a source of suitable images – i.e. the game has been based on a movie licence – images have been digitized. This has been taken a stage further with graphic adventures. Artists are commissioned to produce 'paper-artwork' of the various scenes. These are then digitized and included in the game.

There is a trade-off when it comes to static images. This is between the quality of the images and the quantity. Games that have included digitized images from films have made the mistake of using too few images and too low a quality. It would be acceptable to have a few images if they were of a high quality. It would also be acceptable to have lower-quality images if there were plenty of them. It is important to keep the audience visually stimulated.

To get a photo-realistic image into the computer, there is no cheaper method than digitization. Therefore, digitized images should be used where the integrity of the original subject needs to be maintained in the image. Products that will benefit from this are: games based on films – where a good likeness to the film's star has a direct bearing on sales of the product – and applications such as catalogues and information databases, where the exact form of the image is important.

Reducing Palettes

Scanners and digitizers use every available color to produce the image. If the image is to be included in an application, this is not useful. The application is likely to need a range of colors of its own to produce its displays. The result is that the palette of the image has to be reduced until enough spare colors are created. The palette of a picture is usually a range of shades of the same few colors. It is quite simple to pick out two colors that are very similar, discard one and color all the pixels drawn in that color in the other color. Palettes are commonly reduced from 256 colors down to 32 or even 16 colors for computer games. This is to free colors from the palette, perhaps to create sprites. It may be because the screen cannot display more than 32 colors. Or it may simply be to reduce the storage requirements of the graphics. The picture quality degrades when the palette is reduced but much of the information remains. However, a lot of editing is often required.

Copyright Considerations

Designers should be very wary about digitizing copyrighted material. It is tempting and easy to take an illustration from a book or a frame from a film and use it in an application. However, the originator of the image holds copyright in whatever form the image appears and the designer may be faced with a bill for damages or royalties.

Images can always be edited though. A photograph can be processed to resemble a drawn illustration. Pictures can be formed into a montage creating a new image. There is the good old trick of reversing the image to the mirror image of itself. Artists have always used available images as reference material, but modern technology provides the ability to reproduce an image then edit it.

Many ways can be found to conceal the origin of an image, but it is a matter of personal conscience – or a good lawyer – whether the use of another person's work in that way is acceptable.

6.4   Animated Graphics

Computer animation is the process of generating moving images on the computer display. Animation has many uses: from the creation of movie special effects and cartoons, through computer games, down to moving the mouse pointer around the screen. Full motion video can now be used, shown, and manipulated, by computers – adding a further blurring to the once distinct media boundaries.

Creating Moving Images

If a person is shown a series of still pictures of an object, where the position of the object changes, they perceive the object to be moving. This is because the images of the individual pictures are not immediately erased from the viewer's visual cortex. The pictures merge, appearing to be a seamless flow of action. This concept is called persistence of vision, and forms the basis for the illusion that is animation.

The number of images, or frames, shown per second affects the smoothness of the animation. Less than ten frames per second seems jerky and unconvincing. Television displays 25 or 30 frames per second depending on the system, while standard motion pictures use 24 frames.

With the introduction of visual display units, computers gained the ability to display animation. The computer's screen display can be altered by writing data to a bank of memory. This means that to achieve animation, a series of different images must be sent to the screen memory at a fast enough rate.

Computer animation can be placed into two categories: full screen animation and overlaid 'sprites.' With full screen animation the screen is filled for every frame that is displayed and it looks like a normal film or TV picture. This type of computer animation is used in CD ROM games and to produce sequences of animation for broadcast. With 'sprite' animation the computer alters just a part of the screen, leaving the majority of it intact. This is used in arcade games and GUIs.

Several factors make computer animation difficult. The amount of data needed to create an image is the first problem. A 320 x 200 pixel screen that allows 256 colors to be displayed uses up 64 000 bytes of memory. Older, slower computers struggled to transfer this amount of data quickly enough to get convincing animation. Newer, faster computers have been saddled with even bigger display memories; these give higher screen resolutions but have eaten up the gains in speed. The result is: the quality of the graphics has improved but animation programming is as difficult as it has ever been.

With full screen animation, the large amount of data necessary to create a single picture is multiplied by the number of frames in the animation. So it is usual for an animation to take up a very large amount of storage space, probably exceeding the memory capacity of the computer. Files are therefore stored compressed and then uncompressed during the display of the animation. This type of animation has only become practical since the introduction of CD ROMs with their greater storage capacity.

The advance in compressing full motion video allows for easier storage. Compression techniques make use of the fact that in almost all video sequences individual frames can be derived from other frames, either because there is little change or the change is regular; a talking head consists of very few moving parts. The natural changes of light in scenes can also be understood in terms of algorithms that can aid in compression. Thus 100 frames of video may be stored as twenty to thirty key frames, with information about moving elements referring to the key frames. The compression process itself requires a great deal of computing power that may be beyond the standard machine. There is also the problem that once completed, compressed images are hard to edit because they are stored in a scrambled format.

Sprite animation has its own difficulties. Animation is achieved by using a background screen equivalent to a movie's painted backdrop. The sprites, which are the actors in the scene, are drawn on top of this. They obliterate part of the backdrop, which has to be replaced when the sprite is moved to a new position. Sprite animation, therefore, involves the management of piecemeal screen construction and reconstruction. Games consoles get around this problem by providing hardware sprites. These are held in a different screen memory to the backdrop and are combined, by the video electronics, before being displayed on the screen.

Sprites

Using sprites

The basic technique in software sprite animation is a cycle of three operations. These are called: store, draw and restore. In the store operation, the area of the screen where the sprite is to be drawn is saved into a buffer in another part of memory. This doesn't alter the screen display and is invisible to the viewer, whereas the other operations do alter the screen and are visible. The next operation is draw, in which the sprite is drawn onto the screen. The last operation - restore - is used when the sprite must be moved to a new location; the original section of the screen is restored, overwriting and erasing the sprite. The sprite is therefore a temporary thing that appears only briefly over the screen display.

Most of the difficulties with sprites arise from eliminating flicker. There is a point after the restore operation and before the next draw operation when there is no sprite on the screen. If this is not concealed, the eye will see the sprite disappear for a fraction of a second. This disappearance, when repeated, is seen as flicker. Two techniques to combat this - double buffering and frame fly back - are outlined later in this section.

The store, draw, restore technique sounds very simple. Indeed it is for a single sprite application like a mouse pointer. However, it gets very complicated when more sprites are involved, as in games or applications where icons are dragged around the screen. When two or more sprites overlay each other, there is a possibility that the store and restore operations will use sections of the screen containing other sprites. This leads to parts of sprites being left behind and parts going missing when another sprite gets near. The only way to eliminate this problem is to give the sprites a hierarchy, working down and up the hierarchy when a sprite is moved. To understand this, imagine creating a picture from squares of sticky paper. As the layers are built up, to move a piece of paper overlaid by several other pieces, it is necessary to first remove all the overlaying pieces.

Figure 36 Multiple sprites need to be given a hierarchy. To move the lowest priority sprite, the other two sprites must be erased, then restored after the operation

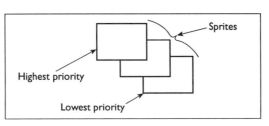

Masking

Displaying an irregular shape on screen so that the background remains intact

When photos come back from the developers they are always rectangular. It would be very surprising if the photoshop took a pair of scissors to a picture of Auntie Ada and cut around her profile. However, if Auntie Ada were a sprite in a game that is exactly what would need to be done.

Most graphics are held in the computer's memory as a rectangular block. To cut an irregular shape from that block, it needs to be put through some processes. Sprites use the concept of a transparent color. It is usual to make the color that will be transparent palette-color zero. When the sprite is drawn, the previous contents of the screen will show through any pixel set to zero. The technique to do this uses the bitwise arithmetic operation – Or.

A Brief Explanation of Bitwise Arithmetic

Bitwise arithmetic is invaluable for low-level screen manipulation. There are three operations, 'OR, AND' and 'EXCLUSIVE OR' ('XOR') that are of interest. These are used to combine two values, creating a result. The calculation is done in binary arithmetic and can best be illustrated by the following:

```
 1010          1010            1010
 0011 OR       0011 AND        0011 XOR
 ----          ----            ----
 1011          0010            1001
```

The digits in each column are compared with the digits above. Don't think of school math in decimal here. With the OR operation the result digit is one if 'the first or the second digit is one.' With the AND operation the result digit is one if 'the first and the second digit is one.' With the XOR operation the result digit is one if 'the first or the second digit is one but not if both digits are one.' In all cases, if the digit is not a one it must be a zero.

If, in the above calculations, the 1 is thought of as ink and the 0 as a transparent paper, it is possible to see how the different operations can be used graphically. The OR operation is a simple overlay. Layers are combined and the inked sections create a solid image. The result that each operation would create when combining two characters is shown in the illustration that follows.

So much for single-color combinations. A computer screen often uses more than two colors. How does this change things? An extra layer of complexity is created when the values being combined are greater than one. A pixel value of 6 OR-ed with a value of 3 creates a value of 7. Thus

Figure 37 The black areas would be the ink colour 1 with the white areas 0

a green color combined with a blue color could combine to make a red. Looking at graphics combined this way, it is easy to imagine that the result is random and not useful.

It is not simply a case of using the OR operation to combine the graphics with the screen, however. This would lead to the colors of the sprite being mixed with the colors of the original screen data, creating an unsightly mess. The screen needs to have a sprite shaped hole punched in it, containing the colour zero. This will make it possible for the OR operation to combine the sprite data with the screen.

To create the hole in the screen, a mask is created from the sprite. This is done by setting all the bits of all the transparent pixels to 1 and all the bits of all the remaining pixels to 0. This mask is then AND-ed with the screen. All the screen pixels combined with the transparent color will remain unchanged while the other pixels will be set to zero. So each sprite requires the actual sprite data and a mask to display it. It is largely a matter of choice for the individual programmer whether the mask is stored separately or generated as it is needed.

Collision Detection

Checking whether one sprite is touching another has long been a bugbear of games designers. In games, as in life, when two things meet something usually happens – so the event is important. The term 'collision' is perhaps more relevant to games as interaction tends to be more catastrophic. The touchstone of good sprite interaction is good collision detection.

Collision detection can be done in several ways. The simplest is to check for proximity. Mouse pointers have an (x, y) coordinate that is associated with one pixel of the sprite. This coordinate is tested to see whether it lies within a particular area, a button for example. In games, the sprite may be given a bounding box. This is equivalent to the area designated for the button, except it moves with the sprite.

The best way of checking collisions often depends on the type of screen being used and the drawing method involved. This is because detection

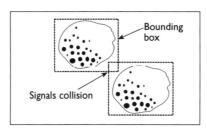

Figure 38
Primitive collision detection achieved by testing whether one of the four corners of the first sprite lies within the bounding box of the second

can be - and usually is - incorporated into the sprite drawing process. Many ways of doing this are possible, but they all rely on checking for the non-transparent data of one sprite overlapping another. Checking for overlap gives the advantage of accurate detection. Only when sprites are seen to touch do they signal a collision. On the other hand, the bounding box method can signal a collision when it looks as if the sprites are not in contact.

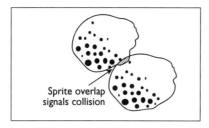

Figure 39
Testing for sprite overlap is a method that provides the accuracy necessary for games

Smooth Animation

How to stop animated graphics flickering

When programming computer animation it is important to eliminate the flickering caused when the image is updated. Flickering is visually distracting and it ruins the animation effect by revealing the magician's trick behind it. Here are two techniques that are used to eliminate flicker:

Frame Flyback

The image on a computer screen is created in lines from left to right, from the top down. The whole screen is redrawn this way, 50 or 60 times a second. The electron gun that scans across the screen has to stop at the bottom right and return to the top left. The period of time in which it returns is called the frame flyback period. Anything drawn on the screen at a point the gun has passed will not be displayed until the gun passes that way again. This can be a 50th or 60th of a second later, allowing the computer to carry out many instructions - enough time for the old image to be erased and the new image to be drawn in without the process being visible.

If the position of the electron gun is disregarded when updating the screen, two effects will be seen. Animation, where the old image is erased before drawing the new, will look flickery if the change is not completed within one cycle of the gun. Alternatively, a change made when the gun is only half way past the position will lead to a tearing or splitting effect.

Programming languages sometimes allow the programmer to call a function that waits for the frame flyback. By allowing a small delay – after calling this function and before calling the drawing routine – the programmer can create seamless screen changes. However, this method can be tricky. The delay needed before drawing the sprite may need to be different at the bottom of the screen to the top. This can be an awkward thing to program.

Double Buffering

A disk jockey's desk usually has two turntables on it. Just before the last record finishes, the DJ readies the next one. In this way the listener hears a smooth flow of music uninterrupted by preparation. One way of dealing with flicker is to prepare a screen in the background before displaying it in a similar way to the DJ. Thus for two screens A and B, screen A is prepared internally before being displayed. While A is visible, screen B is drawn to and again not displayed. When it is ready, it is then displayed in place of A, and the process repeats. To do this, there needs to be enough memory to hold two screens worth of information – not easy for a high resolution display. Also, functions that usually draw directly to the screen need to be redirected to its memory image instead.

Although double buffering is complicated, it produces impressive results. Many fast arcade games rely on this method to produce their smooth animation

Some systems allow the video memory used for the display to be changed by simply changing the base address of memory. Other systems don't allow this. In systems that don't allow different pages of video memory to be used, a routine must be written to copy the contents of the buffer to the screen memory.

Further Techniques

Animation doesn't have to be very complicated to program or involve a lot of low level programming. If the application is quite simple such as creating a flashing logo or moving a few symbols around the screen, some short cuts can be taken.

**How to
implement simple
animation effects**

Color Cycling

In paint packages, there is often a facility to 'color cycle.' Color cycling means changing the actual colors associated with palette colors. So an image might have a palette of 256 different colors all set to black, except for one palette entry which is set to red. If a picture contained all 256 colors, by setting the red to black and making another entry red, the red pixels of the image could be made to move around. This is useful for simple repetitive animations such as flashing signs and pointing fingers.

Palette switching is a more accurate term for color cycling. And palette switching can be used in a variety of ways. Single palette entries can be changed to different colors. This gives a pulsating or flashing effect often used in games to represent fire or rocket exhausts. Another way of using it is to change a range of palette entries and cycle a range of colors between them. This can be used to create the effect of water flowing in a pipe – perhaps for a diagram of a cooling system. It is sometimes used to animate rain falling from cloud symbols on TV weather reports. Fading effects are also created by changing the colors of the palette entries.

XOR-ing

It is useful to be able to use sprites in applications, but sprite animation is complicated to program. For simple applications there is a method of producing a kind of monochrome sprite. Most programming languages allow the use of bitwise arithmetic operations when drawing to the screen. By using the Exclusive OR (XOR) function, data can be combined with the screen data. A further XOR command to overlay the original sprite will erase it. This makes it very simple to program, as only one drawing routine is needed and no storage of the screen needs to be done.

If used carelessly, XOR-ing produces ugly graphics where overlapping sections are transparent or displayed in the wrong colors. However, if careful attention is paid to setting up the palette, it is possible to create a limited number of sprites that do not create these side effects.

See the case study at the end of this chapter for further explanation

The Uses of Animation

The moving image is a unique product of the twentieth century. It has progressed from celluloid film through to television, creating a revolution in communications. The latest stage in that revolution is the moving computer image. However, things haven't changed that much. The images are still communicating the same things but it is now possible to do so in new and interesting ways.

Moving images convey information. It is easier to demonstrate how an engine works if the pistons can be shown moving. It is easier to show a dance step or how to tile a bathroom with moving images. However, it has been the newsreels and archive footage that has led the revolution. Images from the first World War, the Hindenburg disaster, the assassination of John F. Kennedy. These are images that capture a brief segment of a real event. They provide the viewer with the opportunity to witness at first hand something that may have happened before they were born.

Using animation as feedback

Moving images can be used to draw attention to something. The human eye is attracted to motion. It could be a waving flag, a flashing sign or a movement behind the curtains. Therefore animation can be used in an application to draw attention to a part of the screen, a newly available function or some important information.

People enjoy movement. All applications can be enhanced by including more animation and moving graphics. This is because humans are visually stimulated by movement. Whether it is the flames of a fire, the breakers crashing on the beach or crowds milling in the street, people will watch it. Static images are boring. People do not like to stare at the walls.

6.5   Interactive Graphics

How to use interactive graphics to communicate information

Graphics can be used to clarify, and make more interesting, information and data displayed by an application. For example, an application to control the output of a page scanner might have a control to adjust the brightness of the output image. It might have five different levels of intensity. This control could be a simple text input that asks for a number between one and five. This is rather dull and gives an impression of sloppy design. A number doesn't mean much to the user, something more explanatory would be better. A more 'GUI' alternative would be a display of the current level with two buttons, that can be clicked with the mouse, to increase or decrease the value. Even so, this still doesn't give the user much of a clue about the function.

Figure 40
Two dull ways of entering a value

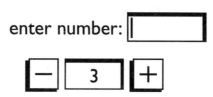

A better interface might use a slider where the level could be set by dragging a pointer up and down a scale. This can be taken a stage further. The application could display a picture of a light bulb in a panel, at five different stages of illumination. Then, as the slider was moved around, the bulb would glow brighter or go dimmer. This approach has the advantage of both communicating exactly what the control does and making the interface with the application more attractive to use.

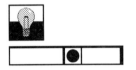
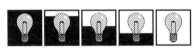

Figure 41
A graphic way
of entering a
value

Interactive graphics can benefit most applications. Wherever there is quantifiable data or variable settings for controls, graphics can be used to illustrate them. Users can assimilate graphics easily, therefore feedback can be quicker.

6.6   More Presentation Issues

When there is More than Will Fit on a Screen

There is a limit to the amount of information that can be displayed on a computer screen. An application may need to show a map, or perhaps a spreadsheet, where the data exceeds the space available to show it. In this case it is necessary to create a virtual display area and use the screen as a view port through which it can be seen. It is usual to allow this view port to be moved around the map. The movement of the map in the view port is termed scrolling.

An important aspect of scrolling is visual continuity. In some applications it may be necessary for the user to keep their eye on the display and have an uninterrupted view of the information. For example, following a route on a map or a sprite in a game requires the user to keep their eye fixed on a central item.

Scrolling

Screen scrolling can be implemented in many ways. Differences arise from the amount the display area is moved, the direction and the control the user has over the scrolling.

An easy way of scrolling the screen is to use a flip scroll. With a flip scroll the displayed information is moved perhaps 50% of the screen width at a time. This is a large jump and it requires the user to assimilate the whole screen with each jump. While this is fine for some applications it is not suitable when visual continuity is an issue.

The flip scroll can be enhanced to get around the visual continuity problem. Instead of a large move, the screen is moved in small increments until the display has reached the 50% position of the flip scroll. This type of scroll is commonly called a burst scroll, because it scrolls in bursts.

The other type of scroll is the push scroll. With this method, the screen is scrolled in small increments as required to see particular information. For example, push scrolls are used in games where the player has control of an animated character. The character always remains in the centre section of the screen. As it moves to the right, the screen is scrolled so the character remains central. Push scrolls are also used in word processors and text editors. When the line length exceeds the width of the screen, inserting new words at the cursor pushes the display to the left.

Sometimes the display is under the direct control of the user. They may be able to scroll the display any amount they like to adjust the area of information on display. This can be controlled either by cursor keys on the keyboard or by using a mouse to manipulate sliders or some other screen device. An alternative is to use the pointer to push against the edge of the screen and make it scroll.

Some word processors use a combination of push and flip scrolling. Push scrolling is used when text is entered at the cursor, to keep the visual continuity, while flip scrolling is used to quickly move the display backwards and forwards.

Different applications require scrolling in different directions. GUI file selectors usually scroll vertically. A video game may scroll vertically, horizontally or both and diagonally as well. Therefore, scroll directions are usually 2-way or 8-way.

The amount the screen is scrolled by depends on the application. For most applications, character sized increments in the screen position are acceptable. However, for arcade games it is thought desirable to use a small increment of one or two pixels to produce as smooth a movement as possible. For this reason many games consoles and games computers allow the screen to be scrolled using hardware.

Different Perspectives

There is always more than one way to show information. In computer games the game is usually played on a map. This may be a large area, greater than the screen size that the player can explore. If we think of a conventional paper map of roads and cities and how it would be displayed on a screen, we would expect it to be displayed flat, as if it were inside, pressed up against the glass of the screen. Games designers are constantly on the look out for new and exciting ways of presenting game maps. This has led to many different angles being used. The conventional map might be analogous to the top view used by the arcade game Gauntlet. The most popular angle has been sideways on, where the world is presented like a cross section of a block of apartments. Figure 42 shows some of the ways games present this simple model of the world.

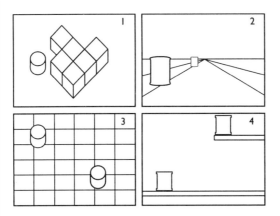

Figure 42
Games designers have various jargon names for different games formats. These are four of the most popular:
1 'Isometric,'
2 'First person,'
3 'Top-down,'
4 'Sideways-scrolling platform.'

Finding a different way of presenting mundane information is a way of making an application more interesting. By exploring alternatives, the designer is able to show information clearly and in a novel way.

6.7 Case Study: XOR Sprites

How to implement simple sprites

There is often a need for some simple animation within an application. It may not be worth writing complicated code to do the animation if the elements are simple shapes or only require limited colors. If this is the case, the XOR facility that most programming languages provide within their graphics commands can be used to draw simple sprites.

Here is a way of setting up a palette of 16 colors for XOR sprites. The palette numbers should be set to the example color:

Sprite	Palette numbers	Example color
Background	0	Black
1	1	Red
2	2,3	Blue
3	4,5,6,7	Yellow
4	8,9,10,11,12,13,14,15	Green

This allows four different colored sprites to be moved over a black background. The sprites should be drawn using the first number in the palette number list, i.e. 1,2,4, or 8.

The programmer proceeds by setting the palette to the above. Of course any colors can be used, but they must be assigned in the same way. To display a sprite, the programmer uses graphics primitive commands for drawing blocks of data setting the 'write mode' to XOR. The data must use color 0 as the transparent color of the sprite and colors 1,2,4 or 8 as the color of the body. To move the sprite the programmer prints the sprite in the same position still using the XOR write mode to remove it. Then prints the sprite in the new position.

When overlapping, the sprites will go behind each other with sprite 1 having the lowest priority and sprite 4 the highest. What is happening on the screen is that the overlap area is being drawn in one of the secondary colors of the sprite but because it is set to the same as the main color, the overlap has no visible effect.

An alternative way of using these sprites is to have only one sprite, number 4, and use the palette 0-7 to create a full color background.

D: One thing always interests me about images. Is it better to have a bad realistic image, or a good unrealistic one? What I mean by that is how effective is a bad photo realistic animation? What about speech that isn't lip synched properly? I think until you go all the way, it's better to use primitive images that don't tickle reality quite so much.

A: I'd agree that cartoon characters can be more believable than a cutout photo of a real person whose chin moves when they speak. Probably because we don't distinguish between images, but gain a general impression of what is realistic from the way something moves. Say an artist draws sprite frames for a beat-'em-up game. They will draw a series of perfect pictures of the figure in different poses. However, if you look at a film of a figure making fast moves, like kicks and punches, you would only see a blur where the figure's limbs were.

D: There is something compelling about a cartoon's ability to parody reality. They surely should not work so well. Rather interestingly there appears to be a meeting place in terms of imagery in both action films and animation. Special effects are designed usually not to make things look realistic, but more like cartoons. Cartoons are improving in order to look more like action films, the Japanese Manga form is a good example of this. Some of the best quality computer generated animations also seem to use subject matter from the cartoon. Living standard lamps and escapee desk weights feature in some highly developed examples.

A: Is that perhaps because cartoons exaggerate reality? Emphasizing certain actions in order to make the overall action clearer. When a cartoon character starts to run, for example, it is often moved into a ridiculous pose before taking the first step. If you look at silent movies they used exaggerated movements in live action. Is this relevant to software? Under what circumstances would this be useful in an application?

D: Software communicates in short hard bursts of high information content. The philosophy behind application software is speed and efficiency, thus most programs move at a brisk pace. It may well be that to get the message across, exaggeration is a useful short-term goal. For instance, one simple puzzle game uses an icon of a key and sound effect of a starting car to indicate that the puzzle is being reset. The concept is 'ignition.' This is comic in a way but works well. Have I got something here or is this not relevant? Does the mind prefer to see interacting with a program as a comic activity?

A: Exaggeration equals emphasis. It's a useful tool in comic books and cartoons to make what is happening crystal clear to the audience. Why not use it in software?

D: Ah, but the problem is that many people cannot relate to this cartoon quality. It makes software seem very immature; all those noises and bright colours. I think older users appreciate a little more sobriety and don't like their tails yanked.

6.8 Picture This; or Perhaps Not

Here is another problem in technology outstripping its own resources. Both memory and screen resolution are being increased in standard machines. To store a 16 bit colour image on a 480 x 640 screen takes over half a million bytes. A 32 bit colour image on a 800 x 600 screen takes nearly two million bytes. Until the day when the problems of storing and manipulating images are solved, graphics will always stretch the resources of the computer.

Much time and effort go into creating attractive and aesthetically appealing displays. However, graphics are merely a vehicle for communication between the computer and the user. The designer needs to remember that graphics are the messenger and not the message.

7

Sound

While you may never have used a computer without a screen, it's very likely you have worked with a silent machine. You may think that sound is just a distraction best left to noisy arcade machines. However, compare a silent movie — with no accompanying music — to a radio play. Most people will agree that the radio play can quickly and easily tell a complete story, while the film struggles to communicate ideas with over-dramatic gestures and captions. It seems strange that so much technology has gone into visual aspects of computing while so little has gone into audio.

It is rare to find sound used well in an application. Until recently the best examples have been found in games, but multimedia applications have begun to advance the frontiers in this area. Sound is still seen as an unnecessary gimmick in the business world, but as more computer systems replace human operators, this major communication channel will undoubtedly become more important.

In this chapter we will examine why and where you can place sound in standard applications.

147

7.1 How Sound is Produced

The following section starts at the beginning of the sound story, and continues to the present day. As sound is a relatively new addition to the computer's output armoury, its evolution is characterized by a small number of technically large steps.

Basic Sound

Sound is such a useful output that it is unusual to find a computer that doesn't provide a facility for sound. However, the early computer designers underestimated the demand for better sound facilities that would emerge as computers developed. As a result, add-on devices to give better sound became popular to support computers that had limited sound facilities. Now it is usual for a newly designed computer to include hardware to provide high-quality sound output.

Toggling the Speaker

The most primitive sound facility that will be found on a computer is a speaker connected to one of the output ports. A varying voltage is applied to a coil within a magnetic field. The coil pulls on a cardboard cone causing it to vibrate the air in front of it. The vibrations are what we hear as sound.

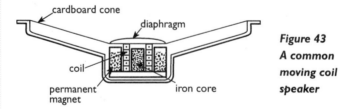

cardboard cone

diaphragm

coil

permanent magnet

iron core

Figure 43
A common
moving coil
speaker

Alternatively the output may be through a piezo-electric beeper.

The output port of the computer is a digital device. It can only provide two levels of voltage: on or off. When a speaker is connected to an output port, it has only two positions: in and out. So to create sound, the computer has to switch (or toggle) the speaker from one state to the other at a fast rate. The frequency that the speaker is toggled affects the pitch of the sound that is heard.

Although this system is very primitive, quite complex sound can be created. Many of the sound effects from early arcade games were made by toggling the speaker. By increasing the pitch as the sound plays, a swooping up effect, or laser shot, can be made. Decreasing the pitch makes a swooping down sound. Two different pitched sounds, repeated, create a siren. A sound produced by a randomly generated pitch will give a white noise or gunshot effect.

Interrupts

A computer processes instructions much faster than a speaker needs to be toggled to create sound. However, The speaker must be toggled regularly to maintain the sound. To produce the correct pitch, it is necessary to create delays between toggles. A simple code routine to create a sound can use up all the processor time. This gives programmers a problem: how to make sounds without causing the computer to 'freeze up' while they are made, especially as sound often accompanies a visual event.

The answer is to use the interrupt system of the computer. An interrupt is a regular and frequent pause in the normal operation of the processor. The computer is forced to halt its current task and execute a different piece of code before returning to the main task.

To create sound, an interrupt is set up and called frequently. A counter is decremented by each call to the interrupt code. When the counter reaches zero it is reset and the speaker is toggled. By using a small value for the counter, a high pitched sound can be created. To make a lower pitched sound a larger number is used for the count. For simple applications this is fine. However, games programmers have found that frequent calls to interrupt code use too much processor time, particularly in games that rely on animation, as this is processor intensive in its own right.

Sound Chips

The first step on the road to better sound was the introduction of dedicated sound hardware into the computer. This took the form of the 'sound chip' or programmable sound generator. The chip was either custom built or one of the general purpose chips - such as the AY-3-8912 - that appeared in many devices.

Usually the chip provided three channels - or voices - allowing three different sounds to be played at once. Multi-channelled sound enabled melodies to be accompanied by bass lines or percussion. It also dealt with 'polyphonic' music, allowing chords to be played instead of just single notes in melodies. Multiple channels make it possible to use sound effects and background music together. Another possibility is the division of sounds to create a stereo effect.

A sound chip has the advantage that once told to start making a sound, it continues to make it until told to stop, so sound can be produced without causing a major overhead in processor time.

The sound chip has one more advantage over toggling the speaker. It is capable of outputting variable amplitude levels, so instead of there being just two positions that the speaker can be moved to, there may be sixteen or more positions. This enables a greater variety of sounds to be produced.

A diagram showing the soundwave created by a toggled speaker would look as shown in Figure 44.

Figure 44 The squarewave output of a simple 'beeper.' Each block represents the speaker cone being thrown out when a current is supplied to the coil

Sound chips are capable of producing different shapes including sine waves and triangular waves (Figure 46).

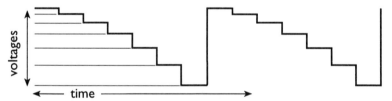

Figure 45 A 'saw tooth' wave created by supplying a range of voltages to the speaker

These give different tones – or timbres – to the sound produced.

The height of each peak determines the volume or amplitude of the sound. As mentioned before, sound chips are capable of setting this height. This allows sounds to be faded away or faded up. More importantly it allows sounds to be enveloped. An envelope is the profile of a segment of sound. At any point during the sound, the volume is determined by the height of the envelope profile. An envelope for an explosion, for example, is a fast rise to maximum volume followed by a slower fall in volume. A piano note or drum hit is similar. A violin, on the other hand, slowly reaches its peak volume, stays at that level and then cuts off very soon after the bow stops moving.

Chips often have their own enveloping facilities, but interesting results can be achieved by implementing an enveloping system in software. This is done by using an interrupt routine to drive the sound chip directly – altering the level of volume as the sound plays. However, the interrupt to change volume level does not need to be as frequent as one used to toggle the speaker.

7.2   Advanced Sound Production

The demand for high quality sound has led to hardware manufacturers following two routes. One route is the further development of the early sound chips, to create imitation sound using its basic components. The other route is to record real sounds and manipulate them.

Synthesis

Sound can be synthesized from the basic components of pitch, timbre – sometimes called tone or color – and volume. The earlier sound chips were primitive synthesizers providing basic control over these things. Modern sound hardware provides more channels and effects.

The various parameters that can be changed to create a synthesized sound are collectively called a patch. To create a patch, a wave form is chosen. This defines the sound's basic timbre.

A square wave has a reedy sound for woodwind instruments such as oboe and clarinet, or for mouth organ or accordion. A sawtooth sound is used for brass and strings. A triangular wave can be used for soft sounds like a flute.

Some synthesizers allow these basic waveforms to be combined, creating more complex sounds.

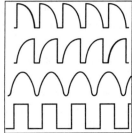

Figure 46
Different
wave forms
produce
different
sounds

The next stage is to define the volume envelope of the sound. This is sometimes called Attack, Decay, Sustain and Release (ASDR). Attack is the ramp the sound goes up when it is first made. Having reached its peak volume, the sound will start to decay or fall back to zero volume. With an instrument such as a trumpet, the sound continues to be made while air is blown into the mouthpiece. This period of time is the sustain period and the volume during the period is the sustain level. Some sounds have no sustain period, percussion instruments for example. As soon as the trumpet player stops blowing, the sound falls away. This is the release part of the envelope.

These two stages are enough to define a simple sound. However, synthesizers can often do more than this. During the sound, the basic waveform can be altered - or modulated - by combining it with another waveform. This may have the effect of changing the sound's tone color, or creating a vibrato effect. By adding a noise - or random - waveform the sound can be made to resemble a drum or other percussion instrument.

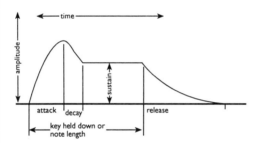

Figure 47
The shape of this typical amplitude envelope defines the volume of a sound at different stages, during the period in which it plays. The various points and levels can be adjusted to imitate real sounds

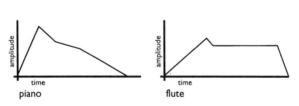

Figure 48
Two amplitude envelopes for different instruments. Note that the sound of the struck piano dies away quicker than the blown flute

This kind of sound production hardware is powerful. It can deliver full orchestral music, using realistic sounding instruments. For the musician-programmer, the synthesizer represents a blank page. In theory, there are unlimited possibilities to create any sound imaginable. In practice, it is difficult to create realistic sounds by trial and error. To synthesize a real sound, it is necessary to know the make up of the sound, its waveform and envelope. Sadly, this means that few musicians experiment beyond using the default sounds provided by the manufacturer.

Sampling

The difficulty of creating a synthetic sound has been resolved by using real sounds. This process is known as sampling.

Sound is input from a microphone or other sound source. The analogue voltage from this device is converted to a value that can be stored as a digit. The conversion is done at a fast rate, typically around 16 kHz.

This results in a stream of numbers representing the sound level at a particular fraction of a second. It is not a complete picture, just a sample of the sound. If the sampling is done at a slower rate, perhaps 8 kHz, less data is recorded and the picture is even less complete.

Having recorded the sound, it has to be possible to play it back. This is done by setting the speaker to its maximum voltage and then using the stored numbers to change the speaker output. Usually the sound chip will have a register to set the volume level. The stored value is converted and the register is set. This changes the voltage supplied to the speaker and recreates the voltage level of the sampled sound. This use of the volume register, to manipulate the speaker directly, stops it outputting other sounds.

If you are having trouble understanding the relationship between wave length and frequency, remember the simple physics equation:

speed = wavelength x frequency

Frequency is measured in hertz (Hz) which is equal to 'per second'. Thus a 16 kHz sampling rate is 16 x 1000 times per second.

To change the pitch of a stringed instrument, the musician places his finger higher or lower on the string, creating a longer or shorter length of string to make a wave form. The longer the string, the lower the note we hear. This is because wavelength and frequency are inversely proportional for a constant speed of sound.

If the sampled data is not output at the same speed that it was sampled, the effect is a change in pitch of the sound. This means that using a sample of a single piano note, a whole octave of piano notes can be created by playing the sample at different speeds. Sampling allows any sound to be used as a musical instrument. This has been overused. Against the belief of many toy manufacturers, there is a limit to the number of times 'Old MacDonald's Farm' played in pig noises, is amusing.

If the advantage of sampling is realistic sound, the down-side is the overhead it causes. Sending data to the sound chip at frequent intervals sends sampling back to the technology of toggling the speaker. Much processing time is wasted just to produce a sound. The problem of overhead, and the other problem of being able to have only one sound at a time, has led to the development of hardware purpose built for sampled sounds. This hardware may allow several samples to be played and combined before being output to the speaker. Sample data is read using a Dynamic Memory Access (DMA) chip that can read data from the computer's memory while other processes are occurring.

Another overhead is the amount of data required. Even short samples can use up a lot of memory space. An obvious solution is to compress the data. However, sample data does not lend itself to simple compression schemes like run length encoding as two consecutive bytes are rarely the same. More complex compression schemes are useless, as it would be impossible to uncompress the data quickly enough to use. For this reason sample files are often stored in a raw state.

Using sound samples in applications

Collecting Samples

Collecting samples is a life's work. Keep an ear out for interesting noises around the house. Squeaky doors or strange refrigerator noises can be recorded and sampled from tape. Slowed down, speeded up or mixed with other sounds, mundane noises can produce weird effects and unusual musical sounds.

The sound of the 'Millennium Falcon' attempting to engage its hyperspace drives in the science fiction film 'Star Wars' was derived partly from a sample of an old shuddering water pipe found in one of the back rooms in the studios. The laser effects were produced by hitting a taut cable holding up a radio tower and recording the resulting twang.

It is possible to buy tapes and records of sound effects. These were originally produced for theatre productions but are useful for both sampling directly and as a source of ideas. However, professional movie sound men would shun such sources as too derivative, preferring to seek out their own sounds.

There are libraries of public domain sampled sounds to be found on bulletin boards and on shareware disks. These are sometimes useful, but beware of using recognisable sound effects from cartoons and dialogue from films. The original sampler may have disregarded the copyright considerations when they created the sample.

As samples are often stored in their raw state, it is possible to 'borrow' the data files from other applications. While it would be wrong to use these directly in your own application, they can be useful sources of 'sound bites' to edit into your own sample files. For example, a gunshot could be taken from a shoot-em-up, reversed, cut and used as a percussion instrument in an avant garde piece of music.

Samples for Sound Effects

Samples can be mixed together. Some sample editing tools allow two samples to be merged. This can be used to put shattering glass noises into an explosion, for example.

Merge the sample with a copy of itself. If speech is slightly offset, this can create a fuzzy sound for intercoms or robot speech. A wider offset will create an echo.

When editing sounds, cut the sample between peaks where it crosses the central line drawn across the editor. This will prevent the sound from giving a distinctive click when it starts or finishes.

Some sample editors have a fade-in or fade-out tool. Use this to soften abrupt cut-offs where a long sample has been shortened.

Record sounds onto tape and then sample from the tape rather than recording through a 'live' microphone. The tape has a much longer recording time, giving you more opportunity to get the sound right without worrying about starting the recording. The recording can also be done far away from humming computer equipment.

Combine sounds in pairs to create a connection in the user's mind. For example: birdsong and tractor noise would create a rural farm atmosphere. Tractor noise and power tools would create a construction site.

Try to create a 'sound picture' by using offbeat sounds and sounds of things not shown on screen.

Be careful to avoid recording a sample with unwanted background noise. Tape hiss and high pitched noises can often be heard at the start and end of samples.

Don't use up memory and media space by storing gaps in the sound. Pauses between speech can be achieved with a programmed delay.

For a deep, authoritative voice effect, record normal speech at a high frequency and replay it at a low frequency.

Wave Synthesis

The latest development in computer sound is wave synthesis. Wave synthesis is a hybrid of sampling and sound synthesis. It works by storing the basic waveform of a sound as a sample. The sample is used instead of the simple waveforms the older sound chips use. However, modulation effects and enveloping can be applied to the sampled waveform. This gives the best of both worlds. It provides the sound designer with a realistic sound as a basis on which to experiment with effects.

Tips on creating and editing sampled sound effects

7.3   Using Sound

Applications run with or without sound effects. They are not a vital part of the operation of the program. However, they are a vital part of the interface. An application with no feedback through sound has an incomplete interface. What sound should be added to improve computer to human communication?

As is everything else in computing, sound is becoming standardized, so there are a few accepted rules that need to be considered.

**How to use
sound as feedback**

Using Sound as Feedback

Dropping a coin down a well – to tell how deep it is – proves that we trust our ears to tell us essential information, but most of the sounds we hear we are already expecting. The click of keys on a typewriter, the screech of tires on a braking car or the thud of footsteps are natural sounds produced by our actions. These sounds are processed by the brain to double check that things have happened as expected. The lack of these sounds would be very disorientating.

Listening to these sounds are even more vital when a novel action is attempted. If you press a lift button and it doesn't light up, or it doesn't go 'ding!' how do you know the lift will respond? Sound feedback happens at an unconscious level. We do not recognize that we have been hearing a sound until it goes missing. For example, a city dweller who stepped outdoors and heard no rumble of distant traffic would immediately sense something unusual in their environment.

**How to create
feedback**

Beeps and Clicks

The most basic sound output is the click, which is produced by just turning the speaker on and off. Further unappealing noises can be made with a little more effort. Noises of this quality cannot imitate natural sounds, but they can be used for simple feedback. The simplest feedback device is just to add a click to key presses. In a more refined use, a click can be added to keys that have a particular effect, such as moving a cursor around the screen.

**How to use sound
as feedback**

Sounds of Warning

In a famous experiment, the Russian physiologist Pavlov could make his dog salivate by ringing a bell, because the bell and feeding were so closely associated. It may seem a bit cruel to treat the user as a dribbling dog but sound effects make for very good associations without the need for description.

If a particular tone is played each time a warning message box appears on screen, the user will look for the box as soon as the tone is heard. This conditioned reflex helps to ease possible confusion when this otherwise unexpected box halts the user's progress.

A different tone can be used to acknowledge an action, for feedback, another for illegal or impossible actions that the user tries to carry out.

Beware of using feedback sound in places where its continuous repetition would become annoying. In these cases try to use a soft non-disruptive sound. Some users habitually try to continue scrolling past the end of a document for example, and a series of angry beeps for doing this can seem offensive. The only intention here is to warn the user that his actions no longer have an effect.

Consider programming an effect to only sound once, preventing the warning tone from being repeated by setting a flag.

Sound effects are particularly useful to indicate the completion of a background task such as a document being printed or an E-mail message being received. Any process that takes time to run and is left running should have the option of an audible 'finished' message. It can be reassuring when running a process to hear that it is continuing as well as seeing it. This is the equivalent of checking on a washing machine, or dishwasher, by listening to it.

It is polite to offer a silence option when any sounds or voices are used regularly.

- Task interruption by an information or warning box.
- Pointer clicking on an invalid area of the screen.
- The program has understood the command it has been given.
- The program has not understood the command it has been given, i.e. an illegal or currently impossible action or selection.
- Warning that the next action is irreversible, such as program exit.
- The completion of a task that may have taken some time, e.g. database search.

Actions that can be associated with a sound effect

7.4   Adding Sound Effects to Actions

If the target computer has adequate facilities, sampled sound effects can be added to software. As a first step, improved quality sounds can be used to represent the feedback devices mentioned above.

How to arrange the priorities of sound effects

Once a program generates good sound, it will be obliged to use it heavily. The user will expect to hear a sound whenever something is initiated and whenever something happens.

The ability to produce more than one sound effect at a time cannot be taken for granted, so it will probably be necessary to think about priority. When two events occur that both have associated sound effects, which effect gets played? In almost all cases sound continues independently of other processes, so conflicts have to be dealt with.

1) What is the priority of the effect, compared to others? Each effect can be given an arbitrary number that represents how important it is that it should be heard. Background effects are usually lower in priority to user-caused effects, as feedback cannot wait.

2) Should the effect interrupt a lower order effect already playing? Some effects may be made pointless if the user's attention is focused on another sound.

3) Should the effect always finish, or can it be interrupted without sounding stupid? The default is that a higher priority effect will always interrupt.

4) Can the effect be interrupted by itself? A repeated effect may not benefit from continuous restarting.

Note that the last two rules can be used even if effects are not awarded priorities.

Some of the actions or events that produce in game sound effects used by a clone of the William's arcade game 'Defender':

    The player shooting.
    The aliens shooting.
    A smart bomb exploding.
    The player's engines producing thrust.
    The player restarting a new life, and re-entering the battle.
    A congratulatory jingle to indicate a bonus ship after 10,000 points.
    Characteristic sounds for different aliens, when they are near.
    A civilian cry for help
    A civilian death.
    A civilian rescued.
    A civilian dropped safely back to the ground.
    In between level counting of bonuses.
    Player death explosion
    Enemy death explosion.

As an example, a warning bleep accompanying a system failure box must have the highest priority, and always interrupt.

There are two ways a sound priority system may be set up: with or without a queue. If there is a queue, a lower priority sound – to the one playing – will be placed at the back to be played later. A higher priority sound may muscle its way to the front and start playing. If there is no queue, much the same thing happens except the lower priority sound that is started – after the higher one already playing – will be discarded.

The questions above may seem familiar to some readers. This is because conflicting procedures in all areas of computing have to be sorted out by priority of interruption. In any multi-user system these problems occur regularly.

7.5 Using Music to Add Atmosphere

Using music within an application

It is natural to score a film with music relevant to what is happening in the film. In many cases the music conveys all the emotion in a scene. An example of this is readily found by watching the Steven Spielberg film 'Jaws' with and without the music in any scene where a character is swimming.

Very early computer games came with musical tracks to accompany the titles and sometimes background tracks to accompany the game. The quality of the music varied from single poorly defined notes to four-track harmonies. Initially the habit of using title tracks came from arcade games which had characteristic 'attract mode' tunes. These were not always atonal or harsh, indeed Beethoven's *Für Elise* made a thoughtful start to one popular shoot-'em-up.

As the multimedia capabilities of most machines increase, music is no longer seen as the preserve of games, and it is a presentational medium nearly all applications can use. It is essential to software that is supposed to engage the audience.

Themes

Using musical themes within an application

Thematic music such as that used in Prokoviev's *Peter and the Wolf* can be used to identify with a particular character. Musorsky's *Pictures at an Exhibition* uses a musical theme for each picture, plus a theme for the gallery in general.

Musical themes set up an air of anticipation, and can be applied at strategic points in an application to prepare the user for changing context. As an example, consider how musical themes might be applied to an integrated office package. The software suite has a word processor, a database and a spreadsheet. By associating a theme with each tool, context changes become more defined. This may be especially helpful for mixed data, e.g. when a spreadsheet section appears in a word processed document.

In computer adventure games, music can be played that reflects the mood at the current time. It is not sufficient to simply attach one theme for each location, as the time at which a location is visited and who might be lurking in the shadows may surely change the mood.

The latest adventure games usually have event driven changes to the sound track. This means that a fight will trigger fast tempo exciting music, which continues until the battle is over. The music playing before the fight will be related to the scene the player is moving through. Care should be taken that the changeover of musical styles is as smooth as possible.

Appropriate Choices of Music

Obviously music is culture specific, which is why it is better to use snatches of well known classical pieces as these have a greater spread of acknowledged meaning, accentuated by re-use in films and adverts. Fortunately, most of these pieces can be paraphrased by a few bars, sometimes with as little as four or five notes.

Music and its Associations

Piece of music	Associated with:
Chopin's *Funeral March*	failure, end.
Mendelssohn's *Wedding March*	success, celebration, completion.
Tchaikovsky's *1812 Overture*	victory, success.
Wagner's *Ride of the Valkyrie*	beginning, undertaking.
Rimsky-Korsakov's *Flight of the Bumble Bee*	complexity, industry, speed.
Bach's *Toccata and Fugue in D minor*	foreboding.
Beethoven's *5th Symphony*	profundity, expectancy.
Beethoven's *9th Symphony*	euphoria.
Strauss' *Thus spoke Zarathustra*	discovery, wonder.
Holst's *Mars* from the *Planet Suite*	war, awe, impending struggle, strife.
Clarke's *Trumpet Voluntary*	introduction, entrance.
Vivaldi's *Spring* from *The Four Seasons*	optimism.

7.6   Using Speech

It has always been hoped that one day computers will accept speech as an input – perhaps making the keyboard redundant. While this remains in the middle distance for now, what we can do is use speech for output.

Text to Speech

How to use speech for feedback

Speech packages work both with a dictionary of words and with a set of rules for pronunciation. An example of this text-to-speech facility is used by famous theoretical physicist Stephen Hawking, who cannot control his own voice due to motor-neuron disease. The clipped robotic accent that represents him is bizarre but much better than having no voice at all, and can be called upon by typing the text that needs to be said.

There are a number of ways in which speech can enhance standard applications. When the screen is dedicated to a particular task, sound is always a useful way of conveying information. Speech can offer a more refined effect than a beep.

Humans can also accept speech 'in the background.' Most people can carry out a conversation while driving, because we have our own ability to 'multitask' in varied environments. Thus incidental information, especially that at a tangent to the information currently being shown on screen, can be conveyed by speech.

In a WIMP environment, it is usually possible to put a clock somewhere on the screen. An alternative would be a speaking clock that announced the time at various regular periods. Warnings that memory space is running low, could also be spoken, as these do not require immediate attention. The same goes for status reports from peripheral devices such as printers. Speaking diaries can warn the user of impending appointments without otherwise interrupting the current task.

To summarize, the use of speech 'over the top' of the screen display allows two channels of information to be open at once. In effect, double the information can be communicated to the user.

Phonemes versus Sampling: Which is Best?

Computer-generated speech can be produced using two different methods: by sampling a complete message or by creating each word from phonemes – fragments of speech sounds.

Both methods are commonly used in everyday applications. Sampled speech is used in recorded messages such as station announcements and dial-up scrvices like the speaking clock. Phoneme based speech is also commonly used in applications such as telephone answering machines and vending machines.

Each method has pros and cons. Sampling produces a high quality result. The tone, inflection and pronunciation of the human voice are accurately recorded. However, samples take up a lot of storage space, limiting the amount of speech available. Samples are also inflexible. Messages have to be recorded on an individual basis. Also, every possible case has to be anticipated. For example, a message to provide a personal greeting to a telephone caller – along the lines of: 'Hello, Mr Smith,' – would need to be recorded and stored for each possible caller.

Phonemes, are more flexible. Any word can be created from basic speech parts, enabling applications to provide personal greetings, read out input text and generally respond interactively to input. As phrases are stored as a simple list of speech parts, a large number of phrases can be used. The drawback with phonemes is the poor quality of the speech. Users complain of garbled and robotic speech. Phoneme speech is synthetic and sounds it.

The deficiencies of both methods can be reduced. Sampled phrases can be broken down into constituent words. Sentences can then be constructed from the words. This provides some flexibility and reduces the data storage overhead. The results are not as good as a straight sample but can be more convincing than phonemes.

Phoneme speech sounds bad because the tone, pauses and inflections placed on a phrase are wrong. The rules to get this right are very complex and it is impractical to use them within a program. However, basic phoneme speech can be enhanced if the programmer can preset the tone and inflection of a phoneme for a phrase. Sentences are then stored as strings of mixed phoneme and inflection data. If storage space is too limited to use sampled phrases, phonemes used in this way should be considered.

Where phonemes are being used to speak text, they use a set of generalized rules to pronounce the written word. This causes problems when the pronunciation is different to the spelling. The problem can be improved by using exception libraries. An exception library is a list of words that the program checks against the word it must say. If the word is found, the program reads the correct pronunciation instead of using the general rules.

D: The first thing I do with in-game sound is usually to turn it off. At least that way I can't hear it for a thousand times and go bananas. Yet theme tunes for television programmes, however many times you hear them, never become quite that annoying. Is it quality, use of music, or the length of time played that makes most soundtracks annoying?

A: I'd say it was the repetition. Also the random nature of its use. Music in TV is used for atmosphere. It's not much better than game music, often it's just a long bass chord or a burst of notes. But it is closely fitted to what is happening on the screen. In games, the music just wraps round like a musical box with no brakes. What about sound effects? Ever turn those off too?

D: No, I normally want those. They tend to be more part of the interface and gameplay. I don't always get the idea they were added on by a third party who never even played the game. I like the fact that Windows allows for its sound effects to be reconfigured. This on its own has caused a large awareness of sound.

A: I guess when the sound is relevant to what's happening it adds. Sometimes music adds to games. In Wing Commander the theme follows the plot and isn't intrusive. In some platform games you get a short tune, when you reach the end of level, played at a manic tempo. I've seen people dancing round the room to that kind of thing.

7.7 Case Studies

Case Study 1: Music Programming in an Application.

The following assumes a computer with some sound facilities. These should include the ability to make a sound at a set pitch and for a set length of time.

Programming an application to produce music

There is nothing difficult about programming a computer to make music. Musical notation is a type of programming language. It allows a musical performance to be stored onto paper and recreated time and again. In this context, music is simply data. A closer look at the data reveals that notes are combined pitch frequency values and time values.

Therefore to create music, the code must be able to read the data and interpret it in terms of pitch and time. The easiest way of doing this is to store each note as two values. The pitch could be stored as a frequency value to be fed directly to the sound output device. Many computer games store musical data in this way. On the other hand, pitch may be stored as a value between 0 and 127 where 0 represents the lowest note of the lowest octave available. This is how notes are stored in programs for use with MIDI keyboards and other musical instruments.

The length of the note is stored as a value representing the number of time units the note should be played for. For example: a crochet lasts one beat and may have a value of 10 time units and a quaver lasts half a beat and has a value of 5.

In this way, a piece of music is broken down into a list of paired values. This fragment of music

 **Figure 49**

might be held as a list like this:

    x,10, y,5, z,5

To play the music, the pitch value and note length of the first note is read and the sound played. The next note is read and played, and so on until there are no more notes in the list.

Sound output may work in one of two ways. The system that outputs the sound may wait for one note to finish before starting the next note. On the other hand it may be set up so that any note that is sent will overwrite the preceding note. It is not difficult to create a tune with the first system, but the second system will require some additional programming to avoid the melody being garbled.

In the second case, the programmer will need to keep track of the time, issuing notes at the correct intervals. Using the note length from the data, a delay could be set up. This gives the first note time to be played before the next note is issued.

It may also be necessary to control the sound in this way if more than one channel of sound is being used to create a bass line, harmony or accompaniment. This is because notes of varying lengths can lose synchronization with each other, causing a horrible row. There are two simple ways of controlling the note output. The first is to include a control value to be included with each note. So the data list above would look like this:

    x,10,c, y,5,c, z,5,c

Where *c* is the control value. This value is used to indicate whether to wait for a note in one of the other channels to finish, or to go ahead and play the note regardless.

The other method of time keeping is to have a separate list of data that is read for every time unit. The tune would need to be divided by the size of the smallest note in it. There would have to be a byte of data for each. If the smallest note were a quaver it would be necessary to store eight bytes of data for a four beat bar of music. Each bit in the byte corresponds to a channel. This provides eight channels or alternatively eight lists of data that can be read. If the bit is set to a one, this indicates that the next note on this channel should be played. If it is a zero the channel is ignored. Using this method, the note length value in the data list is no longer needed.

The programmer should remember that music is often used in a context where it can be interrupted by user input. It is therefore important to incorporate routines that check for user input and make sure that the music can be stopped quickly and cleanly.

Case Study 2: Sound Track for a Haunted House Game

Including sound in an application

Until now we have considered music and effects separately; in this example we pull them together. There is usually a limit to the number of sounds that can be heard simultaneously – decided by the hardware and software methods of sound production. We will assume that we have two tracks, one for music and one for effects, thus we do not need to interrupt the music to play an effect.

How to create feedback using sound

The sound track will be used with a game involving a haunted house. The player wakes up at one minute to twelve and stands outside his upstairs bedroom on the landing. In the hallway are a Grandfather clock, a side table, a staircase and the door way to a deserted room. In a drawer of the side table is an old newspaper article describing a mysterious death in the house. As twelve strikes, the ghost stalks. The player has freedom to walk around and examine any areas described above.

The aim of the soundtrack is to enhance the game, add atmosphere and provide feedback. The first job is to compile a list of sounds and music that could be effective:

Feedback effects:

These only occur when an object is manipulated.

Opening/shutting door: This should be a short sampled sound.

Opening the drawer on the desk: A simple scraping noise will do. The door would not work as a substitute.

Walking on the stairs. A creaky stair sound could be played at different pitches to indicate steps. Going up and down stairs can be indicated by using a rising or falling scale of sounds. However, this may ruin the atmosphere by giving a jokey feel to the situation.

Character-based effects:

These effects depend on the state of the character the user is playing, and should be reflections of it.

The ghost: A wail would seem appropriate. This would not sound good interrupted, so it should have a high priority. Another approach would be to use the ghost cliché started in the 1970s, made for TV films. This is a sort of random tinkling sound. Something like a glass wind chime being brushed against the strings of a harp.

Time events:

The Grandfather clock strikes at 12 o'clock game time.

When there is nothing else happening, the clock could be ticking loudly. Background noises, heard almost unconsciously, add plenty of atmosphere. In radio, background noises are used to set the scene. Clinking glasses tell the listener the scene is in a bar, humming machinery – the scene is a factory.

Music track:

Walking around: This would be a passive but foreboding piece of music because we are expecting something spooky to happen.

The ghost: When the ghost appears, we need an excited frantic piece that reflects the player's state of mind at seeing a ghost.

The newspaper article: The letter represents a mental switch of context to a previous time, and should have its own musical interlude. The music should reflect the emotional content of the newspaper story. The mysterious death may be tragic; in this case the music should be sombre and sad. It may be a grisly murder or an assassination of a notorious villain. Each might require a different musical treatment.

7.8 Sounding Off

Support for sound output continues to be improved with each new computer developed. However, for any single computer, it is unlikely that its sound resources match its visual resources in any way. For some reason, many software programs emit no more than a bleep.

Sound is an important part of the human environment. A large part of the information that we assimilate is in the form of sound. The most efficient human to human communication is verbal. In contrast, the information that comes from a computer is mostly visual. Perhaps this is why some humans find computers unfriendly and arcane.

Sound in applications has often been neglected or ignored in the past. The best applications use sound to the full and it is now an inexcusable flaw in the applications design to leave sound out.

8

Presenting Text

There is no way of overstating the importance of the written word to the development of civilization. Computers add an extra dimension to text, making the information that was previously imprisoned on the page dynamic and interactive.

Although there are other ways for the computer to communicate information to its human user – such as sound and graphics – the majority of communication is done through text.

169

8.1   An Introduction to Text

Why do We use Text?

While we use words and letters for signs and symbols, we can define text as information supplied by – in our case – English language sentences. This distinction is necessary because we do not mentally process symbols and text in the same way.

We do not 'read' simple signs, unless there is more text present than can be recognized. Consider a road sign displaying a list of places and distances left to travel. The driver scans the list for the place he is going to and then reads the miles or kilometers marked next to the place name. This place name acts merely as a pointer to the required information.

People only read text word by word when it is new to them, and it forms no recognizable patterns. Text in books, newspapers and manuals is understood to be formal communication, and is the best way to state rules, facts, etc. This form of text is impersonal and makes no attempt to empathize with the reader.

Text is good for conveying general information, instructions, orders or any information that can be understood as a one way communication. On the other hand, having a two way conversation through text is cumbersome.

Computer text is formed not in words but in strings of letters or symbols known as characters. These are represented in the computer's memory as a number – ASCII value – between 0 and 255. For example, the capital letter 'A' has the ASCII value of 65. When text is printed on the screen, the character associated with the number is drawn at the cursor position and the cursor position is incremented. Therefore, the printing of a string of text on screen is a series of minor graphical operations.

Some characters do not cause a symbol to be printed but have some other effect. These are called control characters and they perform functions such as moving the cursor position up or down a line, or to the left margin, for example.

The History of Onscreen Text

Chapter 2 outlined how computers evolved from using screenless terminals to the high-resolution graphical display devices of today. It was explained how the high cost of memory chips limited the amount of RAM available to be used as screen memory. This, in turn, limited the facilities for showing text.

Computers now have displays that can show text as it will appear when printed on paper. Modern GUI-based systems provide these facilities as standard. However, they are not universal. It is more likely that the text facilities available to the applications programmer will be based on older, tried and tested technology. Probably a system based on eight pixel by eight pixel sized characters, spaced evenly across the screen. For this reason, let us look at how this technology has evolved and some of the problems that have been encountered.

There are two kinds of screen display that are commonly used for personal computers. One is the bitmapped screen, while the other is the character-mapped screen. The bitmapped screen uses one memory location per screen pixel displayed. The character-mapped screen uses only one memory location per character displayed. It achieves this by displaying a whole character at once rather than building its image pixel by pixel. For a character built from a grid of eight by eight pixels, the bitmap screen uses 64 bytes of memory for every byte the character-mapped screen uses. There is also a speed dividend gained by using a character map. It is easy to see why, when memory chips were expensive and processors slow, character mapped screens were the order of the day. However, the use of character mapped screens has declined, over the years, because they have some serious drawbacks.

Character-mapped screens are used in games consoles. There are several good reasons for this. Storing background graphics as character maps is efficient. More 'bytes per buck' can be squeezed onto a cartridge. Character maps can be displayed quicker than bitmaps. This means that the main processor does not need to be so fast. This enables the console manufacturer to use slower, cheaper chips in the machine.

Early personal computers commonly had screens 40 characters wide by 25 characters down. But this was considered limiting for applications such as word processing. A screen width accommodating 80 characters was more desirable. This is close to the 80 odd characters that a standard typewriter can print across a sheet of A4 size paper. Eighty character width screens enable a typewriter to be emulated, without needing to scroll the display.

If computers could now emulate typewritten words, the typeset text of newspapers and books was more of a challenge. Print is proportionally spaced, that is to say: each character printed moves the cursor position on in proportion to the space it takes up. So an 'i' takes up less space than a 'w', for example. This variation in the width of characters isn't possible on a character-mapped screen.

A further problem with character mapping was the vertical spacing of characters. Characters that touch each other look wrong and can be confusing to read. Therefore each character formed from an eight by eight grid needs to have a line of blank pixels down one side and across either the top or bottom – creating space between characters. This limits the effective size of the grid to seven by seven pixels.

Using lower case letters shows up a further problem with character mapping. Lower case letters have 'descenders' these are the tails that are found on 'g', 'j', 'p', 'q' and 'y'. If the grid is already limited to seven by seven pixels, how can the tail be fitted into the image? Usually, it cannot be fitted in and the result is uneven, difficult to read text.

All of these problems can be solved by using bitmapped screens. Bitmapped characters can be displayed at any pixel position on screen. It is therefore possible to display characters of different sizes and unnecessary to store blank spacing pixels. Displaying a character greater than eight by eight pixels – and at an arbitrary screen position – is complex to program and slow to display. For this reason, the operating systems of most computers default to use of eight by eight character sizes, displayed non-proportionally.

As the resolution of computer displays improve, text can be presented more realistically. The jagged edged characters of the past have gone. Modern computers can display text in many variations: size, type style, boldness, and italic lettering can all be displayed on screen as they appear printed on paper. In addition, computer text has the potential to go beyond paper based text. It can be made to interact, to animate and to change, according to circumstances.

Basic Typography

Unfortunately, the terms font and typeface are sometimes used interchangeably within the computing community. The printing community refer to the generic character set as the typeface, from which a font of sizes and styles are produced. Most software refers to a typeface as a font, with bold, underlining and italics as 'styles'.

The most noticeable thing about any typeface is whether it has little feet and arms – serif – or not – sans serif. The effect of a serif is to enforce the horizontal linearity of the font. A typical serif typeface is Times New

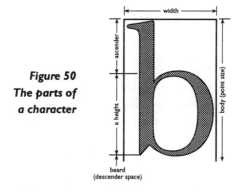

The parts of
a character

Roman, which is highly legible because of its exaggerated x-height. A more recent development is the sans serif face, Helvetica being a well known example. This looks clean and unpretentious.

Whereas the operating system typeface will always allow a set number of characters per line, a proportional font recognizes the difference between the width of different letters. This implies that extra information about a letter has to be held. The process of adjusting the gap between pairs of characters is known as kerning. In communications programs, or in any other application where text may be passed between different systems, it is important to use non-proportional typefaces, otherwise tables and simple diagrams that depend on constant widths between characters may be ruined.

The standardized system of typeface measurement is named the point size. The Anglo-American system works with a 12 point measurement of 0.166 inch, one point being 0.014 inch. When choosing the point size of the text, the choice is a balance of legibility against space available. A good typeface looks good even at a small point size. Where a scalable font is available to a software designer, these considerations can easily be experimented with. Scalable fonts are stored as vectors that describe the letter's shape, thus allowing size changes to be considered as an operation on a single set of vectors. The space between lines of text, known as the leading, is the other important factor that dictates whether the text feels crowded or not.

Early typefaces were restricted by the mechanics of printing presses. Today there are thousands of faces and many are available in software. The first faces were like handwriting, which explains the Gothic style. It is possible in software to graphically extend the presentation of typefaces – e.g. have animated text. Teletext services use colored and flashing text to good effect.

8.2   Using Text in Applications

Legibility

The most important factor to consider when using text is legibility. For text to be useful it must be possible to read it and to read it without effort. Three factors that affect legibility are: the text size, the text style and the text layout.

The size of the text displayed on screen will affect how much text can be displayed. The designer may be tempted to use the smallest characters posible to put as much text as possible on screen. It is important to remember that people with poor eyesight have difficulty reading small print. Children also find larger print easier to read. The limitations of computer displays prevent characters from being as well formed as they would be on a printed page. The smaller the text that is displayed, the worse this effect is. The best size of text to use will depend on the application. For a word processing application it is useful to be able to see a complete line of text across the screen and the text must therefore be small. On the other hand, small text would not be appropriate for a home shopping application on interactive TV where the user may not be sitting close to the screen.

Text style can be broken into further categories: typeface, color, emphasis and case. Clearly, the legibility of a script style typeface will not be as good as a more modern plainer style. Using too many different typefaces can create a cluttered and visually tiring effect.

Color can be used to emphasize text but certain colors interact together, creating a distracting display that becomes difficult to read. (See chapter 6.2 for more about color).

Emphasis is added to text to make its meaning clearer. It usually takes the form of a graphic change to the text such as underlining, emboldening or italicizing. Again the limitations of the computer display can cause problems. On paper, these effects can be quite subtle but on the screen there is little scope for graphic subtlety and sometimes the text gets obscured. Italics can be a particular problem, even on high resolution monitors, because the computer cannot easily display diagonal lines.

It is a habit with some programmers to start their working day by pressing the Caps Lock key. This sometimes results in messages being displayed entirely in upper case. Text written entirely in capital letters is not as readable as correctly punctuated text.

When reading, the reader's eye skips along the written words. From one word it must move to the next word. On reaching the end of a line of text the reader must locate the beginning of the next line. The text layout dictates how easily the next word or line is located. The reader's reading speed is affected by the time taken to locate the next word. Inconsistent gaps between words add difficulty, while even gaps help the reader. Longer lines of text are more difficult to read as the reader can less easily locate the start of the next line. The reader subconsciously uses landmarks in the text to navigate by: capital letters at the start of sentences, indentations in the margins of the text and so on. Although the applications programmer rarely has control over the vertical gap between lines it is worth mentioning that this also has an affect. Lines of text cramped together are more difficult to read. San serif typefaces need additional space between lines as the eye doesn't have the benefit of serifs to follow.

Choosing a Typeface

When selecting a typeface to use in an application, remember that the majority of text that people read is in newspapers or articles, and is usually in a classic face, such as Times Roman. When the intention is not to appear formal or authoritarian, try to avoid this sort of face. User-application help-text, for example, is better in a sans serif face, as help should not appear to be over formal. Sans serif is also suitable for children's books, especially as 'a' and 'g' are closer to handwriting.

As mentioned before, non-proportional fonts are necessary when the numbers of characters in a line must remain constant. Special faces such as script are excellent for setting atmosphere for a historic period. Stencil always suggests military or undercover operations. On the other hand, these can be a bit cliched so experiment with other faces too. Intelligent use of italics, bold and underlining help to increase variety as well as meaning. However, the more detailed special faces can be difficult to read on some types of screen.

Creating Fonts and User Definable Character Sets

Games developers often design their own font to use within a game. Why do they go to the trouble of doing this when there is always a 'system font,' the default character set used by the operating system? The usual reason is to make the style of the text match the game's other graphics. This is clearly the case where the game has a space theme and a modern style is chosen, or the game has a historical theme and old fashioned script is used. For a contemporary theme the motive is less clear. In the game developer's mind, the system font is an anathema. He feels that the game should be unique and have its own identity. Games try to suspend reality and create an artificial experience. Therefore the system font would be a constant reminder that the familiar and everyday operating system lay behind the game.

A character set usually contains 256 characters. The simple messages that games use can be communicated with a minimum character set of A-Z. Numbers 0-9 are needed for scores and some punctuation is useful. Period, question mark, space and exclamation mark are common. Lower case characters are not required. This uses up 40 of the 256 characters, leaving 216 characters that can be used for other purposes such as: creating display panels and icons.

The system font is displayed in two colors: text color and background color. By creating a character set and implementing a separate text printing routine, the designer can produce multicolored text. This is useful for including shadows and highlights to make the text stand out by looking three-dimensional. It also enables text to be made more readable by smoothing curves, using mid-tone colors.

It is not only games developers who scorn the system font. Many business applications use their own font. This may be for a number of reasons. Use of a particular style, over several applications, will give a corporate feel to the products. By not using the system font, the application gives the impression of being more in control of the computer. It makes the application seem more professionally produced and as if it doesn't depend on the computers operating system. Another reason may be that the system font doesn't contain certain characters or symbols needed by the program.

Designing an 8x8 pixels per character font

A non-scalable font is designed using a paint package or a dedicated character design tool. The designer will usually start by drawing out grids of the intended character size. For the majority of systems, these will be eight pixels by eight. One side and either the top or bottom row of pixels are left blank in each grid. This provides a gap when characters are printed next to and above each other. If an application never requires more than a single line of text, a top or bottom gap isn't necessary and the addition line can be used to make the characters clearer. While it is best to keep these margins clear, the designer should not be afraid to encroach on them to make a character easier to read. Specifically, the tails of lower-case letters will nearly always have to use the eighth line.

The effective seven by seven pixels is not a great deal of space in which to design an interesting typestyle. However, small differences in individual characters can make a big difference when seen together as a complete font.

For example, the uprights in letters such as 'H' and 'F' can have a width of one or two pixels. This will make the text either bold or light. For higher-resolution screens, a width of two pixels is better as a single pixel can be difficult to see.

Figure 51
Different styles in
an 8x8 character
cell

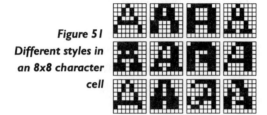

The key to successful font design is consistency. A mixture of single width lines with double width would look odd. However, using single width in the horizontal plane and double width in the vertical is acceptable. Loops in letters such as 'P' and 'R' should be as similar as possible. 'O' and 'Q' should also look similar. The height of letters is important. Text is easier to read if all the letters are even heights. The lower case letters 's' and 'e' are difficult to squeeze in, but if they appear above the level of other lower-case letters the text will appear odd.

Consistency with the typestyle is also important. Lower case 'a' can come in two varieties: with or without a loop that folds over the top. A 'y' can be like an extended 'v' or it can be a 'u' with a tail. Similarly, 'g' can be a loopless 'a' with a tail or it can be a strange squiggle. The position of any serifs is also something that should be consistent.

While designing the set, the designer may invent a number of little rules to make the style consistent. For the majority of letters these will be fine. However, there are a number of letters that cause difficulties. These tend to be the letters with diagonals such as 'K' 'M' 'N' 'V' 'W' 'X' 'Y' and 'Z'. It can be difficult to get these characters right. For this reason, computer character sets often contain compromise characters such as a 'v' with straight sides or an 'x' that is not a proper cross. Other compromises are: make 'M' and 'W' straight-sided with a shallow 'v' in the center, give the 'Z' a shorter top line than the bottom line, make the 'N' blunt at the top joint and pointed at the bottom.

Diagonal lines can be a problem. Pixels that adjoin corner to corner create a line that looks too thin. A kind of open plan staircase effect.

Diagonals can be made to look more solid by putting an extra pixel at each joint.

     Figure 52

One other problem that may be encountered is with symmetry. If uprights of two pixels are being used, symmetrical characters such as 'T' 'I' and 'Y' can't be centered in the seven pixel grid. Again the designer must compromise. Either by moving the character off center, which can look odd, or by encroaching on the gap.

Punctuation and other symbols should be designed to the same rules as the alphabetic characters for consistency, but it is important that they can be seen clearly. The text presentation of many applications has been marred by single pixel full stops.

Character set design is a series of compromises. Even when a large grid is used, and there is plenty of space to design the characters, there will be a number of trade-offs the designer must make.

8.3   Presentation of Text

A well-designed title banner of a magazine, or newspaper, is recognizable even beyond a readable distance. Indeed, if a few letters were swapped around in the title, it is quite possible that the readers wouldn't notice.

Conversely, if a paragraph is accidentally repeated at a later stage in a book, the reader will recognize it only after reading it all for the second time. In order to avoid the re-reading of text blocks in a software application, it is important to give these blocks titles. When placing a text box on screen with a paragraph explaining an error, warning or user help, a short title will stop the same message being re-read. This is important, as unlike other media, text that appears in front of a user does not come in a controlled order. It is only in a software program that you may be confronted with the same text you saw a minute ago. Presenting text so that it becomes recognisable without re-reading the whole block will therefore aid the user.

Superimposing Text

One thing that is easy to achieve on a computer screen is the superimposition of text over a background image. This has to be handled carefully if the text is to retain its legibility.

In recent years, TV has begun to use computer effects to create a shaded area where text is shown. This only changes the underlying image where there is not enough contrast between the image and the text. Before TV companies could do this, they had to show the text in black strips that obscured the image, or transparently, where the image merged with the text and made it difficult to read.

Text superimposed over an image will need either a separate background, a shaded area that modifies the underlying image or some other method of creating a contrast. Those other methods could be: displaying the entire underlying image in subdued colors and the text in a bright color or using a 'drop shadow' or contrasting outline around the text.

Scrolling Text

Modern text is designed to be read in lines, from left to right and top to bottom. When presenting the user with a large quantity of text, the application can choose to show it as a set of static pages, or as a scrolling list as if written on toilet paper. The GUI method of scroll bars and text windows implements the most common form of scrolling. The method used is also dependent on the size of the viewing window, which may be restricted. Scrolling should be as smooth as possible, to emulate a human reader scanning down a page. Unfortunately most text scrolls an entire line at a time. This seems reasonable but is really quite jarring.

Page flicking, the equivalent of storing text as a set of flash cards, is useful if text can be split into sections without losing meaning. Indeed this may well be more meaningful than scrolling if the text areas are truly not related.

A horizontally scrolling message bar is a form of extreme solution if space is at a premium. This form of scrolling can be seen by electronic gadgets that use LCD calculator-type displays such as radio pagers. It was used in early games, usually to give status information.

Justification

Laying out text

Text can be made visually more interesting by laying it out in different ways.

Different layouts can also be easier to read. One aspect of text layout is justification. Text is aligned to a margin, creating a visible contrast with the background. This contrast is information that is additional to the text and can be used creatively.

The most familiar text format is left-justified. This is where rows of text are aligned on a left margin. As the rows are different lengths, the right-hand margin remains ragged. Left-justification is also called 'ragged right.' The rows of text placed in alignment create a visual marker for the beginning of the lines. The ragged 'coastline' at the end of the line provides helps the reader recognise their position in the text. This makes the text easier to read. The output from an old fashioned typewriter is typical of left-justified text.

The opposite of left-justified is right-justified text. All the text is aligned to a right-hand margin and the left margin is ragged. This layout is useful where text accompanies something, perhaps an illustration, on the right-hand side of the screen. By aligning the text next to the item, the words can be associated with it.

Centered text is useful for presenting lists of unrelated items, credits or titles. Each row of text is aligned so that its middle is at the center of the screen. This emphasizes that each item in the list is separate and that the list of items may have priorities associated with their position in it.

Newspapers and some books use another form of justification. This is where both margins are justified, creating, in the case of a newspaper, a column of text. This layout looks neat and tidy. Like a smart suit and polished shoes on a businessman, it gives authority to the written words. However, the uniformity of the text makes it more difficult for the reader to distinguish between lines and so, more difficult to read. Another problem may occur when the text is justified into too narrow a column. This may cause the gaps between words to create a 'river' – a gap that runs all the way down the column – creating an unsightly fractured effect.

Where text is justified to two margins the computer has to space out the words to fit. This involves taking the line of text, counting the gaps between words, measuring the excess space in the line – where the next word won't fit – and dividing it between the gaps. If a word processor can format text this way, it will insert 'soft spaces' between the words, to supplement the 'hard spaces' inserted by the writer of the document.

Word Wrap

On an old fashioned typewriter, when the typist is getting near the right-hand side of the page – the margin – a bell rings. This tells the typist to start a new line at the end of the current word and prevents having to split a word in the middle, or having to hyphenate it badly.

Printing text on screen is done in a similar way to the old typewriter. Each character printed advances the position where the next character will be placed. When the edge of the screen is reached, the next character is printed at the start of a new line. To avoid words being broken in the middle, it is necessary for the computer to detect when a word will exceed the margin. The word must be brought down and printed on the next line. This process is called word wrapping.

Word wrapping is not usually included in the text printing routines that operating systems provide. This is a pity, as it can make the development of a text application far easier. When displaying text without word wrap, the designer has to edit the text so that the lines break at the right point. If the routine that displays text performs word wrap automatically, the designer can use a raw text file with no additional formatting. Also this allows the width of the text area to be changed, either as part of development or within the program, without needing to re-edit the text.

Text and Numerical Data

Using text to make numerical data meaningful

It is so easy to display lists of numbers on a computer screen that it is often forgotten that numbers can be meaningless without interpretation. Sometimes information can be better presented by converting it from raw data into meaningful sentences.

Text can be used to describe what may initially be thought of as numerical. To describe conditions, many games replaced a numerical representation with a lexical representation. As an example, in a classic adventure game, a character may lose 'damage points' from his health. Thus a character with 20 points is fully fit, but if his health points dropped to zero he would be technically dead. As damage was absorbed, the health points decreased, depending on the strength of the attack.

Points	Text equivalent
20	'Hale and hearty'
19-15	'Healthy'
14-10	'Lightly injured'
9-6	'Badly wounded'
5-3	'Weak'
2-1	'Barely conscious'
0	'Dead'

In the game, instead of saying 'Our hero has x health points' the text would read 'Our hero is x' where x is the representative string. Note how the health- point range, that the text describes, reduces exponentially after the maximum is recorded. This is to insure that as the character grows weaker, successive injuries cause more changes in the text to alert the player.

Abbreviating Text

There is less space available for printing text on a computer screen than on an equivalent sized piece of paper. The limited display space, combined with limited space to store data, has led designers to abbreviate messages and text based selectable options. Cutting down the size of words and sentences can solve many problems in an application that uses a lot of text. However it must be done carefully, if the information in the text is not to be lost.

To see how text can be abbreviated, with little loss of information, the following example sentence will be shortened:

'To make a phone call pick up the receiver and dial the number.'

There are some obvious cuts that can be made:

'To make a phone call pick up receiver and dial number.'

How about:

'To make a call pick up receiver and dial.'

At first glance this seems to be a fair cut of the original sentence. And for somebody familiar with the activity it is. However, as clear instructions on how to use a phone, it is not too good. First it is no longer clear that the instructions refer to making a phone call. The message could be talking about making a house call. Second, it could imply that the reader should pick up both parts of the phone.

How about this alternative:

'To use phone: lift receiver and dial number'

This is almost as short as the previous message but much clearer. It assumes that the reader is familiar with the purpose of the phone. This is a more reasonable assumption than assuming they understand the context of the instruction.

If space is so limited that more drastic abbreviation has to be made, it may be better to rethink the design. There is a point where a sentence cannot be reduced any further without losing a piece of vital information.

The loss of vital information is effectively what has happened when a single-word option is used in a menu. A menu option such as 'preferences' is all that remains from 'change the parameters of the application to those that you prefer.' It is only because the option 'preferences' is commonly used that it is understood.

Text Formatting Characters in Text Files

Most text editors and word processors will output a data file in ASCII format. These files are sometimes called raw text files or text only files. This type of file is extremely useful, allowing the exchange of data between applications that have incompatible data formats.

Many applications will use raw text files. It is the application's programmer who must decide how the text information is interpreted. A raw text file is made up of standard characters and control characters. The standard characters are the letters of the alphabet, numbers, punctuation and scientific symbols. If the application displays the file, these characters are printed to the screen.

The first 32 characters in the ASCII set are control characters. They are not printed to the screen but interpreted as instructions that control the text layout.

The ASCII codes were defined in the days of the old teletype terminals and many of the codes relate to printer functions. For this reason there are only a few control codes that are consistently used by applications to lay out text. These are:

Code Description
9 Tab (move the cursor to the next tab position)
10 Line feed (move the cursor down a line)
12 Form feed (start a new page)
13 Carriage return (move the cursor to the left margin)
32 Space

There are other text file formats, less common than ASCII. These have minor differences in the layout and functions of the codes. However, the principles remain the same.

So far we have looked at abbreviation of sentences by cutting out words. Words can also be abbreviated into shortened forms or acronyms - best used where the long form can be seen at the same time. This is an example:

Options for setting page length and width:

    Pge lng
    Pge wid
    Use default sttngs

Although all the information is not available to the user, they can guess that the abbreviations used relate to the things mentioned in the introductory text.

Abbreviating text without losing information can be achieved by careful scrutiny of the context in which it is used. Users are capable of expanding abbreviated text if they have already seen the full information. They have no way to fill in the gaps where this is not the case.

Displaying small amounts of text

- Center the text in a box.

- Underline a short and unique title.

- If you must use an icon, use it on the left-hand side.

- Left-justify the text so leaving a ragged right margin.

Common Text Presentation Pitfalls

Points to consider when writing an application that displays text

Text formatting is never as easy as it appears to be. Text can be a mild-mannered string of data that sheepishly goes where you tell it to, or it can be a wild animal that stubbornly refuses to do what it is told and wanders off where it wants.

Perhaps the commonest problem that can be encountered is the 'line break misunderstanding.' This is where text contains the special characters that tell the text printing routine to start a new line. Text files come in a couple of different varieties. The file may be long strings of text with a single carriage return character to indicate the start of a new paragraph. It may have a carriage return and linefeed character at the end of every line. This format is useful if the text is to be displayed at the width it was created. If the screen width is narrower, however, the text will wrap onto a new line, then break a few words into the line with a resulting mess. If the text is to be displayed on a variable screen, it needs to be in a no line-break format.

The Tab key, on a typewriter, advances the print position to the next Tab stop that has been set up. A Tab stop is an absolute position, whereas normal characters are positioned relative to the last character. This allows lists and figures to be tabulated. In a computer application, what happens when the typist presses the Tab key depends on the program. Some applications will insert enough spaces to move the cursor to the next tab position. This becomes apparent when the user tries to backwards delete after pressing Tab, discovering that it takes 20 key presses to delete the work of four. Some applications will insert a single space as if the Tab key were an alternative Space key. The correct action is for the program to insert a Tab control character – ASCII code 9. The application should interpret this code as an instruction to move the print position to the next tab stop. If the programmer is unwilling to allow individual Tab positions to be set, they should choose a good set of default positions, such as every four spaces. A good compromise is to allow the default number of spaces to be set.

It is important to remember that in a proportional typeface, where characters are not the same width, only Tab stops will ensure column alignment.

A reason why programmers are reluctant to implement Tabs properly, may be because Tabs only make sense when they appear in text that has been started on the same line. When a Tab character is embedded in a block of text that is broken, and word-wrapped by the application, it can have 'unpredictable results.' A euphemism for 'a bug I can't fix.'

Perhaps another reason is that a text file created by one application and displayed by another may have different Tab settings, with the result that tables and indents are incorrectly formatted. This is a problem even with files created on the same word processor. Substituting multiple spaces for single Tab characters solves the problem. However, if the file needs to be edited later, it is much more time consuming to edit spaces than to change tab settings.

Other problems with text come from making assumptions about the format of the data. Text data will always surprise the unwary programmer. Perhaps they assume that text will be separated by a single space. Perhaps they assume that a word will never be longer than a certain length. If this is true they will be surprised by the phrase: 'a-very-very-long-bit-of-text-that-doesn't-have-any-spaces-in-it.' Do all sentences end with a full stop? No! And another assumption is that text will never fit exactly into the width available. This can lead to line breaks being inserted when they are unnecessary.

Text as More Than Text

It is the nature of computing to enhance the things that it emulates. Whereas some graphical enhancements of text may make it more visually appealing, the contents and meaning of text remain paramount.

The ability to 'cut and paste' text in a GUI allows the user to break up and renew the form and function of text in – hopefully – a creative manner.

The concept of 'hypertext' involves gaining text information in a non linear manner. That is to say: by clicking with the mouse on highlighted key words, more text related to the keyword is revealed to the user. Of course, it may not always be text that is revealed. Hypertext certainly adds something new to text presentation but whether that something is truly useful, or just a way of making dull text more interesting, is open to debate.

8.4 Manipulating Text

Using a computer program is a repetitive experience. The same displays and messages are shown time and time again as the same functions are accessed. This repetition is one of the things that underlines the difference between humans and computers. Humans rarely say exactly the same thing over and over. It is possible to humanize applications by varying messages and using more description in the presentation of data. This obviously requires more programming effort than is currently given to this area and also more storage space for additional text.

A program with a large number of text messages can eat up available memory and also become unmanageable. If this is a problem it can be solved by using one of the many text compression methods. A simple one is outlined below.

Getting the computer to produce humanlike responses is both interesting and rewarding not only for the programmer but the user too. For an idea of how this is done see the following section 'Compound Strings' and the earlier section 'Text and Numeric Data.'

Simple Text Compression

A simple method of text compression

Text is stored as a series of characters, each taking up a byte of space. As a byte is 8 bits – that can be used to represent values up to 256 – clearly there is a certain over capacity, as the language can be represented by half as many symbols.

A simple substitution can be used to code common combinations and translate them back when needed. Let's just think of ten common two-letter combinations:

```
th, ea, ch, ck, gh, es, an, ed, er, in
```

Working on a random text such as:

```
'Videoconferencing technology is being assessed by educa-
tion organizations around the globe as a way of stamping
out
illiteracy'
```

Freely substituting using the above combinations would yield:

```
'Videoconferenc*g te*nology is be*g ass*s* by *ucation
org*izations around *e globe as a way of stamping out
illiteracy'
```

Each of the stars represents one of the weird symbols beyond ASCII 128 – foreign characters or more usually graphics for text boxes. A saving of eight characters has been made. This quick test gives insight into the problems of compression. Clearly, a more informed choice of combinations would have faired better, but success is dependent on the particular text. Commercial compression routines use far more complex algorithms but must still tackle the same problems.

The logical extension of this method is to store complete words and index them in a similar fashion to the above. Of course the index must not be so big that it is longer than the text it replaces.

More about text compression can be found in Section 3 Chapters 2 and 3.

Compound Strings

The essence of using text is to convert raw information into something that can be read. Consider the sentence:

How to convert raw data into readable text

> 'Today is Wednesday 2nd, and its unusually hot outdoors'.

This is what we may expect to hear from the radio while driving in the morning. The information that the presenter has transformed to a pithy statement involves the date, the temperature and a comparison between this and the usual temperature for this time of year.

How can a program dynamically produce this text from a date and a temperature reading?

To start with, most computers store an internal date, but it is unlikely to be in a nice text format. The program would also have to store a text conversion for temperatures, as well as an average for the time of year.

Let's assume that we can extract the date, month and year from the internal numerical time format. If we can calculate the day, we can express the day of the week from a string table:

Day of Week	String
1	'Monday'
2	'Tuesday'
3	'Wednesday'
4	'Thursday'
5	'Friday'
6	'Saturday'
7	'Sunday'

This means that the application can index the table with the value 6 to extract 'Saturday.'

However, we are not quite finished. We now need to express the date as a cardinal number. By default we add 'th' to the end of the date, but we need these exceptions:

Date exceptions	Append with string
1	'st'
2	'nd'
3	'rd'
21	'st'
22	'nd'
23	'rd'
31	'st'

This gives us 'Today is Wednesday 2nd, and ..'

Comparing the temperatures from a table of monthly averages may give us this table:

Difference From Average	Resulting String
-10	'there's a chilly day ahead of us.'
-5	'it's a bit cold for this time of year.'
0	'it's just another day.'
+5	'it's unusually hot outdoors.'
+10	'what a scorcher!'

This we can now append on to the first part of the string to give us the final string. Note how analysis aids the process of giving the computer a human face.

8.5 Case Study: A 6x6 Pixel Font

How to fit more text on a low resolution screen

Games often use fonts that use a small grid. In the past it was common to use a font four pixels wide in games that used low resolution screens. This would typically increase the number of displayable characters from 20 to 40. At this size many of the characters are unclear. With only three pixels to define an 'M' or a 'W,' compromises have to be made. The use of these fonts relies heavily on the human ability to fill in gaps in information. Seeing a message in context enables the user to guess what the badly defined characters are. After several years of using these character sets, certain conventions evolved. The positions of the pixels in the centre column became significant, distinguishing an 'N' from an 'M' from an 'H' from a 'W.' If the resolution of computer screens had not improved, these symbols would undoubtedly become as recognizable to us as the normal alphabet.

Figure 53
The problem with fitting a character set into 4x8 pixels

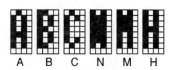

Here is a 6x6 font that uses the first 127 characters of the ASCII set:

Figure 54 Note the 'e, s' and 'z' characters. The designer has a difficult choice to make, between using consistent dimensions or making the characters legible but too big

```
 !"#$%&'()    ,-./0123456
789:;<=>?@ABCDEFGHIJKL
MNOPQRSTUVWXYZ[\]^_`ab
cdefghijkl mnopqrstuvwx
yz{|}~▓
```

Characters 0 to 31 are not defined as these are usually non-printing control characters.

Using this set it is possible to fit 53 characters across a 320 pixel wide screen instead of the normal forty. A custom print routine is needed to print the characters at pixel positions. Having gone to the trouble of writing a custom print routine, it is a simple matter to check for certain characters while printing. The 'I' and 'i' characters are treated as special cases. For these the cursor is moved forward two pixels instead of the normal six. This gets rid of the unsightly gaps caused by the narrow letters and it allows more characters into the line. The space character is also checked for. By moving the print position four pixels, instead of six, more room is created for text. In a line of text the width of the screen, these savings can create enough space for 60 characters, an increase of 50 per cent.

8.6   Information is Power, If You Can Find It

Real information, hard facts and figures, are communicated by text. Because of the way that text information can be compressed, it is the most efficient electronic transfer medium. The amount of text that is being passed via the world's electronic information highways (i.e. the Internet) at any moment in time is immense. Now the presentation of that text is beginning to come to the fore with the burgeoning of the World Wide Web. This text retrieval system also looks good. It can handle sound, voice and graphics – but not in useful amounts as yet.

New problems of text retrieval and text storage are inevitable. If you read periodicals, you may be in the habit of throwing out the old issue when the new one arrives. In contrast, we now expect electronic information retrieval systems to extract information of any age and in any location using a variety of search criteria. Even if I did have 2000 back issues of Time magazine, stored in various rooms around my home, I still wouldn't be able to find all the references to Michael Jackson within a reasonable amount of time. And on a larger scale, computer systems will begin to suffer similar problems.

Being Intelligent

The term 'Artificial Intelligence' has lost most of its glamour since it first came to the fore with the onset of the computing revolution. It is becoming increasingly obvious that we have failed to define 'real' intelligence – does a Grandmaster strength chess program play an artificial game? Is 'AI' just a buzzword, and a gimmick to attract research grants, or does it have a use in the real world?

9.1   Introduction

In this chapter two aspects of application intelligence concern us: smart behavior and task awareness. Smart behavior may be defined as human-like responses used to aid or advise the user. Task awareness is the ability of an application to know what the user is doing.

The suggestions made by a spelling checker as to what the user intended are attempts at smart behavior. Provision is made for new words by addition to a dictionary that can be called up in future references. Note that this example is 'passive' behavior – the application waits to be asked to make suggestions. An example of 'proactive' behavior would be the typo checker that operates as you work, correcting 'teh' to 'the'.

Transparency and designing for the first time user

Here is a further example. Imagine that somebody goes into McDonalds for the first time and orders a milkshake. McDonalds allow their customers to take their own straws and paper napkins. If the person left without picking up a straw, it would be very difficult to drink the shake without one. Lack of knowledge of the system leads to the error. If the person is handed a straw when ordering the shake, as they are in Burger King – for example – this error is eliminated. McDonalds system is passive, leaving the user to take action. The Burger King system is pro-active – intelligently assuming that the customer will require a straw to drink the milkshake – the task is removed from user control.

Intelligent behavior is sometimes useful in sustaining an illusion. Old arcade games would allow characters to stand suspended over a platform with only one pixel actually on the platform, impossibly balanced. Today's arcade games have an improved understanding of the rules of nature, and a large library of animated frames to call on. Characters run and jump under the player's control in a realistic way, thus extending the illusion.

9.2   Understanding User Behavior

We would normally recognize truly intelligent behavior as being independent of the circumstances; the process of understanding, for instance, is usually considered to be a form of synaptic re-programming. If I can truly understand German then it follows that I can read it, write it, speak it and teach it. A software application only has to understand the user and his or her foibles, so this is a very limited form of understanding.

What Did the User Do Last Time?

The simplest element of intelligent behavior is memory. It is memory that allows us to compare and modify our actions accordingly. The last time I went out it rained and I got wet; the next time I go outside I'll take an umbrella.

Applications that use intelligence should record the user's actions for later reference. The assumption that a user wants to do something similar to last time is, at the very least, a good way for an application to go about setting defaults and displaying task awareness.

Incorporating intelligence into applications

When re-starting an application, the user should be presented with the default option of restoring the last file they saved, because this is likely to be the one they want to get back to now. Better still, offer the last four different files that the user saved.

An ATM is different from an application on a personal computer. There are many users not just one. But an ATM can still record data on transactions with customers and respond intelligently. It will offer eight or so set options for withdrawing amounts of money. It would be more sensible if just one option was offered; the amount the customer withdrew most often in the past. This does require some thoughtful processing.

For instance, suppose the last five recorded withdrawals in order were

$10, $50, $50, $50, $30.

$50 is the most common choice, though $30 was most recent. Instead of offering just one option, a range of options based around the default choice could be used. Clearly, for example, $500 is not a withdrawal amount that this customer is regularly considering.

It is assumed that the user wishes to save information to a chosen file. But if the last three file saves have been:

```
my_doc1.txt
my_doc2.txt
my_doc3.txt
```

shouldn't the application automatically suggest my_doc4.txt as a name?

Learning on the Job

Children usually learn by example, and in many instances applications can use this method. When a child first writes, it is shown an example of the letter – or ideogram – to be learned and a place nearby to copy it. The teacher can then correct errors or acknowledge good examples. This virtuous feedback loop ensures that the child's skill improves.

Voice recognition can only succeed if the application recognizes the correct voice. The user can speak a sample phrase many times for comparison on future occasions, and like a child the application must be corrected when it produces the wrong result.

As yet only a few applications learn: those that are designed to recognise something, an image or a smell; specialised artificial intelligence programs; robot factory workers. Whereas, more or less, any normal child can learn to read handwriting, it is notable that very few computers have mastered this skill.

The Basics – Variables and Testing Them

To understand how intelligence can be included in an application, the designer should be aware of how the computer is able to make decisions. There are two things that allow computers to be made smart: variables and the ability to test them.

The computer has the ability to test two values and choose one of two courses of action according to the results. For example, it can say:

If 5 is a larger value than 3, do action A otherwise do action B.

Clearly 5 will always be a larger value than 3 and the computer will never do action B. To make the statement work properly one or both of the values must be variable. The new statement would be:

If 'first_value' is a larger value than 'second_value',
do action A otherwise do action B .

In the above statement 'first_value' and 'second_value' are both variables. A variable is a name associated with a value that can alter. It allows the computer to refer to the value indirectly. Another way of thinking is to consider the variable as a storage vessel.

The tests that computers can do are all arithmetic. This limits the scope of the computer's intelligence to making decisions based on numbers. So a simple decision like:

If the day is Thursday, do action A otherwise do action B

requires the days of the week to be held as numbers.

A: Talking about smart software, I like the way the Windows screen saver knows that you've wandered off and switches itself on.

D: Yeah, though I don't know why anyone needs flying toasters. It's a good example of pro-active behaviour. A similar time-based idea was the auto-save facility in word processors, especially on computers that suffered regular crashes. Every half an hour or so the application would wait for a 'quiet' period (say 10 seconds without a key action) and make a back up.

A: I've always thought an auto-save feature was admitting an application has fatal bugs in it. Do you remember if it was smart enough to know what to do if it hadn't been given a file name? I was using a DTP package with the autosave switched on, it crashed and I had lost my work simply because it didn't know what to call it.

D: As soon as the intelligence goes pro-active it has do everything as intelligently as a user, so I guess that's why it's rare to see this sort of thing in an application as much as we may expect. How about moving a character towards a door in Knightlore? Just to explain: in this arcade adventure game, if you moved your character into a wall near a door, the game would move it closer to the door, anticipating that you had simply 'missed' the door. As the game used a 3D perspective in a low resolution, it was an easy mistake to make.

Did this bit of pro active behaviour cause problems at all, or was it also just correcting a problem in the game itself?

A: The door intelligence was a neat way of getting around just one of the problems with the game. Had the designers fixed all the problems with it, there might be more isometric games and less platform games. Certainly all games could have a lot more intelligence put into the input routines. However, some would argue that the computer would be interfering and 'deskilling' the game if it corrected all the human user's mistakes. I would argue that no one chooses to make mistakes, and if a mistake occurs that could have been avoided with a bit of computer intelligence, the person is likely to transfer blame from themselves to the designer of the program.

D: OK, so this was successful pro-active intelligence, smart behavior. And already we are worried that it's doing too much. So this begs the question – if the computer is just a tool are we quite sure it should be doing anything beyond the user's immediate wishes, however stupid?

A: Man has always invented machines that make life easier. Intelligent machines are just an extension of that. Some machines are better than others. The intelligent machines we have at the moment are just not very good.

Too Much Intelligence

A couple go into a super store to buy the week's groceries. They both have credit cards for the same joint account. They each fill a trolley with goods and one of them takes their shopping through the check-out and uses the joint account credit card to pay. When the second person tries to pay for their trolley load, their card is rejected by the check-out operator. This causes much embarrassment and delay at the check-out. Why has this occurred?

When the card is presented, the check-out operator swipes it through a reader. This dials up the credit card company's central computer, which stores data about cards and transactions. The system is designed to prevent invalid or stolen cards from being used. It also has the function of preventing mistakes in transactions. One of the possible mistakes that it checks for is a transaction being accidentally made twice. Clearly intelligence is being used to ask: Have any transactions been made at this site in the last few minutes? When the answer is: yes, the transaction is disallowed.

This example shows the paradox created by intelligent systems. It can be argued that too much intelligence has been incorporated into the transaction process. On the other hand another level of reasoning, to ask if this is a different transaction, might eliminate the problem. Is the system too intelligent or not intelligent enough?

This kind of intelligent application is based on rules:

If situation A occurs, take action B

The problem is that for every rule that is introduced, there is likely to be an exception. And an exception is a rule added to a rule. This leads to an increasingly complex program structure where it eventually becomes difficult to predict the action of the computer to any given situation.

Some versions of the BASIC programming language come with a syntax checker. This checks a line of code, to make sure that it is valid, whenever the user moves the cursor from the line. This pro-active intelligence can be very useful for highlighting problems before the program is run. On the other hand, the programmer will get half-way through writing a line of code and then need to refer to another part of it. To remind himself of a variable name, for example. When the programmer moves the cursor to scroll the screen back, the syntax checker automatically reports the incomplete line as an error.

Syntax checkers sometimes reformat the code to make it more readable, inserting spaces between commands. The text 'total+1' becomes 'total + 1.' This means that programmers, using a text search feature will not be able to find the piece of text just typed in, unless they remember to expand the text as the syntax checker has.

Another problem with implementing too much intelligence is that control is removed from the user. This is fine for functions that are not a direct part of what the user wants to do. Automobiles with automatic transmissions intelligently change gear according to speed, road conditions and the driver's foot on the gas pedal. Some drivers prefer a manual transmission because it gives more control over the car. If a car was given intelligence and the ability to control speed according to perceived danger, it would be very frustrating to drive. The car would never take any of the risks that drivers have learned to take as part of normal, everyday, driving.

9.3   Intelligent Systems

The academic pursuit of Artificial Intelligence has formed the basis for the exploration into human intelligence. While the discipline and methods are worth understanding, it is down to the application programmer to apply theory to their own programs; this area of research has a notoriously bad record for producing useful results.

Rule-based Programming

Many real jobs can be understood in terms of a series of rules. The study of human professionals applying their skills to different situations has led to the attempt to mimic these skills in so-called expert systems. Via a long-term partnership with an expert, a programmer may be able to extract a set of rules that can simulate the judgement and decision-making process of that expert. Simply put, a rule is a piece of knowledge. By checking a number of conditions, the application may come to its goal state, which varies depending on the application.

One well-known rule-based analysis system is MYCIN, a bacterial infection expert developed by Edward Shortliffe. MYCIN's goal is to recognize a particular bacterium by requesting information about a patient's symptoms, condition and history. MYCIN follows its current hypothesis until it is disproved, or it is sufficiently sure to make a comfortable recommendation.

An example summary of MYCIN's questions and the operator's answers is:

```
Patient's sex? Male.

Age? 55

What type of infection is it? Primary Bacteremia

When did symptoms first appear? May 5th
```

```
From what site was the first culture taken? From the blood.
When? May 9th
Is the organism a rod or a coccus or something else? Rod
What is the gram strain of the organism? Gram-negative.
```

The program contains approximately 500 antecedent-consequent rules on around 100 causes of infection.

An example of one of those rules is:

```
Rule 88: IF   the infection type is primary-bacteremia the
              suspected entry point is gastrointestinal tract the
              site of the culture is one of the sterile sites
         THEN  there is evidence that the organism is bacteroide
```

This program does not ask any open-ended questions in order to home into the correct conclusion more quickly, as the interface to this sort of system would be far more tricky. It is fairly obvious that there are not that many professions that can easily be reduced to a set of rules. However, it is not the case that 'artistic' thinking is not reducible. It is well known that Bach's sonatas follow strict mathematical form, and that Shakespeare's sonnets also have a tight structure.

Learning as Induction

For a computer to effectively learn anything, it has to be told facts directly, or it must try to ascertain facts via observation. Some facts, such as the amount of available memory, can be directly gained by 'asking' the machine. The speed that the user types however, must be gained by observation.

Observational learning has many problems. Consider a fictitious robot that has observed that cats are often stroked. It forms the rule:

>   IF cat THEN stroke it.

However, the definition of cat may be from a list that includes lions and tigers. By trying to follow the rule in this case, the robot will be mauled. If this is correctly viewed as negative behavior, the robot should deduce that the rule is incorrect.

The rule, however, does not need to be thrown away. By adding another quantifying or restricting rule it may be amended:

>   IF cat AND small THEN stroke it.

This should prove less injurious. The ability to specialize this rule is only an option if the robot can define 'small' in the first place. After noting that dogs are also petted, the robot may wish to generalize the two rules:

IF carnivore AND small THEN stroke it.

Again, this requires the definition of 'carnivore' to exist in its database.

Natural Language Parsers

The process of deconstructing a sentence or text is known as parsing, and the software components that do the job are known as parsers.

Understanding text requires that language has a set of defined structural rules that an application can use to extract meaning from a sentence. In fact, humans only use grammatical language as a support structure to aid expression. Poets and novelists often change convention altogether to extend meaning.

Science fiction movies tended to accept the idea that computers will have no trouble understanding human language in the near future; unfortunately the example of HAL in the novel and film '2001: A Space Odyssey' will certainly not be fulfilled in time.

The reliance that software parsers place on grammar means that they are always somewhat limited. There are plenty of examples of software language translators completely misunderstanding the original text, usually due to an important word having more than one meaning. Once these limitations are accepted, text is quite a good way to give computers simple instructions.

As an example:

The boy stood on the burning deck.

parses as:

The (noun) (verb) (preposition) the (adjective) (noun).

By parsing this structure, the application can in theory 'answer' questions such as:

Where did the boy stand?

or:

Who was standing on the deck?

No attempt is made here to say that this 'answer' is a form of cognition. This form of rule-based behavior is merely reflecting the structure already present.

The application could in theory 'answer' similar questions about the following statements:

The chef cooks on the hot stove.

The soldier shoots at the enemy aircraft.

The girl eats inside the old cafe.

Variations: The big chef, the hidden soldier, the small girl, indicate that further rules can be used to pull in more.

The best-known applications for short sentences are text adventures. These define a limited set of nouns and verbs to describe a number of allowable actions. The main advantage is that no clues are given by the existence of menu options or icons to the possibilities. One of the entertaining aspects of adventures is their ability to accept experimental commands from the player, beyond the scope the designer had intended, appearing to respond to them intelligently. Unfortunately, the inability of most limited parsers to understand simple spelling errors, and even the most basic sentences, soon finished off the text adventure in its most open form.

A limited parser for all its shortcomings is still a very flexible tool. For example, it is probably easier to write: 'there is yellow smoke coming out of the bonnet' in an automotive expert system, than to express this problem through a chain of icons.

Brute Force and Ignorance – Neural Networks

If there is one branch of AI studies that is finding increasing application in technology, it is the neural network. This section will not tell you how to implement a neural network but it may help you decide whether your application needs one.

The neural network is a concept that grew out of early AI research carried out in the 1950s. AI studies are divided into two approaches. The approach of one group is to mimic the reasoning skills of the mind, while the approach of the other is to mimic the working of the brain itself. This second approach started with scientists building simple brain-like machines. The best known of these was the perceptron built by Frank Rosenblatt at Cornell University. A machine designed to learn and recognize patterns, it had an array of photo-sensitive resistors that made up the retina of an artificial eye. The sensors were connected to circuits that combined their signals and fed them to outputs. Typically, the machine was shown photos of faces and asked to identify whether the subject was male or female. If the output was incorrect, the circuits were adjusted until the machine gave the correct answer.

The dedicated hardware devices of perceptrons were soon abandoned in favour of the more flexible digital computer. The result, twenty years on, is the development of the neural network. This is a software equivalent of the old perceptron. Inputs are fed in and combined producing an output. After 'training,' the neural network is able to produce a particular output in response to a given input. So, shown the input from a grid of sensors for example, a square can be distinguished from a circle no matter what the orientation of the square may be.

How is a network taught to produce certain outputs? In broad terms, the neural network emulates cells. The inputs are 'nerve cells,' detecting and reporting changes in their state. These are connected to 'brain cells' – neurons – that give a particular output when stimulated by a combination of different inputs. All the input cells connect to all the output cells, so the whole network responds when it receives an input. As well as input and output cells, there is another kind of cell. This is the 'hidden' cell that is connected between two inputs. The task of this cell is to act as an inhibitor, altering the value being fed to the output cell if both inputs are being stimulated. Initially this unit feeds random values to the output, producing incorrect results. When training the net, these incorrect results are subtracted from the correct values and fed back to the hidden cells, so that, next time, they provide the correct values to the output units.

It is difficult to see how this produces a system that can recognize images in different orientations. The secret lies in the net's ability to fill in the missing blanks, given only part of the information. For example, we could define a kitchen as a room with a sink and a stove. A network for recognizing rooms could be given inputs for sink, stove and refrigerator and when stimulated, would give the result: kitchen.

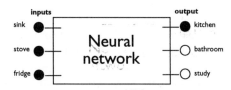

Figure 55
A neural network is 'taught' to produce a certain output when it 'recognises' an input

Stimulating only the stove and refrigerator inputs would still produce kitchen, whereas a room where only the sink input was stimulated would suggest a bathroom.

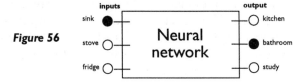

Figure 56

Neural networks are finding their way into more and more applications. They are used to recognize the faces of known shoplifters as they pass department store security cameras. They are used to recognize the unique odors of people's hands in security systems. Neural nets can be used for handwriting, signature and character recognition. They have been taught to learn the patterns of stockmarket trends and scrutinize loan applications.

The prominent word here is 'recognize.' And that's what nets do. They recognize a particular set of complex conditions and signal whether the conditions have been met. This is not too different from the simple IF..THEN program statement. In that context they are a useful addition to the range of techniques available to the applications designer.

9.4 Problem Detection

An important area of application intelligence is how the program behaves when a problem occurs. Programs can be made 'aware' of problems when they happen and they can take appropriate, intelligent action. In this section we look at error detection and processing.

Exactly what constitutes an error depends on circumstance, but there are three basic areas:

1) The program has not got the type or amount of data or input that was expected, and to continue execution would be hazardous.

2) The program becomes corrupted due to an error in the code or a problem processing data. The data may have caused the problem, but was not in itself erroneous.

3) The program does not have the resources to carry out a certain operation.

When an error is recognized, the program must follow a recovery strategy to avoid the system crashing, or producing spurious results. Early recognition of problems, and handling problem input, can help stave off serious application errors – especially those in the first category.

Actions that Prove the User Doesn't Understand

How an application can intelligently monitor the users actions

The structure of a computer program is a collection of paths that branch off to new places, loop back to earlier places, or connect two different places. Like a child's puzzle, there is a start and then paths that lead to the final goal. The application should be quite capable of monitoring the user's progress along these paths.

It is unusual for applications to keep an exact record of how many times a user has accessed a certain function or attempted a certain action. However, keeping track of this information can provide the program with an insight into how well the user understands what is happening. If a loop is entered repeatedly, when it should be executed only once in a while, this shows that the user is going round in circles – lost in the application. For example, a user wishes to change the size of the text in a word processor, and selects the option to 'change text size' and enters the value 7. The word processor is unable to display text at that size and ignores the user's actions. When the text continues to be printed at the old size, the user tries again, perhaps with a different size. By keeping a record of the number of times the program has to reject the user's input, and what the user input is, a picture can be built up of what the user is trying to do. If the user is trying different values, clearly more information is required about the values the program will accept. On the other hand, if the same value is tried each time, the user doesn't understand why the value is not being accepted. Either way, the computer can provide extra and specific information in the form of on screen help.

Monitoring the user: things that an application can intelligently respond to

- Actions that are not normally repeated, such as settings and changing defaults.

- Trapped errors, such as attempting to enter an invalid value or carry out an invalid action.

- Use of functions that correct errors such as the delete key or undo facilities.

An example would be to monitor those words the user regularly used the delete key on. When people are typing, they regularly transpose letters of certain words. By tracking the word before and after correction, it is possible for the computer to correct the transposition before the user has to.

An application that has been revised a few times may well have the facility to convert old data into the current format. Consider this loop for a user attempting to load data of an unknown origin into the application:

1. Open File – the user selects the file from a list.

2. Choose format – the user guesses which format the file may adhere to.

3. Not the right format – the program doesn't recognize the format.

4. Goto 1

After the user has tried and failed to open a file in three or four formats, it is time for the system to offer some further help. The application should try to open the file in as many formats as it recognizes, listing the ones that have worked. This saves the user turning into an automaton.

Whether to Parse Errors or Report Them

A useful skill for an applications designer to have is the ability to antici-pate the mistakes of the user. If a program asks the user to enter a number between 1 and 5, it can be guaranteed that eventually someone will enter 7. It is a simple piece of intelligence to check the entered value and ask the user to re-enter the number if it is wrong. Alternatively the program could ignore the value 7 and use the value 5, that being the nearest valid value to 7.

**How to handle
user errors**

This illustrates the two different courses of action the program can take when trapping errors. The error can either be reported, so the user can take some corrective action, or the error can be parsed and a corrective action taken pro-actively.

One problem with reporting errors is that the user may not understand why the error has occurred, and may not be able to correct it. On the other hand, pointing out the error will give the user more understanding of the program. A poor error message, however, will do nothing other than add confusion.

The problem with parsing errors is that the user never knows that an error occurred and may assume that the program is not working correctly. To use the previous example, the user who enters 7 and sees the program operate with the value 5 may assume that entering the value has no effect on the program and will continue entering the wrong value.

A middle way is for the program to pro-actively correct the error when it occurs but at the same time report it. For example, the message might be:

```
The value entered was incorrect and has been modified
to a legal value.
```

This allows the user to learn about the mistake without being punished. Errors can be sent to a 'log' file, that can be examined at the user's leisure. In this way the interactive session is not interrupted.

A: The campaign for smarter software starts here!

D: How do we do that??

A: With any lobbying campaign it is a case of gently persuading people to agree with your point of view. It seems to me that:

1) current software is fairly stupid.

2) all software can benefit from being made smarter.

Therefore it would be 'a good thing' to persuade applications designers to incorporate more intelligence into their designs.

D: But does it make good financial sense? After all the smart behaviour takes extra design work. And at least un-smart applications are predictable.

A: It is a way of adding value to an application. Companies are spending millions developing new products that seem to have more features than their competitors. Here is a direction in which very few steps have been taken.

Most current development goes into making products more complex and difficult to use. Why not keep the complexity on the inside and keep the outside simple?

D: I need to think in terms of hammers. How do you add value to a hammer. Quality, price. Intelligence? Don't forget computers and software are just tools in the same way that a hammer is a carpentry tool. So if intelligence is a value-added bonus, why is it seen so rarely in other tools. Why don't we have cookers that work out how to cook your dinner; videos that record your favorite program automatically; phones that call your mother when she becomes available? Surely it's because people wouldn't trust them. Tools need to be reliable to be usable.

A: There are powered nail guns and tackers. To an ordinary hammer you can add a claw to pull nails. You could say that the governor on a steam engine is a form of intelligence. We have a cooker that knows what temperature the pan is. All the consumer goods, including tools, around us are getting 'smarter.' Think of cameras over the last fifteen years. Yet software applications, where this sort of intelligence can be added easily and without special hardware, is progressing very slowly.

D: I guess you can't get easier than software can you? I think the progression is slow because the user is carried along in a product friendly way. We have 'auto-focus' as camera manufacturers say. No-one wants to be told that their brains are being made redundant by a consumer item. Mature software must carry intelligence with as little fanfare as possible. In fact, where possible, without reference to the idea that anything 'smart' is being done at all.

A: For 'automatic' read 'skill no longer needed.' I don't agree. When I take holiday snaps I still use artistic skills to choose the composition and subject. Using an auto-focus camera simply removes a level of complexity that has no direct relevance to getting an image onto paper. Point-and-click technology has made photography accessible to a wider audience. It is no longer the domain of a skilled elite. Application designers should do the same for software. It's not a case of telling people they are stupid – faced with new software they'll tell you that themselves. It's a question of making software easy.

9.5 Agents

An agent is a process that works for you as an intelligent proxy. In most cases, the agent works behind the scenes, not in front of you. This means that it is far more important that it can act without prompting.

Searching for Things

One of the problems that will face users in the information revolution is that the useful has to be separated from the useless. This may start off as a simple filter process, but as the amount of data expands, problems are amplified.

If a search for references to the word 'coffee' is made in a short document, a small set of word matches will do the job of indexing all the paragraphs that are about the subject. These word search matches are known as 'hits'. Naturally, a reference may appear twice in the same section, or an alternative phrase may be used – 'popular hot beverage' – that may result in losing some potential hits. Some superfluous information may be indexed due to a reference not being of the intended context, e.g. 'coffee colored paintwork.'

If the search domain is widened to include multiple documents, found globally on the Internet, the above errors become a more serious waste of time and resources. The agent whose job is to 'go find all the information you can on the coffee market' needs to apply a lot of rules to mimic intelligent decision making.

- The search terms imply that commercial considerations are important. One could also assume that only current information would be wanted. A list of keywords to help the agent would include 'coffee beans, beverage market' and 'coffee prices.' Some keywords to exclude may be 'coffee machine' and 'coffee color.' It is important that the application has some ability to parse English; a straight word match is far too clumsy.

- An open ended search requires new references to be found, more leads on the right information. Most archived documents include bibliographies or Requests For Comments (RFCs) which can be added to the document search list. Again these must be effectively parsed.

- If possible, a search routine should be carried out locally – fetching a large document from a distant place just to trivially reject it is obviously inefficient.

- When a relevant section is found, it is important to find the true 'beginning' and 'end' of the information required. This is a matter of presentation as well as efficiency. This might require searching for headings, or just the start and end of paragraphs.

Being You When You Aren't There

Some applications work with data that needs to be collected at various times for processing. For instance, a communications package can be programmed to collect messages – maybe E-mail messages from an on-line service – when the lines aren't busy, or when the rate is cheaper. Trusting automatic processes like these lies at the limit of most people's faith in computers.

Looking at the communications program scheduler:

- Flexibility of collection should match the user's normal habits. If there are 100 personal messages to collect, perhaps only the most important ones from a limited set of senders ought to be collected. Who is important, and what exactly defines 'too many messages' could be set initially by the user and perhaps modified pro-actively by the application observing the user's behaviour.

- If the communication was interrupted, it would be vital that the line was closed properly to avoid inadvertent expensive call or on-line service costs.

- If an error occurred during the process, it must be logged for later perusal. Because of the nature of the process, most problems would have a straightforward 'disconnect' strategy.

- Does the sender of the message realize that the intended recipient was not collecting it directly? This is important, as the message may require immediate action that is assumed to have been taken when the message was read.

Only processes that are fairly safe can be attempted continuously. The trading crash of the early 1980s was often said to be caused by automatic trading programs all selling at a pre-set level. If this level was set by the operator, perhaps it follows that a bad workman blames his tools.

9.6   Sensible Defaults and Settings

An area where the applications designer can increase the intelligence of the program is in the defaults and settings that it provides. Sensible defaults can save the user time and help them understand a complicated application.

We have already mentioned word processors that give the option to re-edit one of the last four or five files edited. Other systems prompt the user to say whether they want to start a new document or edit an old one. If editing an old one is the option chosen, the application loads the last file saved.

It has become the convention to provide both a 'save' and a 'save as...' option in file menus. The 'save' option allows the user to save the file using the current filename, rather than re-entering a name. If 'save as...' is selected the user is given the current filename to edit. These conventions have grown out of early efforts to put intelligence into applications.

When a program remembers the last filename used, or other information, it is providing continuity. This is important to maintain the pretense that the computer is an intelligent entity and not just a machine. The effect is achieved by saving a configuration or initialization file – a file that is saved out by the application before it is shut down. When the application is restarted at a later time, the 'config' or 'init' file is read in and the stored information used to set up the system.

Config files are used to save information such as: the last file edited, the position or layout of the screen, what options were selected, and even how many times the program has been used.

9.7   Unintelligence

If programs can operate in an intelligent way, they can also work in the opposite way: unintelligently.

If a person asked you a question, which you answered, then a little while later asked you the same question, you would quickly become frustrated with them and assume they were stupid. Prompting for the same information over and over is an error that some programs make. Installation programs are often guilty of this crime. The user is asked to go through a list of settings accepting or changing the defaults. At the end they are asked to look at the selected settings and confirm that all is okay. If something is not okay, the user is made to go through the whole procedure again. This is simply lazy design, where the programmer is more concerned with their own convenience in writing the installation program than with the convenience of the person using it.

The main failing of the program's intelligence, in the above example, is that it has not placed any value on the user's labor. The programmer has not considered that five minutes of entering new settings is the equivalent of five minutes of typing in a novel, or designing a skyscraper. The data that has been entered is discarded as worthless, instead of being treasured by the program. Anything that the user has taken time to achieve should be valued by the application.

All settings are valuable data, but they are especially valuable in a graphic interface environment. If a user scrolls a window to view a particular area, selects another view, and then returns to the original view, they are irritated if they have to go through the scrolling process again. Losing the users' data is a way of making an application appear unintelligent. The program that does this is the equivalent of somebody who forgets your name.

Applications that don't use the ideas put forward in this chapter can be said to be unintelligent. However, in most cases that is not a serious criticism. Users currently have no expectation of intelligence from the computer. So when they find a smart application it is a bonus. Users will tolerate a degree of program stupidity or forgetfulness so long as it doesn't interfere too much with what they want to do. But some applications overstep the mark, stubbornly refusing to remember any change the user has made, reinitializing every variable at the first chance they get.

9.8 Intelligence and Knowledge

The majority of computer applications play dumb. Others show the first glimmers of being truly interactive, responding as intelligent servants to the requirements of their user. Progress in this area is slow. A designer introduces a new intelligent feature and later it becomes accepted as the convention. The scope for development in this area is still large.

Sometimes, common-sense is what we look for in the design of objects around us. An illuminated light switch is easier to find in a dark room. A kettle that switches itself off when it boils is safer than one that doesn't.

These objects have simple purposes, and the designer knows what the owner needs from them. The intelligence in a software program is a reflection of the designer's knowledge of the users' expectations. Put simply: smart designer, smart program.

10

Learning Curve

Books on computer programming usually explain how to structure a program in terms of its function. Programmers are taught to write code the most efficient way to achieve speed of operation, small program size and readable code. These are all considered more important than the structure presented to the user. This chapter shows how an application should be designed to unravel like a story, revealing new information and features as the user spends time with it.

10.1 What is Learning?

Learning is the process of expanding personal knowledge and skills. It can be broken down into the areas of acquiring new information, acquiring physical skills to the point where a person no longer has to act consciously, and the gathering of experience.

A learner driver is first given basic information about the cars' controls. This lever changes gear, that pedal increases the speed, this pedal stops the car and so on. They are also given information about the rules of driving. Stop at this line, obey this rule. Learning to drive begins, like many other activities, with a period of instruction.

When the learner has acquired enough information they can move onto the next stage, practicing driving skills. Driving involves using both hands and, in the case of a manual transmission, both feet at the same time. At first it is difficult to coordinate the movement of all four limbs, but after hours of practice most drivers master the skill. At this point the interface – the car's controls – becomes transparent to them. They no longer see them or think about them. They are able to carry out the complex sequence of physical movements needed to negotiate a junction yet at the same time be thinking about what's for dinner. However, mastering driving skills to this level does not make a person a good driver.

The third part of learning is the acquiring of personal experience. The learner driver discovers how to handle a skidding car by being in a skid. This is information that cannot be communicated but has to be gained 'the hard way.' You can tell a child that fire will burn them, but until they have put their hand in the flame, they have no understanding of what that means. Personal experience is gathered by the individual and used as reference. When a new situation is met, knowledge gained from past episodes is used to guess the outcome of the present one. There is an element of experimentation and discovery in this. This can all be summarized by the phrase 'we learn from our mistakes.'

The stages of learning

- Instruction
- Practicing skills
- Experimentation and experience

What is a Learning Curve?

The phrase 'learning curve' is often used to describe how difficult something is to learn. An application may be said to have a 'steep learning curve.' This is usually a euphemism for 'it's difficult to use, unless you already know how.'

'Learning curve' is the phrase that best describes this chapter's main idea. This concept is that applications need to be presented to the user in a phased manner. It must be assumed that the user starts with no knowledge and becomes more proficient as time goes on. Plotted as a graph, the learning curve appears as a ramp.

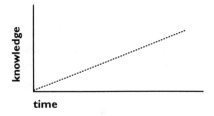

Figure 57 A linear learning curve where knowledge expands in proportion to time

Figure. 58 The shape of the learning curve for most applications

It is easy to picture a user climbing the slope as a metaphor for their efforts to learn. The curve may also take the shape of a stretched 'S', such that plotted against time, the period of greatest learning appears just after the user has understood the basic instructions.

10.2 Affecting the Learning Curve of an Application

Quick Starts

How to design for the first time user

The immediacy of software appeals to people in the same way as a new car. The need to give it a quick spin around the block can be overwhelming. The majority of people are going to have their first contact with an application in this way, and so it is the starting point of the learning curve. To accommodate this, an application has to be able to guide the first time user into an immediate appreciation of the functionality.

As an example, consider a chess program (apologies are made to readers who do not know the game). The human player will just want to start playing, probably with the classic opening move Pawn to King 4 (P-K4).

The player begins by asking:
  How can I start to play?
  How can I play P-K4?
  How do I quit?

These questions are immature, but this is only natural. Note that just like learning to ski, it is important to know how to stop! With a drag and drop interface, moving the pieces should be easy.

To allow the player to start up immediately, the program will need to use intelligent defaults, or pre-selected options. Here are a few:

1) The player is given the white pieces, the computer controls black. This allows the player to start , while also removing the need for the player to know how to ask the computer player to start instead. Most chess simulators allow for each player to be human or computer controlled.

2) The computer's game is set to 'standard' difficulty, this being simple enough not to require too much processing time, but hard enough to impress upon the player that the game will prove a good match. There may exist a multitude of different play level options, none of which the player need use immediately.

3) The board is set up with white pieces at the bottom and uses white and black pieces of the accepted standard design if these are graphically depicted.

   Again, it is unlikely that a player will immediately want to play with novelty pieces, or with the board the other way up.

It is very foolish to deny the need for a quick start facility. Though a user can only be a first-time-user once, everyone is a first-time-user once.

Comparison and Bounds Testing

The next stage that the user goes through is the wish to test the bounds of the program. This may involve comparison to a natural task, or to a previously used product.

> How do I increase difficulty?
> Can I limit the computer's thinking time?
> Does it recognize illegal moves?
> Can I do en-passant?
> Does it recognize castling properly?

The player is still experimenting with the interface, but is starting to wonder about how to achieve the task in hand – a good game of chess. The interface is still not transparent enough for the user to ignore it completely.

By now the user will have seen the standard responses to illegal moves, and will be sensitive to the feedback information that the program provides. This allows for rewarding experimentation. For example, to castle, the player may move his king first – which is the proper way – or the rook. The program must respond by moving the other piece to the correct position. The user will be watching out for a warning if for any reason castling is illegal.

Configuring For Real Use

Only when the player is comfortable with the interface can they actually start to use it fully. Now the player is experienced, they can make use of 'expert' options. In fact a competent user can reach the bounds, outstripping the functionality of an application, remarkably quickly.

> Can I play through a database of famous games?
> Can I change the color of the pieces?
> Will it rate my playing strength?

These questions are concerned with honing the application or getting the most out of it.

Practical Advice when Implementing a Learning Curve

When designing an application it is useful to write out a list of all the things the program will do. The list of functions can then be divided and categorized under the following headings:

1 Have to know how to use
2 More functionality
3 Esoterica

How to design for the first time user

Under heading one should be listed all the basic functions of the application. If the application were a word processor, this list would include 'type into document.' This is such an obvious thing to experienced users that they might not think of listing it. However, for a user moving up to a computer from a typewriter everything is new and strange.

In 1985 when Amstrad launched a low cost word processor onto the British market, they were receiving three or four calls a day asking why typing on the keyboard didn't produce output from the printer. It had to be explained to the callers that they had to load software, open a document, type and then use the 'print document' function. Ninety-nine per cent of the users got by with the manual, but one per cent were still thinking 'typewriter' and weren't interested in learning any more than that.

The 'have to know' functions are the controls that have to be used every time, or nearly every time the application is run. These include parts of the program that are used commonly, but not often by new users. Some elements need to be set up before they can be used, but are essential to run the application. With a word processor, it is necessary to have an open document to type into. This is why modern word processors usually initialize with an open, untitled document.

With a new application, the nursery slopes of the learning curve are dependent on the 'have to know' functions. The steepness of the slope depends on how easy it is to find the functions and how complicated it is to use them.

Basic Functions, Feedback and Modification

The basic functions of an application must be consistent throughout, while being capable of modification as the user becomes more proficient. These building blocks must have a simple, though non-intrusive, feedback mechanism.

How to use feedback

When users attempt to access a basic function, they may be in doubt whether they have succeeded, so the function must have an immediate visible feedback. There are various standard feedbacks that a user will feel happy with:

1) An immediate responsive change in the screen. This is what would happen in an arcade game when a player yanks the joystick. The screen picture reflects a new position or view. This is the most immediate feedback type.

2) A further list of options. As long as some form of title text connects these options with the command that summoned them, users will be content that their actions have had an effect.

3) A feedback sound effect combined with a change in a static status area. A status area is a fixed part of the screen that displays information in a textual or figurative way, like a speedometer. This is the least effective, especially if the status area is small, or the sound effect is not heard. A more experienced user does not require so much.

4) A large text box. This is the most intrusive.

How to use feedback for first time users

Consistency in feedback is also important. New users are very sensitive to slight changes in feedback type. If feedback is usually written in blue bordered boxes but one function returns a beep, this will cause confusion, even if the user isn't consciously aware of it.

Working with new software is very much like being a member of a new club with weird rules. No one explains them, yet you don't really feel you should ask any questions.

More Functionality

The user will eventually grasp the basics of an application and will want to try out new things. Sometimes this will be forced by circumstances. The annual accounts need typing up, a disk becomes full, there's been a change of address, for example. Sometimes it will be the user's natural curiosity and desire to get the most from the application. There is a subtle difference between the two. The user forced to try something new will have much less patience than the 'recreational explorer.' Therefore the designer should cater for the former type of user. Some developers keep a fictional situation in mind, 'designing for the managing director whose secretary has left for the day.'

How to design for a range of users of differing proficiency

It is sometimes difficult to decide what is an essential function and what is simply additional. If the function can only be used after the basic functions have been grasped, it is not itself a basic function. This is very much in the control of the designer. The word processor that starts up with an open document has demoted open-document to a non-essential function. Whereas a word processor that does not allow any text to be input, until a document is opened, has made the open-document command a 'have-to-know' function.

Entire subsystems can often be hidden from immediate use. This is the application equivalent of a clear desk, or a workshop with all the tools put away. If it doesn't need to be used straight away, why have it hanging around cluttering up the place?

It is becoming popular to have expandable menus and button bars. These reflect the user's status as novice, proficient or expert in the number of functions available. This seems like a good idea. Unfortunately it is human nature to immediately select 'expert mode,' to have all the functions available, in case the one that's needed is hidden. Also the 'access denied' aspect of this scheme doesn't go down too well with users, either. It is better to hide everything, but communicate clearly how to access the additional functions.

Esoterica

Some options are only put in because testers or experienced users have bullied the programmer into including them. These are often fairly esoteric, sometimes forming answers to questions that most users wouldn't ask. Not only should these functions and subsystems be tucked away for the novices benefit, but also because experienced users get a kick out of discovering them.

Techniques Used in Games

Part of the entertainment of a computer game is that it presents a new experience to the player. Games often involve exploration and learning. With such games, manipulating the learning curve becomes an important part of the development. A popular yet primitive adventure game called 'Nethack' actually comes with no instructions beyond basic controls: half the game is to work out how to play.

It is sometimes the designer's intention to create a closed environment: a game world in which the player can gradually discover items and work out what the items do. It is more entertaining if discovery is a gradual process. The designer does not want to give the player too much information, making the game confusing, or too little information, making it difficult to progress in the early stages. For this reason, games designers put a great deal of effort into making the game unravel in a self-explanatory way. Games begin easy and get more difficult as the player progresses. Although increasing difficulty is not appropriate in any other application but a game, it is useful to know how this is achieved.

Games designers assume that a new player will not have mastered the controls on first beginning to play. So games often begin with a level that would be very easy for a skilled player. If the game eventually requires the player to use multiple controls it may start off with tasks that need only a subset of those controls. A fine balance is needed if the designer is to make the game challenging but not impossibly difficult.

Games often start with an easy level that provides practice. Some games include a training mode with some of the game hazards turned off. A flight simulator may include the option to practice landings, if this is a difficult part of the game. Practice is an important part of learning. A few general applications allow the user to do a 'dry run.' The inclusion of an 'undo' function allows a change to be seen before data is altered permanently. This aids experimentation and can help the user gain a fuller knowledge of the application.

The perfect learning curve for a game is said to be stepped, rather than a linear progression. This may only be true for arcade games where hand-eye skills are important. Each step of the curve is a new goal that must be achieved. Once the goal has been reached, the curve flattens out, allowing the player to practice their skills at the new level before going on to the next.

The best games contain a large degree of experimentation. Well designed games will allow the player to experiment with little or no penalty. Games that punish experimentation, by ending the game or making it impossible to progress, become frustrating. This is true when applied to general applications. An application that punishes the user's experiments by throwing away their data, or not providing enough feedback, will be frustrating and difficult to learn.

Games often have additional features - it may be a different type of weapon or, in the case of a simulation, some new item that can be built - that only become available as the game progresses. This has the dual purpose of making the game less complex in the initial stages, while providing more entertainment later on, when the player's interest may be flagging .

How Games Reward Learning

Criticism has been levelled at some games companies. They have been accused of setting out to design addictive games in order to make more sales. Addiction is too strong a word. Games are made compulsive, just as books, TV and movies are. And much the same techniques are used. What happens next? The player's curiosity and desire to learn keeps them playing. They want to see something new. Games often provide clues that there will be something new to see if the player progresses a little further. In fiction, this is done with an unresolved question. If the player has already progressed through several stages and each has been different, then it is logical to assume there is more to come. Each new item or feature is a reward for getting so far.

Rewards are an important part of learning and it is useful to know what application users find rewarding. Achievement of goals can be rewarding, as can some special piece of entertainment which marks progress made. Educational software for young children contains the best examples of these kinds of rewards. Simple animations and catchy tunes mark the successful completion of a task. In applications for the more mature, similar things are happening at a more subtle level. People prefer to use GUIs not for greater productivity but because they are more rewarding in the way they give feedback to tasks achieved.

Training Screens

Due to their complexity, some games have started to overlay text descriptions of all the components on a screen - something that would previously

How to use feedback to aid learning

How to use feedback to reward learning

only be seen in a manual. The best method is to write underlined text in a clear area of the screen, with a connecting line from the text to the subject. This is a graphical version of the more familiar help screen that usually lists keyboard combinations or 'hot keys.'

A training screen is particularly effective when explaining the symbols on a status bar or other dynamic screen information area.

To save space, a word processor may limit its status bar information from:

>   Page 1 of 4   Line 364   Column 10

to:

>   1/4   364   10

This is reasonable, as an experienced user won't need the text strings, the numbers themselves change as the cursor moves round the screen, making it obvious what they represent. To a novice however, this is not true. If a 'beginner mode' were to insert the full text, the status bar might become cluttered. Superimposed text would explain the meaning of the numbers at the same time as seeing their position on the screen.

Hiding Options in Menus and Dialogues

There are three ways of making more options available to a WIMP inter-face. You can introduce extra menu topics, add extra items onto menus, or add 'advanced' buttons on dialogues.

Expert Menus

How to design for
users ranging in
proficiency

The application initially shows the user a 'novice' menu. This offers a limited number of menu items. The user can choose to see the 'expert' menu, which displays all the available options. By limiting the options, the user is not necessarily presented with a simplified version of the program – it is truer to say that non-essential functions are left out.

When an entire set of functions is to be left out, a menu title can be removed from the menu bar. More often, menu items are left out – or grayed out – in individual menus. In the chess program example, all the functions that offer options for championship play can be left out.

Advanced Dialogues

At a basic level this involves adding an 'advanced', 'additional' or 'more' button onto a standard dialogue. A 'file-find' function may produce a dialogue that simply asks the user for the name or 'filespec' of the file to look for, and the places in the computer system to search. As well as the 'cancel' and 'OK' buttons there also lurks a 'more' button. Pressing this button extends the dialogue, which also asks about the date and instances of the file to be searched for. The reason for hiding the advanced options is mainly to make the search seem simpler to the user. Asking superfluous yet logical questions can cause a user to become frustrated with program 'bureaucracy.'

Standard find:

What is the name of the file?
In which directory(s) should I look?
On which device(s) should I look?

Extra options:

Shall I ignore instances of the file older than a certain date?
Shall I stop looking after finding the first instance?

10.3 How Users Learn About a Program

It has already been explained that learning in general involves instruction, practice and experience. How does this figure in the way people learn about a new application?

Just like learning any other new activity, learning an application follows this pattern: first the user receives instruction either from a manual or from someone who already knows how to use the program. Next the user practices, becoming familiar with the layout and structure of the program. For example, they might learn the position and meaning of icons. The final stage in learning an application is experimentation with the program and gaining experience in using it.

The mind uses many methods to remember information. Association is one. Mnemonics is another. Rhythm and rhyme aid retention of data. Also 'clustering' can help. This is a concept where large amounts of items are broken into smaller, easier to remember clusters. For example, if you were to fix drinks for eight people it would be easier to remember what each wanted if you broke the group into two smaller groups of four. With smaller numbers it is easier to pick out a pattern: three want coffee, there-fore the other wants tea.

Applications can be designed to make use of these methods by displaying items in groups and naming functions creatively. Icons and other graphic devices can be used as mnemonics to support the learning process. It may not look elegant, but the user would certainly remember that a tartan screen was used as the print menu.

The Role of a CUI

One advantage of using a common user interface (CUI), for example Windows, is that the user brings previously acquired knowledge with them, leaving less work for the application to do. The user does not need to be re-taught how to use windows, icons, etc. There are a large number of input devices whose behavior the user is already comfortable with. A user learning about a Windows program effectively short cuts the learning process. This does mean users become proficient more quickly.

To gain this benefit, applications must adhere to the CUI's standards, and improvements or enhancements will not be immediately welcomed by the user. One disadvantage is that users can be led to believe they know more about an application than they really do. An application that looks familiar but does not work in the way it is expected to will frustrate them and appear cranky.

How to design for the first time user

Things That Users Find Tricky to Learn

If an application can be made easier to learn, it can be made more difficult too. The most difficult to learn application is one that hides all functions from the user, even the simplest ones, and gives no guidance as to what the user must do now, or do next.

There was an early word processor that started up by presenting the user with a blank screen. Typing on the keyboard produced warning beeps. It was necessary to open a new document before the program would operate and this was achieved by pressing a control key combination – Ctrl+F for File.

If the program gives no clue as to what the user has to do to operate it, they are forced into the position of experimenting. If experimentation is punished by silence or cryptic messages, the user is unable to progress.

Other things that can make a program difficult to learn include:

Changing things dynamically. The user navigates around an application using landmarks that they have remembered and recognize. Changing the position of these things will cause confusion. The same applies to procedures and messages.

New physical skills. An application that requires some form of input that is unusual will take practice to learn. People using a mouse for the first time, find it difficult, particularly double clicking which is an unnatural action.

Too much information. GUIs are supposedly easy to learn and yet they contain a lot of visual clutter. A brief look at children's books will give a good idea of how information can be presented simply.

10.4 Learning What You Know

If you view the application user as a growing and learning child, their education must take place over a period of time. The problem is that users learn at different rates and start from different levels of understanding.

The learning curve of a program is a neglected area of its design. Little thought is put into how the user gets to know an application. For this reason, many users get no further than a very basic understanding of an application, learning only the minimum that they need to. Sadly this means that much of the effort that has gone into developing the product may be wasted.

Users find out how to use a program via brief instruction and a process of discovery. Experience cannot be replaced by reading the manual. One law of learning, Martin's Law (no relation), states that you only learn what you almost already knew. If the application does not allow the user to steadily increase knowledge of the program, simply by continuous contact, then it is flawed.

11

Little Helpers

'When there's something wrong in the neighborhood, who ya' gonna' call?' So said Ray Parker Jr in his famous 80's hit song 'Ghostbusters.' There is a point at which every user gets into difficulties with an application and it is at this point that they look for a help system. Help systems vary greatly from being non-existent to 'nannying.' If a help system is working properly the user will hardly notice it. If it is not providing useful information it becomes an irritant.

Programmers consider adding help a chore. They are happy to put in help for the easy stuff like moving the mouse and clicking the go button, but when it comes to explaining something complex, it becomes bothersome. The help system should not be neglected, it should be an integrated part of the design, supporting the other methods of communicating with the user.

**How to provide
help information
in an application**

11.1 The Perfect Helper

What is the perfect helper? Well, imagine you are in front of an application, trying to feel your way around it. Wouldn't it be useful to have a technical boffin sitting next to you to interject useful comments? Your helper can advise you of what you are doing, what related functions are connected with your current operations, and warn you of failed or problematic outcomes. The boffin knows where all those useful functions are, and how to access them. And to save space, the boffin can take the form of a parrot and perch on your shoulder, squawking advice while keeping a beady eye on what you are doing. This is the idealized perfect helper.

What Are the Essentials of Our Perfect Helper?

- The helper is a third party, separate from both the application and the user.
- The helper is always there to make (context-sensitive) help suggestions.
- The helper can react to what the user does with respect to the application.
- While not interfering with the applications execution, the helper becomes an alternative focus or reference point.

It is hard for an application to replicate all the features of our imaginary helper; the application cannot, of course, be truly separate from itself. The nearest that an application gets to providing perfect helpers is by the implementation of status bars and help functions.

11.2 Keeping Users Informed: The Status Bar

A status bar is any area of the screen that constantly displays information about the program's state. Like a clock on the mantelpiece, it always reflects some useful information about something and usually stays in the same place. The status bar may be movable, or its presence at all may be optional.

The status bar does not have to be a bar. A program may well display different information in different places. This idea first surfaced in arcade games, where part of the screen was reserved for displaying the players score, and how many lives were left.

In general:

- The bar should not be interactive: the information it displays is probably not alterable directly, in a meaningful way.

- The information would naturally be expected to change during the use of the program.

- The information may be displayed in any mixture of text, numbers and icons.

| Input mode: type in value and press ENTER | INS 4/12 |

Figure 59 A typical status bar.

How to give help with the function of icons

A status bar can be used to précis what a particular menu option or icon might do. In a GUI system, while the mouse is hovering over the icon, or while a menu item is in focus, the status bar can switch from its normal display to show this form of information.

One problem with status bars is that they may force the user to scan up and down in order to get info. For example, if the status bar is used to summarize the menu items and icons that are currently in focus, the user may be forced to switch attention from one part of the screen to the other in rapid succession. This is particularly so if the status bar is at the bottom of the screen and the toolbar icons and menu are at the top. One obvious way around this is to use a movable status bar that places itself directly beside the focus object. This bar, or 'tooltip' can be a little messy on screen as it may appear in a variety of places possibly covering other areas of the screen.

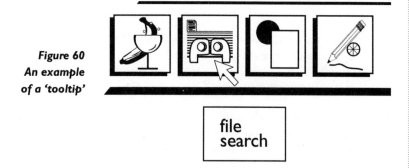

*Figure 60
An example
of a 'tooltip'*

A more help oriented status box can be used to hold a variable amount of text that explains the current mode of operation, and what further functions are possible. For example, a drawing program usually has one particular tool in action at any one time. If the selected tool is a draw-rectangle tool, the status box may contain an explanation of how a rectangle can be created, as well as which keys to press in order to draw the rectangle from the centre outwards, or to constrain the tool to drawing squares. If the length of the text is variable, then the status box needs to have a scroll bar and probably be a mini, movable, sizable window in itself.

Single line reminders of essential functions are still popular, especially in non-WIMP interface applications. A typical line may remind users of the function key settings, e.g.:

> F1=SAVE F2=LOAD etc.

Some applications use a status line to provide instructions. When a function is selected, the status line displays what the user must do next. When that is done, the next instruction is displayed. The status bar may have space for two or more lines of text, allowing the previous instruction to be displayed in a dimmer color above the current one. This communicates the idea that a procedure is being processed but is as yet incomplete.

Toolbar Buttons Indicating Status

When a toolbar button is pressed, it can remain depressed and thus indicate a change of mode. In a word processor, a depressed 'B' button may indicate that text from this point in the document is written in bold. Instead of just depicting a button as being depressed or not, an alternate state can be shown with another icon in the bar button. Thus a button that turns a grid on in a drawing package may depict this directly with one icon representing a blank sheet, and another a sheet with a grid on.

Using a Focus

While a status bar keeps the user informed of the current way the program is functioning, what is often needed is a focus for the program. The focus is where the user's eye is first drawn when looking at the screen. Perhaps a better definition would be that it is where an onlooker's eye is drawn – one who isn't actually using the program.

If you were to switch channels and see the middle of a tennis match, the first thing your attention would settle on would be any superimposed information telling you what the game and set scores were, and who was serving.

Unfortunately it is quite easy to design a program with no focus or 'centre'. While not fatal, it can elicit a feeling that the software is unfriendly, or produce the common complaint that 'I don't know where to start.'

One of the best examples of a simple focus is the smiley face on the Minesweeper game that comes with Microsoft's Windows. Why does the game use a face? Perhaps because humans spend most of their emotional attention looking at faces, and can recognize even the smallest changes.

The game involves the player trying to guess where mines are hidden in a grid. If the player guesses wrongly, a mine explodes, ending the game. When the player probes a mine, the face winces in anticipation. If you do get it wrong, it frowns in anguish. If you manage to finish the game by clearing the minefield, the face dons a pair of shades and looks smug.

By clicking on the face, the game is reset.

To summarize the face's reactions:

Smiles – Default.

Winces – As you test a mine.

Frowns – if you get blown up.

Wears glasses – Cool! You finished.

Press it to reset the game.

The smiley face reacts to what you do, as opposed to just reflecting the status of the game variables. One could criticize the fact that what is essentially a status bar also accepts input, but it seems natural enough in use.

The important point is that this little helper is seen to be acting on a level 'above' the game. It is not much of a status bar in this case, more of a back-seat driver.

11.3 'On-line' Help Systems

Here, the term 'on-line' just means that the help files are being called from the application, as opposed to a written manual. Help systems are not primarily written to replace manuals, though they sometimes incorporate all the text that would otherwise be printed.

The main function of the help system is to explain what functions do, or how particular problems are dealt with by the application. The help system may be called up or invoked by pressing a special key combination, by a menu option or even by a dedicated key. Clearly for immediate convenience, this beats looking things up in a separate printed manual that may not be to hand. The extra size overhead that they place on an application is no longer considered to be much of a problem. Help systems can also provide 'hyper-text' or the ability to navigate the text by selecting a subject, as opposed to viewing a sequence of pages.

Help must address several of the user's requirements. A user may want to browse the keyboard mappings, look for a particular function name in an index or step through a tutorial.

Context-sensitive Help

How to design for the first time user

'Help me NOW' is the shout that a user makes when he or she becomes stuck. Coming back to our perfect helper parrot, we want advice on how to get out of a troublesome situation, when we are in it. But a standard help system is like a book; you have to find the information you need – it doesn't know what you want.

A context-sensitive help system limits the help to entries relevant to what the user is doing when it is invoked.

Many programmers use development systems with context-sensitive help. The system allows them to highlight a word in the language code and then bring up an explanation that refers directly to it. Thus by highlighting the term 'goto' in my program source code, I can see how this statement should be used. This is much quicker than manually referring to an index, and then moving to the correct page. The system has 'hidden' the index and allowed the user to link a term and its description without any interposing stages.

This kind of help aids the learning of the application by the novice user. It also serves the purpose of providing reference material to the experienced user.

Graded Help

How to design for users with a range of proficiency

Users at different levels of proficiency need different levels of help. A novice user will require a lot of help with deep explanations and definitions of the terms used. As they progress they will still need help to explain how to use complex functions. However, the user should now be familiar with the terms used, and explanations can be brief and easy to refer to quickly. An experienced user shouldn't need so much help, but it is useful for them to have reminders. Summaries and symbols should be enough to refresh their memory.

One of the earliest applications to have a graded help system was the word-processor WordStar. This allowed the user to have the control keys of the various functions summarized on screen or not. The first level gave a full list, the second a shorter list, and the third no list at all.

Designing for the first time user

In the previous chapter it was mentioned that applications sometimes allow the user to select novice, proficient and expert levels. The same applications often tie in the help system. More help is displayed for a beginner than an expert. However, the actual text doesn't differ between the levels – just how much is shown. The next development should be to provide different help to the beginner than to the expert.

Pointers for Writing Help Text

How to write help text

Help text has two basic requirements. It must contain all the information needed by the user and it must be communicated clearly.

In an ideal world, help text would be like a personal tutor explaining as you go. So perhaps the help text writer should find a guinea pig – someone who doesn't know the application – sit them down, explain the function and listen to their questions. This conversation could be tape recorded and transcribed. Then the help text could be prepared using the important points picked out of the transcript.

This is an impractical solution, life is too short and the value of the result would depend too much on the experience of the guinea pig. The next best thing is to write down as many questions as possible about the program. These should begin how-do-I.. and what-is.. The help text should then attempt to answer them. Use a guinea pig to test out the help text and improve the areas they had problems with.

At an early stage, the help author must decide whether they are providing reference material, a tutorial guide or both. This will affect the type of information they include and how it is presented. If the reference approach is used, the information may only need to be summaries, reminding the user of information they have already learnt but forgotten. The tutorial approach requires more detailed explanation: not only how to do something, but also why it is done, how other things are affected and examples.

Help should cover things in the application that might cause confusion. These could be items not encountered in the program before, or options where the user may not know what the outcome will be.

In general, the most complex, and the less often used functions, tend to get the least help. This is a mistake. If a function is used only occasionally, the user will forget how it works and need to refer to the help system. It should be ensured that the less often a function is used, the more help accompanies it.

The level of expertise of the user should be found. If the program is a general application for beginners, everything needs explaining. If the application is specific to a small group of technical users then it may only be necessary to explain unusual or complex features.

There is no point in putting a lot of effort into explaining basic functions if the application uses a common interface. Effort should be put into explaining the unique features and where the application differs to others in the way it works.

If a concept is difficult to explain, an example should be given. But examples may require the use of other unexplained systems so may set off a long trek into the unknown for the unwary novice. Choose examples carefully and keep them simple.

Jargon, if used, must be translated. If a technical term is explained by reference to further technical or internal terms, the system is effectively building a Tower of Babel that locks in the experienced user and locks out the novice.

The user should be referred to other help text that will aid understanding. This usually means similar functions and their examples. Or it may be useful to mention related functions, so that the user builds up a complete understanding of how the program works.

11.4 Bad Help

Users judge the quality and reliability of an application by all its aspects. After one bad experience, the user will never use a badly implemented help system again. There are several ways of creating a poor help system.

Did you ever stop to ask a stranger directions, and later find yourself three miles down the road totally lost? In the brief conversation at the side of the road, many things can go wrong.

The instructions may be incomplete, leaving out some vital piece of information. The instructions may be good up to a point but finish before the final goal is achieved. 'Keep going for three miles, you can't miss it.' The instructions may have been inaccurate, telling you to go left when you should go right. The instructions may take you to a place you didn't want to go. The crucial point is that the stranger probably based the instructions on a familiarity with the destination that you don't have.

Application help can fail in similar ways. Inaccurate or missing information will confuse the user. Providing help that doesn't answer the user's questions is wasted effort.

Some help systems can be overpowering. Users don't need help with everything, so a help system that insists on explaining every dialogue box and button, no matter how obvious the function, can get very tiresome.

Help shouldn't be used to explain a function that gives no feedback. This is the wrong solution to a design problem. The correct solution is to make the function give feedback.

Don't fill the help system with information not specific to the direct use of the application. It is a safe bet that a user in the middle of using a paint package already knows what a bitmap is, for example.

A popular compiler for the programming language 'C' has a context sensitive help system. This works well when explaining the various 'C' commands available to the programmer. When the compiler detects an error while compiling a file, it prints a warning message to the user. For example:

```
ERROR: 'wages_record' undefined.
```

The programmer can click on the error message with the mouse pointer to see an explanation of this error message. If they do that they will see this message:

```
'identifier' undefined

An attempt was made to use an identifier that was not
defined.
```

Designing error messages for the first time user

There are two likely causes of the above error. The first is that the user knows what to do but has simply forgotten to include an essential piece of code. The second reason is that the user is unfamiliar with the language and doesn't yet know of the need to include the essential piece of code.

The help text assumes the first case, where the user knows what to do.It explains the error message, but not why the error occurred. This begs the question, why on earth would a proficient user read the help text? It would have been better to expand the text for the benefit of the novice user, explaining that each identifier needs to be defined before it can be used and by giving an example definition.

To be fair, the above help text was probably included for completeness, so that there was some feedback when help was asked for. The 'undefined identifier' error is so fundamental to 'C' programming that the help-text author probably felt no explanation was really necessary. This was a missed opportunity. The help system, Instead of making 'C' programming accessible to a wider audience, will reinforce the idea in the novice user's mind, that 'C' is totally impenetrable.

A: Did I ever tell you about the time I was working for a magazine that published BASIC programs as a listing. A guy phoned up one day to complain he couldn't get a program working. He said, "When I run the program I get the message: TYPE MISMATCH IN LINE 30. And I've tried typing MISMATCH into line 30 and it still doesn't work!"

D: That's a lovely story. This is the typical problem with showing errors; there inevitably has to be an interface between the error message and the user. What should that message have said?

A: Good question. This was in the days when BASIC was built into the computer and squeezed into a 32K chip. There simply wasn't the space to fit a long explanation. Perhaps, 'Type of value does not match type of variable,' would give a novice user a clue to the problem. It depends whether you think an error message should just be an error message, or whether it should help the user to learn the application.

D: There are two different problems. First the experienced programmer needs to be quickly warned that he or she has made a typo. Secondly a novice needs to be told what to look for. The expert just needs the line quoted and the minimal error message, the novice needs the line quoted and a few examples of correct matching, e.g.:

```
Mismatch in this line:
10 ANIMAL$ = 24

Here are some examples of correct matching:
CAR$ = "JEEP"
B = 22
Etc.
```

Most likely a mode switch would be most applicable, with the novice setting as default.

Cyclic Help

The ability to create links from one subject to another, as is possible in modern help creators, needs to be understood properly to avoid cyclic descriptions such as the one below and other pitfalls such as help that 'peters out'.

Where is the Old Castle?
The Old Castle lies on the Blue River.

Where is the Blue River?
The Blue River flows under the Stone Bridge.

Where is the Stone Bridge?
The Stone Bridge leads to the Old Castle.

> Where is the Old Castle?
> The Old Castle lies on the Blue River.

If two links exist, one from explanation A to explanation B, and another from C to B, it is no longer clear where the user came from, once he is at B. This means that the text of B must be written carefully to avoid seeming too linear. In the above example involving the Old Castle, the correct format for descriptive help is a general scene and three specific entries in addition:

> Where is the Old Castle?
> The Old Castle lies on the north bank of the Blue River, and can be accessed by a Stone Bridge. The whole area is in the middle of the country.
>
> The Blue River runs from the west side of the country to the east.
>
> The Old Castle was built to protect the villagers from attack.
>
> The Stone Bridge is one of the oldest structures in the country.

Note the use of the term 'country' to mark a relative position.

From the initial enquiry 'where is the Old Castle?' the help system provides a base position with all the relevant information mentioned. From there, the user can seek additional information about the locations by accessing the links to their entries. The original version has the user trekking from entry to entry in search of the information they were looking for.

Internal Terms

If you use application-specific terms, these must have simple synonym equivalents that can be found in a subject index, otherwise the user will get stuck.

If the subject index contains, for example:

> HyperFormat: A complete text formatting system.

but does not contain 'Text,' or 'Format,' users are unlikely to discover the function that has been devised for their benefit.

There are many areas of technical synonym ambiguity that a help index must bridge, if it is to work with people who don't think like the application authors.

Some examples:

- Search, Find, Look up – While the application may associate one term with text and another with files the help system must revert to assuming that a user views all these expressions in the same context.

- Forum, Conference, Topic – all of these mean different things in different on-line services. A help system for a communications package may need to accept that users are unaware that the terminology they are familiar with is used differently in this context.

- Comment, Remark, Annotation – While these phrases are specifically used in program source code, configuration files and word processors, they are nevertheless interchangeable in the real world.

- Field, Parameter, Argument – all of these are associated with stuffing data into functions.

11.5 The Future of Help

The future of the help system as it stands is pretty bleak. It is too easy for help systems to be written in the language of those who don't need help. And just like the old joke about there being only one Monopolies Commission, the user soon comes to the conclusion that the system isn't working for them. Let's get back to our perfect helper. Ideally, what is needed is a voice-activated system, that could talk back. A system that could answer questions like a human instructor. It would be good if the help system knew as much about the user as the application. Perhaps a small camera placed on a helmet would enable a separate system to view the application from the user's perspective – but of course this is an unlikely future for general applications.

Creating a help system is an exercise in guesswork. It is always difficult to anticipate what aspects of an application the user will need help with. The perfect system can only be produced by trial and error – continual evaluation and feedback from users. Help systems are provided to support the application and make its workings clearer where they are obscure. Therefore some might say that providing a help system is an admission that the interface doesn't communicate adequately with the user. However, as help systems become more comprehensive, users are learning to look for help not as the last resort but as the first. There is now the expectation that help will be provided and new applications that fail to provide help will not be viewed with respect.

12

Documentation and Support Materials

This chapter is about the material that accompanies an application: the instruction manual and the other bits and bobs that make up a complete package. Unless an application has been designed brilliantly, and is completely transparent to the user, some form of written instructions are going to be needed. And of course, written instructions will be needed to explain how to install and run the application in the first place. So there is no getting away from it, a manual must be written and it is better to think about it earlier than later.

We are assuming that the application is not running on a site specific machine installation. These are usually active in public places, so space may only be available for cursory instruction. A telephone kiosk, for example, may have a guide for ringing the emergency services, getting through to the operator, or ringing abroad directly – but that's it. So if you have the opportunity to write support material, think about those who don't, before wasting the opportunity to provide something of quality.

12.1 Manuals

Is it still necessary to produce a manual for an application? Users have a new awareness of software; the phenomenon of computer literacy that has been mentioned in earlier chapters. And as interfaces become friendlier, there will be more users who won't need to read a conventional manual.

Despite the decreasing need for supporting text, a manual is still a desirable part of an application. The manual is the best place to explain to the user exactly why the application exists. This is best done by explaining the philosophy of the product in terms of how it solves the problems in the field it operates in, and of course why it may be better than any other alternatives.

The user's first contact with the application may be with the manual and not the software. If there is no documentation, except that found on the disk, the user or potential user will start to perceive the application as unfriendly, even before they start using it. The support materials that accompany the application should reflect the qualities of the program.

There is the simple, practical problem of what does the user do when stuck halfway through using an application. How do they access the online help if they don't know how to? A manual provides a separate course of action. Some areas of troubleshooting rely on actions taken while the program is not in operation.

It is assumed by some that computers can simulate or replace everything. They cannot yet simulate the physical contact between a human and an object like a book. The package needs to contain something the user can 'get their hands on.' A user purchasing an application will be comforted to find a package of components that all work together, combining to provide a complete solution to their problem.

Manuals, being portable and physical, can project the quality of an application beyond the screen of the computer. If the manual is produced as a nicely bound book this will project an image of high quality software.

Manual Considerations

What makes a manual a good manual? There are several things that might make a manual good: the quality of the writing, the depth and clarity of the informat on presented, the layout of the information and the quality of the materials used to produce it. Ultimately a manual is a good manual if it does its job. And there are two jobs a manual does. The first job is to instruct the user how to begin using the application. The second job is to provide the answers to questions that arise from use of the application. So there are two basic structures of manual: the tutorial or instruction manual and the reference manual. These are commonly produced as separate booklets, along with an installation guide.

Manuals must be tailored to the audience for which they are intended. There is little point in producing a 150 page manual for a simple application aimed at a novice user. The audience for this application is unlikely to want to read such a large amount of text, or be able to retain much of the information anyway. Likewise, a complex application aimed at a specialist user will need detailed explanation. Two or three pages will not be enough.

Writing manuals for the first time user

Why not rely on on-line help? Press F1 to find out.

There is another option. A fully written manual can be provided on CD-ROM with a simple reader program that also allows the user to make hard copies. However this is not a good solution. The reader program makes it difficult to refer to the manual and the application at the same time. If the user has a printer it may not print the document correctly; they will not be impressed by a manual with two lines of text on each page. Few people bother to bind this kind of manual, resulting in a heap of loose papers that get lost and muddled up. This method should be avoided, except by dyed-in-the-wool cheapskates.

Most manuals are written after the application has been developed. During development, the designer often has to describe how an application is to work in a written specification. This document can provide a useful basis for explaining how the application works in the manual.

It is possible to take this a step further and produce a manual before the application is developed. This is a useful design technique as it can highlight weak areas in the interface. It will become obvious where, in the application, not enough feedback is given and where procedures are not clearly defined.

Who gets to write the manual? This is a tricky question. It is easy to say the person to write the manual is the person who designed the application, or coded it, as they know the application best. However, being a good application designer or programmer does not imply the existence of writing skills. Also there is a tendency to miss out vital information when the writer is very familiar with an application. This is because certain actions have become transparent and the familiar user is no longer conscious of doing them. The best course of action is to divide the task and the manual into two. Ask someone unfamiliar with the program to write the tutorial or basic instruction section of the manual. The reference section should be written by a person who knows the application inside out.

A Guide to Writing Manuals

How to write a manual

Writing manuals requires skill and care. This is not fully appreciated by product developers, and many manuals end up poorly written. Writing the manual is often a chore to be done at the end of the development project, an extra expense that is sometimes missed off the budget and the time schedule. It is hardly surprising that people find the resulting documents incomprehensible. Instruction manuals, especially those translated into pidgin English, are considered a joke.

The first thing to consider when writing a manual is that people do not read them out of choice. They have to read the manual when there is no easier way to find out what they need to know. Therefore it is important to give clear and concise information, to make finding a particular item as easy as possible and to keep the text simple to read. If that is not done, the reader is being obstructed from reaching the information they require.

Various writers and academics have set out rules for 'good writing.' The ones pertinent to technical documentation can be paraphrased:

Simple rules for writing clear manuals

- Never use a jargon word if there is another way of describing something.
- Use words with as few syllables as possible.
- Keep sentence lengths short.
- Cut out words that add nothing to the meaning of the sentence.

These rules, which are intended to make text easier to read, may need a little explanation. The word jargon is itself a piece of jargon. Jargon could be explained as words known and used by only a limited number of people. Having explained jargon in full, I can now describe it as ' words in limited use' or as ' words known to few.' A word can only be understood when it falls within the vocabulary of the reader.

There are exceptions to every rule. The user shouldn't be separated from jargon so much as protected from it. Using jargon at least once, but providing a good explanation of what it means, allows the user to learn the jargon with the application.

The English dictionary is made up of a mixture of Anglo-Saxon words such as: wood, rock, hand, foot and head, and Latin- or Greek-derived words such as introduction, philosophy and personality. A high proportion of textual subject matter containing expressions of a multi-syllable inclination may increase the cerebral perplexity of the passage. Or to put it another way: too many long words make a sentence hard to read.

It should be possible to read a sentence out loud, without gasping for air at the end, or pausing for breath in the middle. If this can't be done, the sentence is too long. Many concepts can be packed into a sentence. If too many are packed in, the reader will have difficulty assimilating them all at once.

It is normal, when speaking, to include a number of fill words such as: actually and really. These provide time for the brain to process and deliver the next phrase. In writing, these words are not needed and should be taken out. Strangely, these words usually, actually, practically, virtually and literally end in -ly.

When listing the functions of a program for reference, it is useful to structure sentences so that the task comes before the procedure. Consider the sentence 'Press the red button to activate the elevator.' This seems like a reasonable way to explain the function of the red button. However, if this sentence is buried in a paragraph of text containing many similar phrases, the reader will have to read to the end of each sentence before finding the information required. Restructuring the sentence: 'to activate the elevator, press the red button,' puts the important, unique information at the head where it can be quickly found as the reader scans the text.

Technical documentation can be very 'dry' and boring to read. Manuals can be lightened with a little humor or by using an informal style. Humor can be used to create a friendly impression that will hopefully spill over – into the software.

The last, and perhaps the best, reason to include a little humor, is that it provides an incentive to read on. It is the intention that the user should read the manual and thereby get the most from the software and an informal style will help the process along.

Some manuals overdo the jokes and the style becomes irritating. Take, for example, this excerpt from an electronics guide:

```
I am presuming that the board is dead, with no output from
the display adapter, but that the PSU voltages are all OK,
and there is no obvious damage, like steaming great holes
in the board, or blackened bits where the lightning went.
If either of these last two apply, you know where the
dustbin is.
```

There is a fine line between entertainment and irritant. In this case the author oversteps the mark. The last sentence is really only included to amuse and is essentially redundant. It is good to include humor but it is not okay to waste the reader's time with irrelevant excursions.

Writing Tutorials

**How to write a
tutorial guide for
the first time user**

A tutorial teaches a user how to operate an application. This is done by working through an example, providing instructions at each stage and anticipating the questions that will arise in the user's mind. The skill in writing a tutorial guide is in being able to structure the work-through. The example work must be typical of the user's application, it mustn't be too long winded for the user to finish in a single session and it must cover all the information the user needs to continue unguided. A tutorial session should last, ideally, no more than twenty minutes.

On-line tutorials can often be good, but tend to fix the pace of use in a way that a book doesn't. And of course no one has to learn to restart, redo, turn off and reset a book. A tutorial from a book is the ultimate proof that an application can be mastered without previous experience. In this way, the crossing point between the user observing an application and using it directly is visible. This bond, or 'cyber-link' is not something that is easy to explain, but it certainly seems to exist. Some find it difficult to be on 'first name terms' with an application before a formal introduction.

A good tutorial guide, for a complex application, will start by illustrating the core functions of the program. This may involve taking the user step by step through the process of producing and completing a piece of work. At the end of this first session, the user may not appreciate all the functionality of the program, but should understand its basic structure and the procedure for producing a result. It is also important, at the end of this first session, for the user to feel that something tangible has been achieved – something that can be pointed to, saying: 'look what I've done.'

From this foundation, the tutorial should, in further sessions, go on to cover all the functions of the application in more detail. At each stage the guide should encourage the user to experiment and try out the functions that have been demonstrated. This reinforces understanding and provides opportunities for the production of their own work.

Tutorials should be presented in the form of a list of instructions, preferably numbered. This makes it easier to move from the manual to the screen without losing the thread of the tutorial. It is also a good idea to use illustrations and descriptions, showing how the screen should look at certain stages of the session. The user can then spot where something has been done wrong and back up a few steps.

12.2 Support Materials

There are quite a few extra materials that can be supplied to help the user with the application, or complement the program. While some of these originated for copy protection, quite a lot can be put in a small box. One game company produced a map of its game-world printed on a tea towel; others included a free T-shirt. The game company Infocom, were renowned for the imaginative novelties included with their games. These included 3D spectacles, scratch-and-sniff cards and plastic toys. Some novelties were for fun, while others had some purpose in the games.

A keyboard overlay can just be a piece of thin card that fits into the slots in some standard keyboards just above the function keys. In some cases, an overlay can extend across the entire keyboard.

Quick reference cards – which should be made in plastic or stiff card laminated with plastic – are excellent for brief reminders, especially short cut keystrokes. A circular one might be doubly useful, as they inevitably get used as coffee cup mats.

There is plenty of computer paraphernalia, screen wipes, mouse mats, monitor stickers and clips. Any of these can be customized with the logo of the application. Each adds to the 'perceived value' of the product.

It is worryingly easy to 'buy' the satisfaction of the user with a cheap novelty. Even a cut-and-fold cardboard model can make the difference between a good product and an excellent product in the customer's mind.

What You Need in the Box

A standard boxed software package should include:

1) The transfer materials, disks, CD-ROM, tape, or cartridge that contain the application. There should be advice – written or etched on the materials themselves – of what to do in case the material is faulty.

2) An installation guide. Installing is the most vulnerable time for the application, as it is in a limbo state between being in control of itself and being dependent on the user pressing the right buttons. A poor installation will handicap the operation of an application, possibly fatally. Make sure the user can check the following things for themselves in a trivial manner:

   (a) That the software is up to date and registered if this is relevant.

(b) That all files necessary are present and not corrupted.

(c) That the target machine has the capacity to run the program, after it installs successfully.

3) Manuals and technical documentation.

4) Late notes. These are a list of all the known bugs, manual errors, etc. that have shown up since all the materials have been produced. These often come as 'readme' files on the transfer materials, although a separate sheet of paper is easier to stick by the monitor.

5) Producer warranty. This is the legal area of connecting the application with the company that produced it. Apart from the obvious disclaimers, this should include telephone numbers and E-mail addresses for technical support and upgrade information. This may include a form to send to the producing company to prove ownership, thereby registering the product.

6) Promotional details. Just like adverts in a movie, users expect commercial companies to print things that may just be thrown away immediately.

Piracy and Manual Protection

It is unlikely that you have your own printing press, but if you have a computer, you do own your own software press. The ability to copy software at will, in the days when most software came on floppy disks of various sizes, first became a problem for the games industry as this was the first software mass market.

To combat the spread of 'pirated' software, publishers built in methods to verify that the user not only had the software, but the support materials that were not so easy to duplicate. This usually involved asking the user to type in 'the seventh word on the eighth page' of the product manual. This cumbersome method of protection is still employed, but less so as CD-ROMs become the main transfer material for application software. Other methods involve supplying a 'hardware lock' or 'dongle' or some other – difficult to duplicate – device that the software depends on.

If a product is not being sold directly to the public, a reply card and disk serial number is a far less intrusive way of verifying ownership, although it doesn't in itself stop the spreading of pirated software or its use. However, the illegal user knows that the technical support, that a registered user expects to get, will not be forthcoming. This is an argument for including technical support as part of the package, which is now the norm.

Making the Code Available to the User

The choice between using a bespoke tailor or buying off-the-peg suits forces the buyer to make trade-offs between price and style. Unsurprisingly, most customers want software that they can purchase for off the peg prices and later tailor to their own needs. This means that a product has to be designed as a set of interlocking pieces.

Increasingly, large parts of programs and initial data can be altered by the user or customer. This may include data that affects how the program functions from the start, and cannot always be set within the program itself. The package may include a code library that allows the user to utilize pre-built functions to perform a different task.

The documentation to support these more technical issues is quite different from standard documentation, as there is far more potential for problems when attempting to support users pushing your software 'to the edge.' It is better to support these users using E-mail, or better still, dedicate a conference for them on an electronic forum system such as Compuserve or Delphi.

12.3 Silent Service

The manual is an important part of any product and should receive the same effort and attention as the programming and design. In coming years there will be a temptation to produce instructional material in other forms than the traditional book form such as CD ROM manuals, on-line help, interactive demonstration programs, audio and video tape. While these are all perfectly valid, the paper book still has the advantage that it can be referred to independently and requires no other equipment. A book demands little from the user's working environment.

It is a universal law that good manuals go unnoticed, while bad manuals become notorious. The application-manual author should endeavour to produce work that is completely overlooked. If a manual can be produced without criticism or comment from some quarter, the author will have done a very good job indeed.

Section III

Development Issues

The third and final section of this book outlines some of the basic techniques available to the programmer and discusses the design issues associated with them.

Even if you are not a programmer, if you intend to be part of the design process, you need to be aware of how programs are put together. You will not be able to communicate your ideas successfully if they are seen to be unworkable. It is important that programmers are not allowed to dominate a design just because they are programmers, so it is up to the designer to learn the basics.

Basic Program Structure

Whatever the language that will finally be used for your program, the designer must be able to describe the basic idea in a way that can be programmed. This does not mean that the designer must be a programmer; it simply means that he or she must appreciate programming construction. Further to this, a designer must understand the process of expressing everyday problems in programming language.

Any example code in this section will be written in 'C', as this is the current standard programming language. Code is usually represented in fragments which only show the pertinent parts; the ellipses (...) are to remind you of this. Reserved words of the 'C' language are printed in bold. Work through the comments to the right of the double slashes (//).

1.1 The Basics

All programming languages share – or can mimic – basic structures that allow for some form of structured programming.

Functions and Procedures

What is a function?

A function or procedure is a section of code that is designed to be 'called' from elsewhere in the code. Instead of repeating code lines to do the same thing, a function can be written that will do the same thing with different values.

It is clearly beneficial to write functions that can be called as many times as possible, in order to reduce repeated code and also to reduce the likelihood of bugs creeping in; it is easier to check that one function is correct than various similar statements repeated throughout the code.

Here is a very simple example function. It is a function to make a number positive. It does this simply by multiplying any negative numbers by minus one.

```
...
// A function to turn any integer positive
// The function 'make_positive' takes an integer argument
// 'number'
// and returns an integer.
int make_positive(int number)
{
    if (number < 0) number = number * -1;   // Multiply by -1
    return number;                          // Return answer
}
...
```

Now we can use the function in later code.

```
...
int a,b,c;              // Declare three integer variables
...
a = 5;                  // set variable 'a' to 5
b = -3;                 // set 'b' to minus 3
c = make_positive(a);   // variable 'c' is now set to 5;
c = make_positive(b);   // variable 'c' is now set to 3
...
```

An important aspect of functions is the ability for one variable to represent any similar variable. Thus *number* in the above example function is later used to represent variables *a* and *b* to produce a result. The program expects to be given integer values – whole numbers with no decimal part, usually in the range -32768 to 32767 – other types of variable may not produce the correct result. The set of descriptive symbols that are used in everyday life need to be carefully mapped to their equivalents inside a computer.

Loops

A pyramid can be made by stacking levels of blocks on top of each other. A simple pyramid has one block on top of a two by two square base of four blocks. A pyramid with a base length of three blocks has three levels containing fourteen blocks in total.

What is a loop?

The series can be represented as

1
1 + (2 x 2)
1 + (2 x 2) + (3 x 3)
etc.

So how many blocks in total is a pyramid with a base length of 11 blocks composed of? We could write this out in long hand in code, in the same way as we could on paper. However, by exploiting the repetitive nature of the problem, we can use a loop.

```
// A function to calculate the number of blocks in a pyramid
// of base length 'base_length'.
// The loop iterates i until it exceeds base_length
int blocks_in_pyramid(int base_length)
{
  int i,total;                  // Declare two variables
  total = 0;                    // Set total to zero
  for(i=0; i <= base_length; i++)   // Loop
  {
   total = total + (i * i);     // Cumulative total

  }
  return total;                 // Return total
}
```

In the main loop, the loop variable i starts at zero and increases in size until i is more than the base length. In programming parlance, i iterates until the condition

i <= *base_length* is no longer true. While the loop loops, only the statement in the loop's braces *total = total + (i*i)* is executed.

Note how important it is to represent the underlying pattern. After this, a program comes into its own because any size pyramid can now be accounted for. A solution that works in this fashion is called an algorithm. It is left to the reader to verify that the function works. Programs are usually constructed of hundreds of such functions and algorithms.

Conditions and Switches

In the example above, we saw an example of a condition:

```
(i <= base_length)
```

this just means that if *i* is less than or equal to *base_length* then the condition is true and the loop continues to be executed.

How programs make decisions

In the function *make_positive*, we saw an example of the use of the *if* command. This alters the course of execution of a program depending on the condition that follows the *if*. Let's take another look at this:

```
...
// A function to turn any integer positive
// The function 'make_positive' takes an integer argument
//'number'
// and returns an integer.
int make_positive(int number)
{
   if (number < 0) number = number * -1;// Multiply by -1
   return number;                        // Return answer
}
...
```

If the condition 'number is less than zero' is true, the code following the bracket

```
number = number * -1
```

is executed, otherwise it is not. A positive number is simply ignored. The ability of the program to respond differently – depending on the data it is given to work with – is what makes the program useful.

How program functions return errors

Functions often return values that indicate whether they have worked or failed, and testing these values is necessary to keep the program running without errors. In the example below, the *if* statement checks to see if the condition *fp == NULL* is true or false.

```
...
fp = fopen("file.txt","r");
if (fp == NULL)
{
   report_error("ERROR: FILE NOT FOUND");
   return;
}
...
```

A file called *file.txt* is being opened. If the file pointer *fp* is *NULL*, this indicates that the file could not be opened for some reason, so the program breaks away. To assume that the file had opened correctly, when it had not, might have caused severe problems later.

A more complex example of condition testing is the *switch* statement. This is used to test a variable that can have a value of more than just true or false.

How a program can select from a range of choices

In the example below, a fragment of a possible computer version of the popular letters game Scrabble is written. A tile is examined and a score value given to it as it would be in the game. The function *get_letter( )* is assumed to return a character corresponding to a tile. Thus the letter C is valued at 3 points.

```
...
char letter;
int score
...
letter = get_letter();    // Get a letter from the board
switch(letter)            // Look at letter and jump relevant
case.
  {
  case 'D':               // It's a 'D'..
  case 'G':               // ..or its a 'G'
   score = 2;
   break;                 // Leave the switch, we are done
  case 'B':
  case 'C':
  case 'P':
   score = 3;             // Three points for a 'B', 'C' or 'P'.
   break;                 // Leave the switch
  case 'F':
  case 'H':
  case 'V':
  case 'W':
  case 'Y':
   score = 4;
   break;
  case 'K':
   score = 5;
   break;
  case 'J':
  case 'X':
   score = 8;
   break;
  case 'Q':
  case 'Z':
```

```
        score = 10;
        break;
    default:        // If it isn't any of the above
        score = 1;
        break;
}

...
```

Digitization

**How the real
world is defined
for the computer**

When computers talk to computers they speak in numbers. If humans were to do the same thing they would greet their neighbor with a cheery 39, answer the phone with a polite 8 and bellow a belligerent 101 at that pesky road-hog. Just about the only thing that is converted into numbers, ready for use, is the menu of a Chinese restaurant. So for computer use, information from the real world needs to be converted into numbers; a process known as digitization.

How the conversion is done makes a big difference to a program. It can make finding the solution to a particular problem easier or more difficult. The ability to define problems in terms of numeric values is essential to the process of designing and developing a computer application.

The simplest conversion is the concept of true and false. False is represented by zero and true is represented by any non-zero value, and so any yes or no question can be answered with a numeric value. This is usually referred to as binary logic. A basic unit that represents a binary value is known as a flag.

Other 'real world' things can be represented by lists. The ingredients of a recipe could be held as a list of items. The possible cooking methods could be another list. Programming languages always allow lists to be defined and manipulated.

The 'C' language doesn't have a basic type that represents a binary flag, but we can create one from a larger basic type:

```
typedef unsigned char flag;
```

This isn't necessary, but it makes the code more readable. As a memory aid, *true* and *false* can be defined using macros:

```
#define TRUE 1
#define FALSE 0
```

This can be used by a function to return a binary value that indicates its success or failure.

Strings and Things

How text is stored
and manipulated
in a program

The basic storage unit of a character - held in memory as eight bits or a byte - is recognized in most languages. A sequence of characters - or string - is used to represent words and sentences.

It would seem natural that text should itself be a storage unit, but as it isn't, it is sometimes clumsy to handle. Handling strings can put a strain on memory because a string has no set length; 'hello' is longer than 'hi', whereas both 64 and 6400 can be represented as integers. Strings of fixed length are thus much safer to use.

The fragment below shows the use of two standard string functions and how problems occur. The *strcpy( )* function copies the string "JOHN" into the buffer *name*. The string takes up four letters but also one extra character to signify the end of the string - which makes five altogether. The *strcat( )* function concatenates - appends - the string " SMITH" onto "JOHN" to form "JOHN SMITH".

Unfortunately this string has a length of 11 - including the end string marker - which means that it is too big to be held by *name*. Thus the program will overwrite memory in its attempt to carry out the *strcat( )*, probably causing the program to crash or behave erratically.

```
...
char name[10];         // Can hold a string of 10 characters
...
strcpy(name,"JOHN");   // length of 'name' is 4 + END = 5
strcat(name," SMITH"); // length of 'name' now 10 + END = 11;
BUG!!
```

As a string can be constructed from its constituent parts, text output can easily be controlled by the program.

1.2 Design and Execution

A complete
example of a
small application

Listed below is a utility, DATEFIND, which has the simple function of searching through a given text file and extracting any calendar dates mentioned, such as might exist at the start of a letter. This is a complex problem because of the wide variety of formats dates appear in. The example shows a complete solution is arrived at by analyzing the big problem into smaller problems and tackling each individually.

So what is a date? A large number of formulations of words and numbers would be recognized by many people as a date. The following, depending on context, could be accepted as dates:

9/9/99
May 1st
16 December, 1994

but these would never be:

9/99/9
May I stop here
160 December Avenue, Jack City

The first job in program design is to clearly state the problem. In this case it is to define in analytical terms exactly what a date is.

DATEFIND does this by recognizing that a date is constructed from five different entities:

(1)   A numerical date which may be followed by a cardinal quantifier. Examples would be '1st', '2', '31', '22nd,' etc.

(2)   A numerical month, as the '2' represents in 30/2/1995.

(3)   A textual month such as 'September' or 'June'.

(4)   A numerical year, such as '1994' or ' `95 '

(5)   Separators between the above quantities such as full stops (9.6.66) or dashes (9-6-66).

The program does not check that the date is legal for a corresponding month, nor consequently for leap years. This could easily be added – and once more is left for the reader to do.

As with all designs, some things are not catered for, and must be possible to do at a later date if necessary. It is just as important to recognize what a program will not do, from the start, in order to fully define the functionality.

The first part of the listing handles the compiler management, and defines some useful values. Note the data stored as well.

```
/****************************/
/* DATEFIND by David Eastman */
/****************************/
#include <stdio.h>
#include <string.h>
#include <stdlib.h>
#include <ctype.h>
#include <conio.h>
#define TRUE 1
#define FALSE 0
// If it isn't a date, say so.
```

```
// Will not bother with leap year checking
#define NO_OF_MONTHS 12
// A four digit number year is valid if it starts as..
#define CENTURY 1900
// All strings that handle dates must be this big
#define DATE_STRING_LENGTH 40
static char *month_names[NO_OF_MONTHS] =
{
    "january",
    "february",
    "march",
    "april",
    "may",
    "june",
    "july",
    "august",
    "september",
    "october",
    "november",
    "december"
};
```

The pattern buffer stores the various orders of date components that will
be accepted as a date. The pattern buffer has a fixed number of patterns,
whereas the separator list is dynamic, allowing new cases to be put in
more flexibly.

```
#define PATTERNS 6
char *pattern_buffer[PATTERNS] =
{
    "DMY", // 13.6.66
    "MDY", // 6/13/74
    "SDY", // May 2nd, 1994
    "SD-", // March 1st
    "DSY", // 2nd November '95
    "DS-" // 3rd Sept
};
// End with '!'
static char separators[] =
{
    '\\' , '/', '-' , ',' , ' ', '.' , '\n' , '\0', '\t', '\r',
'!'
};
// Cardinal numbers
static char *cardinal[3] =
{
    "st",
    "nd",
    "rd"
```

```
};
// Examples of legal date strings
// March 8th, 1994
// 2/4/89
// 24 FEB 95
// 07-07-77

typedef unsigned char flag;

flag is_this_a_date(char *date_string);
flag is_this_a_month(char *date_string);
flag is_this_a_month_string(char *date_string);
flag is_this_a_year(char *date_string);
void spoon_feed(char *string);
flag is_separator(char letter);
```

The *main( )* routine that follows, acts as the shell of the program. It opens the file that the user names as the first parameter. Note the check to make sure that the file exists, and that the program doesn't need to break off, if this is the case. The file is read line-by-line until no further lines are available. DATEFIND then reports itself finished and prints one statistic: the number of lines read. This minor thing acts as a useful confirmation that the file processed wasn't actually empty.

```
int main(int argc, char *argv[])
{
    FILE *fp;                    // The File pointer
    char buf[256];
    int lines;

    lines = 0;

    if (argc > 1)                // If DATEFIND is called directly..
    {
      fp = fopen(argv[1],"rb");
      if (!fp)            // No file found.
      {
      printf("\nFile '%s' not found.", argv[1]);
      }

      while(fgets(buf,255,fp))      // Loop while lines available
      {
      lines++;
      spoon_feed(buf);
      }

      fclose(fp);
    }

    else puts("Syntax: DATEFIND filespec");

    printf("\n\nDATEFIND Finished!\n%d lines read.",lines);
```

```
        fflush(stdout);              // Useful if called as a window
        getch();                     // Useful if called as a window
        return 0;
}
```

This is the main operating procedure. It accepts a line of input, breaks up words and numbers between separators and tests to see if these chunks are legal date elements. Once three chunks have been processed, a check is made to see if a recognized pattern of elements has been seen.

```
void spoon_feed(char *string)
{
    char buf[DATE_STRING_LENGTH], last_hit[DATE_STRING_LENGTH];
    char pattern[6],*p;
    int i,len;

    p = string;
    pattern[0] = '\0';          // Clear pattern store
    last_hit[0] = '\0';
    len = 0;

    while(*p)
    {
        i = 0;
        len++;
        // Chew up line into chunks
        while(!is_separator(*p) && i < DATE_STRING_LENGTH-1)
        {
            buf[i++] = *p++;
        }
        buf[i] = '\0';
        // Check for validity
        if (isalnum(buf[0]))
        {
            if (isdigit(buf[0]) && is_this_a_month(buf) &&
                    pattern[0] != 'M'){
                strcat(last_hit,buf);
                strcat(last_hit," ");
                strcat(pattern,"M");
            }
            else if (isdigit(buf[0]) && is_this_a_date(buf)){
                strcat(last_hit,buf);
                strcat(last_hit," ");
                strcat(pattern,"D");
            }
            else if (isalpha(buf[0]) &&
                    is_this_a_month_string(buf)){
                strcat(last_hit,buf);
                strcat(last_hit," ");
                strcat(pattern,"S");
```

```
            }
          else if (isdigit(buf[0]) && is_this_a_year(buf)){
               strcat(last_hit,buf);
               strcat(last_hit," ");
               strcat(pattern,"Y");
          }
          else strcat(pattern,"-");
     }
     // Has a recognised pattern been found?
     if (len == 3)
     {

          for(i=0;i < PATTERNS;i++)
          {
               if (!strncmp(pattern,pattern_buffer[i],3))
               printf("\nDate found:\n>> %s\nFound in: \n>>
               %s\n",last_hit,string);
          }

          len = 0;
          pattern[0] = '\0';
          last_hit[0] = '\0';
     }

     if (pattern[0] == '-'){
          len = 0;
          pattern[0] = '\0';
          last_hit[0] = '\0';
     }
     // Mark pattern and continue/restart
     // pattern match?

     // Find the end
     while(*p && !is_separator(*p)) p++;
     // Find a start
     while(*p && is_separator(*p)) p++;
     }

}
```

The following functions parse the text for the relevant date constituents.

```
// Return true if this is a legal numerical date
// Function assumes the first character is a digit
// e.g. 28th, 19, 03, 12-, 29/,
flag is_this_a_date(char *date_string)
{
    int date,i;
```

```
    // First digit
    date = *date_string - '0'; // Converts ASCII to a digit
      date_string++;
    if (is_separator(*date_string)) goto check_number;
    // Second digit ?
    if (isdigit(*date_string))
    {
      date = 10*date + (*date_string - '0');
      date_string++;
      if (is_separator(*date_string)) goto check_number;
    }
    // Only legal thing now is a separator, cardinal or end
    // Look for separator
    if (is_separator(*date_string)) goto check_number;

    // Look for cardinal
    for (i = 0; i < 3 ; i++)
    {
      if (*date_string == cardinal[i][0] &&
          *(date_string+1) == cardinal[i][1]) goto check_number;
    }
    // No good
    return FALSE;
check_number:
    if (date > 0 && date <= 31) return TRUE;
          else return FALSE;
}
// Return true if this is a legal numerical month
// Function assumes the first character is a digit
// e.g. 1, 12/, 2-
flag is_this_a_month(char *date_string)
{
    int month;
    // First digit
    month = *date_string - '0'; // Converts ASCII to a digit

    // Second digit ?
    date_string++;
    if (is_separator(*date_string)) goto check_number;

    month = 10 + (*date_string - '0');
    date_string++;

    if (is_separator(*date_string)) goto check_number;
    // Forget it
    return FALSE;

check_number:
    if (month >= 1 && month <= 12) return TRUE;
      else return FALSE;
}
```

```
// Return true if this is part of a real month
flag is_this_a_month_string(char *date_string)
{
    int i;
    char *p,buf[DATE_STRING_LENGTH];

    strcpy(buf,date_string);

    p = buf;
    while(*p && isalpha(*p))
    {

      *p = (char)tolower(*p);
      p++;
    }
    *p = '\0';


    if (strlen(buf) < 3) return FALSE; // At least three letters

    for(i=0; i < NO_OF_MONTHS; i++)
    {
      if (!strncmp(month_names[i],buf,strlen(buf))) return TRUE;
    }

    return FALSE;
}
// Four numbers or two numbers, possibly an apostrophe
flag is_this_a_year(char *date_string)
{
    int year;

    // Either 96,'97 or 1975

    if (*date_string == '\'') date_string++;
    year = atoi(date_string);

    if ((year > 9 && year < 100) || year > CENTURY) return TRUE;
        else return FALSE;
}
// Is this a valid separator?
flag is_separator(char letter)
{
    int i;

    i = 0;
    while(separators[i] != '!') // '!' marks the end of list.
    {
    if (letter == separators[i]) return TRUE;
```

```
    i++;
  }
  // If we got this far, then we found no match
  return FALSE;
}
```

1.3   Resource Limitations

One nice thing about being an adult is that if you start playing with your toys, you can leave them out and put them away whenever you want. Unfortunately program languages demand: open brackets to be closed; open files to be shut when you have finished with them; and the declaration of any functions used beforehand. When you are programming for a system with shared resources, it is important to put things back on the shelf or the other kids will start crying.

The system that your program runs in probably has limited resources, so it isn't a good idea to design programs that cannot be restricted in memory use. It is best to allocate memory at the last possible moment, and free it immediately afterwards. For instance: if you want to search a file for something, for speed reasons you may wish to store the file in fast local memory, as opposed to slow storage memory, e.g. RAM as opposed to hard disk. In that case, it is important to reduce the number of operations that you do while the local memory is used up. The search parameters should be found before you load the file, not while it is in local memory, as asking for these parameters may involve, for example, drawing a graphical dialogue box – putting more strain on local memory. The order in which you do things does affect the way the system operates.

It is tempting to write tasks that concentrate on efficiently using the machine as much as possible at any one time, whereas it is better to write programs that cut the job up into chunks and allow for periods where the program can pause and give control to other tasks. In some cases, you actually have to instruct the program to lose control or give way, but the point is that a modern system will always be doing more things than just working on your programs instructions, so it is best to design for this.

Managing the resources of the computer

2

Program versus
Data

A computer program contains two essential components: code and data. Code is the intelligence of the program and its ability to process. Data is the raw material to be processed.

2.1   Program Engines

Programs contain different kinds of data. There is initialization data that defines the dimensions and types of elements the program uses. Another kind of data is the user's data. This is the result of using the program; the user's output. It is easy to spot the two types. The first is usually integrated into the program while the second is stored in separate files.

You may have guessed where this thread is leading. It doesn't take a giant intuitive leap to combine the two concepts and come up with the idea of storing the initialization data separately from the program. The code that remains is an 'engine.' Just as a real engine is reliant on fuel to run it, a program engine is reliant on data.

How Engines Work

How to implement a data engine

A program engine consists of a set of standard functions which are passed data and then activated. So far there is no difference between an engine and any other type of program. The data passed to a standard function is data that has been stored as a separate file. Again this is not so different to other programs. The final, subtle, difference is that the stored data controls the calling of the function routines. Usually a program will have a solid chunk of code that controls the calling of subroutines. An engine reads in a data file and it is the data that controls the calls to functions.

As an example, looking at an ordinary 'C' program, you might discover a section like this:

```
...
do_action_two();
do_action_two();
do_action_three();
do_action_four();
do_action_one();
...
```

Whereas the same program working as an engine might be like this:

```
...
int i;
int application_data[5]={ 2,2,3,4,1 };
...
for(i=0; i<5; i++)
{
        switch(application_data[i])
        {
        case 1:
```

```
            do_action_one();
            break;
        case 2:
            do_action_two();
            break;
        case 3:
            do_action_three();
            break;
        case 4:
            do_action_four();
            break;
        default:
            break;
    }
}
...
```

Of course this doesn't show the data being loaded as a separate file which a true engine should do. Even so, changing the second application is simply a case of editing the array definition.

The Advantages of Using an Engine

The use of the engine concept allows development of an application to be separated from preparation of the data. This has several advantages. Programmers are not necessarily the best people to create the data for an application. Defining what the engine must do and allowing the programmer to develop it – in isolation from the data – keeps development streamlined. It also means that data can be prepared by less technical people, but perhaps people who have greater insight into how the application should work.

Why a data engine is useful

Data is much easier to manipulate than code. Having created an engine, all the development can be concentrated on preparing data. It may be possible to use an engine more than once, allowing applications to be defined in terms of data rather than code.

Development is easier if existing tools can be used to create the data. For example, an engine could be designed to read a text file and operate from text commands. Data for the engine can be created with any number of word-processing packages. These allow easy editing, cutting and pasting of the data, until the required effect is achieved. This would be a much better alternative to creating a custom-written tool.

Most authoring packages are in fact engines. Users are building their own applications from data. Perhaps this is one more confirmation that the best person to design an application is not a programmer but the user.

Applications for Engines

The engine concept is universally applicable to all software. It is, after all, merely one more way to structure data and code. However, there are some applications where it is more useful than others.

Clearly, applications which use a lot of data, such as databases, will benefit from the use of an engine. CD-ROM products where there are a large number of items of a similar nature, such as pictures, sound samples, tunes and so on, can also make use of an engine. However, it is in applications where there is a high level of interactivity between things, that the engine concept becomes invaluable. Graphic user interfaces and games – where there are a number of things happening at the same time, in a predictable way but each interacting with one another – are good examples of applications where engines can make a difference (the difference between straightforward development or a de-bugging nightmare.)

2.2   Different Types of Data

Programs work with three kinds of data: internal data that controls the operation of the program, internal data that is inherent to the task, and data that is processed by the program when it is run.

If we look back at DATEFIND, we can sort through the code and separate out data that is still sitting in the code. For instance, in the function *is_separator( )*, this line appears:

```
while(separators[i] != '!')
```

The pling character ('!') is used to mark the end of the separators list. This is an example of operation control data. Because the pling character itself has no meaning it would have been far better to index this using a macro thus:

```
    ...
#define END_OF_LIST '!'
    ...
while(separators[i] != END_OF_LIST)
```

Any number, string, or character that is mentioned explicitly in the code is data, and probably shouldn't be there. Sometimes it is too inconvenient to move this incidental data, but wherever possible data should be placed in separate editable files, or at least placed away from the main code engine.

Data that is part of the task – such as the array holding months of the years in DATEFIND – should be easy to change if needed. It should be a straightforward matter to edit the code to enable the program to operate on Spanish text, for instance.

From the outset, data that needs to be easily adjustable must be maintained outside of the code, in order that a tool can manipulate it without the program needing to be changed. Data that is important to the program, but is a little too technical for a non-programmer to alter – such as the list of separators or the list of patterns in DATEFIND – should be accessible from one place in the code. If, for example, it was thought that a pling may in fact be used as a separator for dates – unlikely as this is – it should not be necessary to go through all the code looking for plings to remove and replace by a new end-of-list marker.

The detachment of data from code is a design point that needs to be incorporated early on, so that tools and files are in place before data is put in the code because 'it seemed the logical place to put it at the time.' Once your data is freed, it is amazing what you can do with it.

Separating String Data from Code

Displaying messages and other text is something that every application needs to do at some point. It is usually so easy to print a line of text, that most programmers treat text in a casual manner. Messages are put into the code wherever they are needed. For a short application or one that uses very little text this is quite acceptable, but for a large application this mixing of data with code is undesirable.

How to reduce the amount to storage space taken by text messages

The simplest solution is to store all messages in one location and use a simple index to access the string required. This has an advantage. When messages need to be changed, it is easier to find the relevant string when they are all in one file than if the whole code has to be searched.

Text can use up a large amount of space and, for an application where space is tight and the amount of text to be used is large, it may be a good idea to tokenize the text. This will involve writing a tool that reads in all the text strings, divides them into single words, compiles those words into a dictionary and saves out the dictionary plus the text strings in a tokenized form. For example the text:

Hey, diddle diddle,
The cat and the fiddle,
The cow jumped over the moon,

Would be converted to a dictionary of:

Hey,	diddle	diddle,	The	cat	and
the	fiddle,	cow	jumped	over	moon,

And the data:

1,2,3,4,5,6,7,8,4,9,10,11,7,12

Note that the dictionary creation tool searches for duplicate words and, if found, doesn't save them again. Also note that punctuation and upper and lower case are included in the stored word. This keeps the code simple and the additional overhead in storing similar words is not too large.

Having created this data, the programmer can then recreate the text by printing each word from the dictionary as it is indexed from the data.

As it stands, the example saves no space at all. In fact it is less efficient than using simple strings. However, when a large amount of text is handled in this way, considerable savings in space can be made.

**How to speed up
slow code**

2.3   Tables versus Algorithms

During the course of developing an application, a programmer may come across a situation that calls for a complex calculation to be executed a number of times. This may have the affect of tying up the processor for a period of time, causing the application to either slow down or pause noticeably.

A solution to this problem is to use the algorithm to create a data table and then access the data table rather than use the algorithm.

Accessing a table is often quicker than doing a calculation. This is because it is basically moving existing data rather than creating new data.

Here are a couple of examples where this technique can be used:

1) Screen co-ordinates. It is often necessary to access screen memory directly in graphic applications. Although screen memory is usually a block of contiguous memory locations, it is not always laid out in a straightforward way. This can mean that calculating the memory location of a pixel using x and y coordinates requires a complex, time-consuming calculation. The table-driven solution is to calculate the address of the start of each screen line and store it as an array. The memory location of a pixel can then be easily found by using the y coordinate to index the table, reading the address and then adding the x coordinate to it.

2) Circle drawing. Drawing circles and other types of geometry require the use of sines, cosines and other floating-point arithmetic. Floating-point code is notoriously slow to execute. So if a lot of geometry is being calculated, as is the case when drawing a three-dimensional object, the code can be noticeably slow. This will be apparent from the speed the object is drawn on screen.

This is a simple circle-drawing routine:

```
...
#define RADIUS 100
...
void algo_circle(int start_x,int start_y)
{
    int x,y,i;

    for(i=1;i<=360;i++){
    x=start_x+(RADIUS*cos(i));
    y=start_y+(RADIUS*sin(i));
    pixel(x,y);      /* library routine to draw pixel at x,y */
    }
}
...
```

This routine will draw a circle of size *RADIUS* at co-ordinates *start_x,start_y*. The alternative to this – using tables – requires two separate routines. The first is called only once and sets up the tables in two global arrays called *table_x* and *table_y*:

```
...
void set_table(void)
{
    int i;

    for(i=1;i<=360;i++){
    table_x[i]=RADIUS*cos(i);
    table_y[i]=RADIUS*sin(i);
    }
}
...
```

The second routine draws the circle using the values stored in the arrays.

```
...
void table_circle(int start_x,int start_y)
{
    int x,y,i;
    for(i=1;i<=360;i++){
    x=start_x+table_x[i];
    y=start_y+table_y[i];
    pixel(x,y);
    }
}
...
```

The *table_circle* routine takes less processing to produce the same result as the *algo_circle*. The same principle can be applied to all algorithms. If fast execution is a requirement of an application, it is always better to use precalculated values wherever possible.

3

Tools and Productivity

Most creative activities would be impossible without tools. Some tools enable work to be done quicker and more effectively. A good carpenter will be able to use a range of equipment bought from the hardware store, but from time to time will also build a tool, perhaps a jig, to hold something together while it is worked on. This is reflected in software development. Ready-made tools for standard tasks can be purchased. Also special tools can be created for a particular purpose.

3.1   What is a Software Tool?

A software tool is an application that creates, or alters, either a program or data. Most people will be familiar with some standard tools such as text editors and program compilers. These are tools that have been developed, perhaps by commercial companies, for general use. They are the hammers, saws and drills of the software world. A saw can only be used to cut, but it is able to cut a variety of materials.

Most application development can be achieved using commercial tools. However, there is always something – and it is usually data – that requires a special effort to achieve. For example, in the early days of computing there were no applications for editing graphics. Any graphics that were to be put into a program had to be designed on graph paper and typed in byte by byte – or 'hand-coded.' Clearly what was needed was a tool to do the job, and so the 'paint program' was born. Hand-coding remains the last resort of every application developer, but the wise write their own tools. Tools written for a specific task are often referred to as custom tools.

Let us look at an example from the previous chapter – tokenizing text. A way of compressing and handling text was proposed. This technique could be both hand-coded or automated with a tool. The method involved creating a dictionary and strings of data from plain text. Several tools, or a tool with several functions, would need to be used. The tools would be: a text editor to create the original text, a tool to scan the text and create the dictionary, and a tool to scan the text and create data strings from the dictionary words. The best solution would be to use two tools. The first of these would be a standard text editor to create the original text. The second, a tool that combines the remaining functions, outputting two files: the dictionary and the string data.

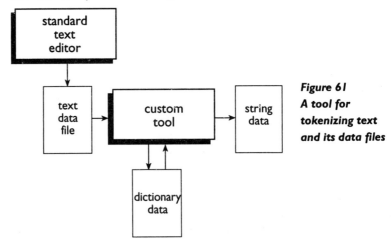

Figure 61
A tool for
tokenizing text
and its data files

Many of today's commercial applications may have started life as tools written for a limited purpose.

3.2   When Should a Tool be Written?

It usually becomes clear when a tool should be written. It is the point when the time taken in editing data exceeds the time that would be taken developing a tool to do it. However, this point is often reached when it has become too late. Developers may not realise they have a problem – that could be solved by developing a custom tool – until they have already got part way into a long winded solution. Tools should always be part of the overall design. At the design stage of every project, time should be spent considering what tools are needed and what tools can be developed that will speed up the process. Time for tool development should be included in the development schedule.

Tools are sometimes seen as an unnecessary expense, a side issue or as a second-rate task to be done by a junior programmer. For this reason, tools are often not written, or are badly designed or inadequate for the job. Managers may not see the need for spending time writing a tool when that time could be spent entering the data by hand. This attitude shows a lack of understanding of the benefits that good tools bring to a project.

It is possible to produce a tool that takes several weeks to write and then only use it for twenty minutes, before discarding it forever. This doesn't seem to be very sensible, but if the alternative is to spend several months doing the same job by hand, it can be very sensible indeed.

How to Gain the Advantages of a Tool

The advantages that a tool brings depend on what the tool does and how it does it. It is difficult to provide guidelines for developing a tool without knowing in advance what the tool is for. However, there are some general principles that all tools should adhere to:

The one thing that every tool does is output data. And it is helpful if the data is in a useful format. Many tools fall short of being invaluable simply because they output data in an obscure format – which then has to be converted. If a tool can output data in a directly usable form, much time and effort can be saved.

How to gain the advantages of using a custom written tool

A tool should allow data to be stored and retrieved. It is easy to build a tool that creates data and then stores it. It will make the tool a lot more useful if that data can be retrieved and re-edited. Creating data is an error-prone business; mistakes don't show until the data is used. If the data can be re-edited, mistakes can be quickly fixed.

A tool should allow data to be manipulated and edited in a dynamic way. It is not always enough that data can be altered. Sometimes additional data needs to be inserted or some global alteration needs to be made. The development process may dictate a change in the data's format. Tools should be able to accommodate these changes without requiring new data to be input. It should be possible to read old versions of files and update them to the new format.

A tool should allow data to be displayed in a way that can be easily comprehended. It is possible to represent and edit a polygon as a series of x,y coordinates. However, it is not easy to see whether the string of numbers would produce a regular shape or a tangled mess. A tool that displays the data in a graphical format, and allows the data to be created by manipulating the graphics, may take more time to program, but in the long run may save more time taken correcting errors.

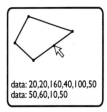

Figure 62
A tool for editing
polygons

data: 20,20,160,40,100,50
data: 50,60,10,50

3.3   Applications for Tools

The primary purpose of a tool is to take the drudgery out of creating an application. It is therefore important that the designer looks for areas of the design where development stages are repeated. This will usually be in the creation of data, but data can take many forms.

Developing a CD-ROM application may require preparing a large number of bitmaps and storing them as compressed data. A GUI application may need many dialogue boxes and menus designing. A game may need levels and backgrounds to be created. In each area there is the potential, if not the necessity, to use a tool.

Building From a Tool.

The creation of a tool can often set the course of development of an application. The tool may dictate the format of data to be used. This in turn dictates how the application uses it. This is not a bad thing. Often problems with the design can be worked out in the development of the tools, leaving the way clear to develop the application.

Quite often, code developed for a tool can be reused in the application. In the above example, of a tool to create geometric shapes, the same code used to display the development shapes in the tool can be used to display the final shapes in the application. This saves time and provides an opportunity to test the code during development.

Having the right tools to do a job can make life a lot easier. However, there are always choices to be made and a tool takes time to develop. The decision to produce a tool will require careful weighing up. On one side there is the time taken by the problem, on the other, the time taken creating the solution.

4

List Processing

List processing doesn't sound like much fun but is such a
basic programming method that a designer should
understand it. As in previous ones, this chapter focuses on
understanding how relevant techniques can be used, as
opposed to understanding the programming behind them. To
follow the example program fragments you will have to be
familiar with the concept of pointers in 'C.' This is
traditionally a bit of an obstacle for tyros. Fortunately, most
of the ideas involved can be shown by diagrams.

4.1 Representing Your Data

**How the real
world is
represented using
numbers**

Like most languages, 'C' has some basic internal storage types such as: integers, characters, doubles and longs. These machine dependent types could not possibly be expected to represent any interesting data on their own.

If we can correctly represent the state of something using numbers, then we can start treating it as data. Once the state of something is in the form of data, it can be manipulated by the computer. By using structures, we can make up an abstract data type to represent an arbitrary object.

Take a television for example. It has 20 possible channels, a contrast slider control, a volume knob and an on/off switch. The slider starts off in the centre but can have twenty positions above the middle and twenty below.

We can use a structure definition to define this:

```
typedef unsigned char flag;
...
struct television              // Stucture for television
{
  unsigned int Channel;        // Channels 0 -20
  unsigned int Volume;
  int Contrast;                // Contrast -20 thru + 20
  flag On;                     // On or off
};
...
```

Now we can represent the state of a television:

```
struct television my_television;
my_television.Channel = 10;
my_television.Volume = 2;
my_television.On = TRUE;
```

Object Oriented Programming

**What benefit does
object oriented
programming
bring?**

We can write a function that turns the abstract TV on, sets the volume low and tunes in to NBC. While we are aware of what the abstract data represents, the code itself just treats the structure as any other structure. It would be legal within the language to set Channel to 1006, Volume to -5000 and On to 'Z'. This is because there is no way to persuade 'C' that there are rules that define how the abstract data type can be manipulated. This can, of course, cause bugs.

Using an object oriented language such as 'C++,' we can prevent the television structure being mistreated by allowing only specially adapted functions – or 'methods' – to manipulate them. We could write a change_channel() method for instance, that sets the Channel variable to a legal value. We can make this the only way to manipulate Channel. In this way we treat the television structure as an object. This term has come to mean that functions are tied to the data they work on. By developing code in an object oriented way, it is much easier to pass projects on to other programmers. Once an object and its methods are defined, the limited access forces others to use the objects only in the way the writer intended.

4.2 Lists

How lists are used in programs

An item of data can be unique or it can be one of many similar items in a list. There are two simple ways of handling a list of data items. The first is to specify that the list has a finite number of entries. This is okay for lists that don't change, such as: a list of the days of the week, or the months of the year. These will be a list of seven entries, and a list of twelve, respectively. For a list where the number of entries changes – the last working days in a month, for example – this is not very convenient. So the second way of handling data is to allow the list to have a variable length, marking the last entry in some way that can be detected by the program. It has already been explained in chapter 2 of this section, how the pling character (!) is used to terminate a list of separators. This is the fundamental technique for creating applications that are expandable during the design process.

Storing data in this way can be complex. Although the pling example would have few problems, a list held in alphabetic or numeric order can be disrupted if data needs to be added to it. Let us look at a technique for handling data lists.

Dynamic Lists

How are lists created?

A task that programs regularly need to do is sort through a set of data elements. For instance, to create a list of available files to load, a user interface would need a list of file names sorted alphabetically. As the program cannot come with an in-built list of available files, the program must read the system information and create the list dynamically, i.e. from scratch. The term dynamic is used to indicate that something can change during the course of running the program.

To say that data is sorted, clearly implies an ordering. However, one piece of data is not normally connected to another in any way, except within an array. But an array is not dynamic, the number of elements and their index order in the array is fixed – defined at the start of the program. In languages such as 'C' where addresses – positions of data in memory – can be manipulated it is possible to 'point' to the next element in order.

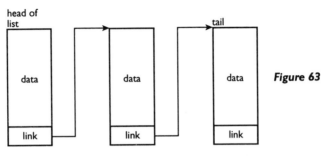

Figure 63

In the diagram, the boxes represent the elements that are fixed chunks of memory. The 'data' is the information – which is probably held in a structure – and the link is the pointer to another element. There needs to be a pointer to the head of the list. The last element, or tail, is marked by having a link that points to NULL, an address that equates to zero.

What is a linked list?

Imagine packing items for your holiday, using a list. It would be much easier to assemble them if each item told you where to find the next on the list. So your passport contains a note to tell you where your sunglasses are. When you find the sunglasses, a label is attached telling you where to find your Canadian dollars, and so on. The obvious advantage is that items can be of unequal size and can be stored anywhere.

Generating Lists

To create and add to an exhaustive list requires using memory dynamically to store the new structure. Initially, a list is just a pointer of the right type:

```
...
struct data_element
{
  int data;                        // Element's data
  struct data_element *next;  // Link pointer
}
struct data_element *list;
...
```

The first element can be created by use of the standard memory allocation calls in 'C', such as *malloc( )*. The data is then copied to the element and the *next* pointer set to *NULL*.

To add a new element at the end of the list, the new element is first created.

Then the tail element of the existing list is linked to – or set to point at – the new element.

The danger of using memory dynamically is that it can run out, thus any additions to a list are not guaranteed to be possible.

Traversing a List

Once we know where the list starts, it is easy to move from the top to the bottom, doing whatever we want to on the way. The program steps through, or traverses, one element at a time, moving by pointing to the next element. It is the pointer that moves, nothing else.

Here, a pre-generated list based on the structure *data_element* is traversed by a simple *while* loop. The loop only executes while the pointer is set to a valid element. The *NULL* value, read from the tail element, is evaluated as *false* and terminates the loop.

```
. . .
struct data_element
{
  int data;
  struct data_element *next;  // Link pointer
}
struct data_element *p,*list;
. . .
p = list    // Point to the start of the list
while(p)    // While still in list
{
  . . .
  p = p->next;  // Move to next element in list
}
. . .
```

List Exotica

The basics of a list can be mixed around in different ways to produce different types of lists.

The circular list just has the tail linked to the head. This can be traversed forever, which may be useful for a program that needs to continually look at a list while operating.

A doubly linked list is harder to set up, but is designed to be as easy to traverse backwards as forwards.

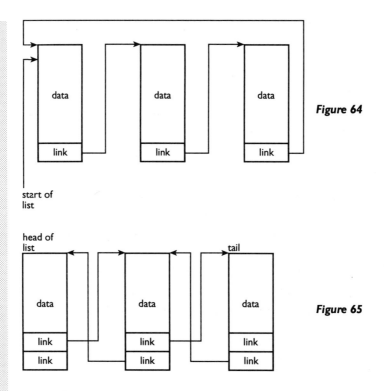

Figure 64

start of
list

head of
list

tail

Figure 65

Sorting and Filtering

When a linked list is established, it isn't necessary to move the data anywhere if the order needs to be changed, just the links.

How is a linked list sorted?

Instead of writing a program, we can show the basics diagrammatically. A simple sort can be done by moving down the list, swapping any consecutive elements that are in the wrong order. When the list is traversed, we repeat the process until no swaps are needed and the list is sorted.

Let us assume that we have formed a linked list of club members, using a basic structure:

```
...
struct club_member
{
    char name[20];
    int membership_no;
    struct club_member *next;
};
...
```

The first of our members to join are Andy, Bo, Chris and Diana. Their membership numbers are based on their dates of birth (Figure 66).

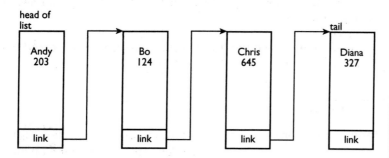

Figure 66

So the question is, how do we produce a list sorted by membership?

By traversing the list, we can see that the head of the list ought to be Bo now, as 124 is lower than Andy's membership number 203 (Figure 67).

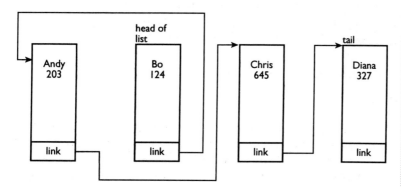

Figure 67

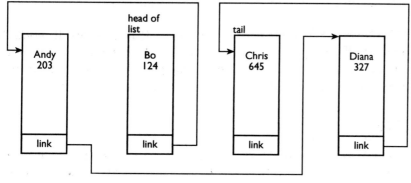

Figure 68

Note that the boxes that represent the data sitting in memory haven't shifted, just the links. We stored Bo's old link to Chris, and gave it to Andy, in order not to lose any data while sorting. After further swapping, we reach Figure 68.

Now if we traversed the list, it would start from Bo and end with Chris. The data, however, is still physically in its original position.

Filtering

Some operations need to be performed on only a portion of data. Let us say that you need to change the telephone number for all people in your address book that live in Jack City because an extra '1' needs to be added to their phone code.

Assuming we have a list of telephone numbers, we can work our way through the list, searching for addresses in Jack City. When found, the numbers can be changed:

```
. . .
p = list        // Point to the start of the list
while(p)
{
    if (!strcmp(p->city,"Jack City")) // If city name is
    // "Jack City"
    {
      strcpy(temp,p->phone); // Temporarily store the phone no.
      p->phone[0] = '1'; // New number starts with a '1'
      strcat(p->phone,temp); // append the rest of the number
    }
    p = p->next;    // Next element in list
}
. . .
```

The above fragment changes the numbers as it traverses. It would be better practice to produce a secondary filtered list and let the user see the numbers that will be changed before doing so, in case the search string doesn't match as expected.

Trees

What is a binary search tree?

When searches are made repeatedly and a list is composed of a large number of elements, it becomes inefficient to traverse the list from its head to find a particular element.

Binary search trees can be created by treating elements as nodes on a tree; a node having two link branches. One branch represents 'less' than the current value, one side 'more'.

A correctly set up or 'balanced' tree is very quick to search. In the example diagram below, any of seven cities can be indexed within two steps, starting from London and branching to the left or right depending on the target cities' alphabetical order. Moscow for example, would be to the right of London but to the left of Tokyo. Note that if the tree were re-balanced, another eight cities could be added with no more than three steps being needed.

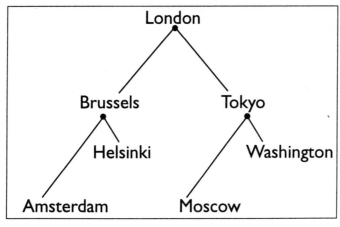

Figure 69

A Final Word

This is the end of the book. In terms of computer games, at this point it is traditional to say congratulations and well done for getting to the end of the book, do you want to read it again? However, it may be better to say we hope you enjoyed reading this book and that you found it both helpful and interesting.

Further Reading

The Art of Writing Made Simple
Geoffrey Ashe, William Heinemann Ltd, 1972
ISBN 434-98496-5

Human Memory: Theory and Practice
Alan Baddeley, Lawrence Erlbaum Associates, 1990
ISBN 0-86377-132-7

Cognitive Psychology: A Students Handbook
Michael W. Eysenck & Mark T. Keane, Lawrence Erlbaum
Associates, 1990
ISBN 0-86377-153-X

**The Complete Guide to Illustration
and Design Techniques and Materials**
Terence Dalley (editor), QED Book, 1980

Sound for Picture
Edited by Jeff Forlenza and Terri Stone, Mix Books, 1993
ISBN 0-7935-2002-9

Keyboards and Computer Music
Philip Hawthorn, Usbourne Publishing Ltd, 1985
ISBN 0-86020-928-8

Hedgecoe on Video
John Hedgecoe, Hamlyn, 1989
ISBN 0-600-57271-4

Godel, Escher, Bach, An Eternal Golden Braid
Douglas Hofstadter, Penguin, 1979
ISBN 0-14-0055797-7

The Icon Book
William Horton, J Wiley, 1994
ISBN 0-471-59900-X

Parallel Distributed Processing Vol 2
Psychological and Biological Models.
James L. McClelland, The MIT Press, 1986
ISBN 0-262-13218-4

The Dream Machine, Exploring the Computer Age
Jon Palfreman & Doron Swade, BBC Books, 1991
ISBN 0-563-36221-9

Designing and Using CBT Interactive Video
Richard Palmer, NCC Publications, 1988
ISBN 0-85012-675-4

Design for the Real World
Victor Papanek, Granada Publishing Limited, 1971
ISBN 0-586-08171-2

Programming Windows
Charles Petzold, Microsoft Press, 1990
ISBN 1-55615-264-7

Psychology at Work
Edited by Peter Warr, Penguin Books, 1987 ed
ISBN 0-14-022654-0

The Animator's Workbook
Tony White, Phaidon Press Limited, 1986
ISBN 0-7148-2439-9

Artificial Intelligence
Patrick Winston, Addison Wesley, 1984
ISBN 0-201-08259-4

Index

C-G

H-R